To Andrea—

Thank you
for taking on
Goosebumps.

Best.

Richard Martin

August 3, 2018

Goosebumps of Antimatter

Richard Martin

SPUYTEN DUYVIL
New York City

Acknowledgements

Many of these stories and poems have appeared in the following publications. Thanks to the editors and publishers of:

Literary Magazines: *ACM, AlteredScale, Big Hammer, BURP, Chronogram, Estuaires: Revue Culturelle, Exquisite Corpse, Fell Swoop: The All Bohemian Revue, House Organ, Impact Magazine, Maelstrom Review, Mid-American Review, Modern Poetry Studies, NEBO, Samisdat, The Bellingham Review* and *unarmed*.

Chapbooks: *Between the Eyes* (Acre Press, 1984), *Sideways* (Obscure Publications, 2004) and *Strip Meditation*, (Igneus Press, 2009).

Books: *Dreams of Long Headdresses: Poems from a Thousand Hospitals* (Signpost Press, 1988), *White Man Appears on Southern California Beach* (Bottom Fish Press, 1991), *Modulations* (Asylum Arts, 1998), *Marks* (Asylum Arts, 2002), *boink!* (Lavender Ink, 2005), *Altercations in the Quiet Car* (Lavender Ink/Fell Swoop, 2010), *Under the Sky of No Complaint* (Lavender Ink/Fell Swoop, 2013), *Buffoons in the Gene Pool* (Lavender Ink/Fell Swoop, 2016), *Techniques in the Neighborhood of Sleep* (Spuyten Duyvil, 2016).

Photographs of Thomas Haines' paintings by Katie Kanazawich
(Habitat Studio, Binghamton, New York).
Photographs of James de Crescentis' paintings by Alan Weller
(Santa Fe, New Mexico).

ISBN 978-1-947980-04-4 pbk.   978-1-947980-46-4 hdc.

Cover painting by Thomas Haines:

"Figures Against the Sky", Acrylic on MDO Board, 18"x 24", 2005

Library of Congress Cataloging-in-Publication Data

Names: Martin, Richard, 1949- author.
Title: Goosebumps of antimatter / Richard Martin.
Description: New York City : Spuyten Duyvil, [2018]
Identifiers: LCCN 2017044324 | ISBN 9781947980044 (softcover)
Classification: LCC PS3563.A7277 A6 2018 | DDC 818/.54--dc23
LC record available at https://lccn.loc.gov/2017044324

for Joel Dailey
and his 34 years
as supreme editor of
Fell Swoop: The All Bohemian Revue

CONTENTS

WELCOME TO GOOSEBUMPS* OF ANTIMATTER**

Since the publication of my anti-memoir, *boink!*,*** in 2005, by Lavender Ink (New Orleans), I have been badgered relentlessly to write a sequel by the five people who have admitted under oath that they have read it. I have resisted mightily, despite the mysterious packages left at my door and the late night phone calls of no one on the line, including but not limited to threatening text messages by those insidious patrons of my art. By some undefined process, at least a process unknown to me, the FIVE in question have decided that *boink!* (**see Appendix A & B**) is a work of genius.

Now it would be inappropriate for me to take a bow and assume that if my anti-memoir is a work of genius, then I am, as the author of it, also a genius. Sadly, this is far from the truth. Early in life my brain was branded with the tattoo "dumbass" (**see Book 2, Meet Ant McGoogle**). I could provide any of a number of a examples as to why those in charge of my upbringing and schooling felt compelled to brand my brain in that way. Perhaps it was easier to say: "Dumbass get me a beer!" or "Dumbass get out of my class!" Easier I say than calling me by my Christian name, Richard James James Martin (computer has offered a red line under the second James but it is not an accidental repetition of a word). I'm not sure why I took "James" (**see** *boink!*, **p.** 144) as my Confirmation name when my middle name was James. But I'm sure the "dumbass" branding iron hadn't cooled yet when I made that "dumbass" decision.

OK, about that example. Years ago, before I decided on an unsuccessful writing career (and it burns me up sometimes that successful writers, those who earn a living through their writing, find the time to label the "unsuccessful" ones unsuccessful precisely because they can't support themselves through their writing) and prior to being chased out of the house by my first wife with a spiked heel, I landed a job at a Cold Storage plant in a rural and toxic town. After signing a document confirming that I knew what "cold" meant in its adjectival position before "storage," I was directed by the manager, one in heavy winter gear (fur boots, leggings, Eskimo parka, thick gloves, ski mask), to Boxcar #2. The Cold Storage Plant was near the railroad tracks that ran through the center of the toxic town and out into the countryside. There were four or five boxcars that rested on a side track adjacent to the main train line. It was early May, pleasant in temperature, and the hillside looming above the train tracks had burst into forsythia. I've always been a bigtime fan of forsythia. I feel closer to the sun whenever I see it.

Once I climbed up into the boxcar ("Dumbass, use the ramp!"), I observed two men busy loading large boxes of frozen food onto a gigantic dolly. A metal ramp was positioned against the boxcar, which allowed either of the men to roll the loaded dolly from the boxcar to the storage facility once stacked to capacity. The men were similarly dressed as the manager. I begged to differ and sported a different style. Dressed in only my khaki jacket, jeans and white Converse basketball sneakers, I nodded to the men and picked up a box of frozen French fries,**** placing it on top of the other boxes on the dolly. It wasn't long before I started to shiver and watch my frozen breath shatter and fall to the floor of the boxcar. Looking at the scattered fragments of my breath, I inquired about the temperature inside the boxcar.

One man said: "It's thirty below zero."

The other man said: "You're going to freeze to death."

I thought it best to leave the car and pursue a job more suitable to my spring attire.

My employer saw me leave the boxcar in a fit of shivers and approached me.

"What are you a dumbass or something? I told you to put on the extreme winter gear before entering the boxcar. It was right there on hooks to the right side of the desk where you signed the agreement that absolved the company of death by freezing."

Genius debunked!

As for a sequel to *boink!*, it just wasn't in the literary cards. And that's exactly what I told my five deranged readers through certified letters, emails and Cease and Desist Orders. So in response to my denial of their incessant requests for a sequel, and after a period of getting to know each other through clandestine meetings, they kidnapped me. For days, they kept me in a beat-up Ford van in an Arby's parking lot (partial to *We Have the Meats*) and after torturing me with Confessional poetry, tutorials on academic networking and selected readings from *boink!*, they issued an ultimatum. Either I write the requested sequel or the time had come to engage in a friendly game of Russian roulette. One of my captive readers said: "Your writing makes me want to kill myself anyway."

It was a tense situation and the gun (snub nose 38) went into my hand first. However, after I explained (pleaded) to them that *boink!* was written under the authority and mandate of pure chance, dumbass luck if you will, i.e. I never intended to write it until a sequence of serendipitous occurrences forced a pen in my hand and led to the ultimate construction of the beloved tome. This appeased the fanatics. At least, they let me lower the "snub nose" from my temple and shoot at my foot. The odds weren't in favor of my foot. Enraged by a spot of blood on the floor the van and the deafening sound within the closed box-like nature of the machine (and a powerful hankering for beef), my book clubbers kicked me out of the van into the street. Once I had my bearings, I hobbled back to my hovel on Turret Street in a southwest neighborhood of Boston.

Years passed. I wrote books of poetry and short story collections, sending them out as Occupant mail to those in my neighborhood and beyond. Heteronyms (smacks of Pessoa…love the guy) of mine wrote many of their own books and found their home in the pages of *Fell Swoop: The All Bohemian Revue* (**see Appendix C**), a radar-less rag run by the ruthless Editor-for-Life, XJ "Pops" Dailey. My heteronyms went on to become quite famous and in high demand, mostly at county fairs and ice cream socials. Very few associated their God-given talents as an extension of mine. I became adept at disguise, and eventually moved beyond pig roasts, chocolate sodas and ribbons, accepting readings across the country and in Europe. You might say I was successful finally without any one knowing about it. A couple of paternity suits were slapped on me due to the heteronyms' successes and reprobate behaviors.

During this time, I also had the opportunity to interview a few poets and artists (not the five readers) I had come to know and communicate with after my kidnapping and bloody foot had made the back pages of some newspapers across the country. At first, these poets and artists thought I might be trying to drum up some enthusiasm for my work by shooting a big toe off in an Arby's parking lot. A number of years ago, a local artist had come to national prominence by taking pot shots (**see poem**) at his body and filming the results, along with some photographs of the carnage. It ushered in a new art movement known as *Carnage and Carnations*. Many of the framed photographs showed a carnation pinned on the artist (usually an undershirt), as well as featuring the bullet extracted from an arm or a leg in a glass case. The show was a big hit and led to other artists maiming themselves in the name of art. Art had suddenly become super real. Thinking back on it, I'm sure I could have promoted the Arby's "Big Toe" incident into something to my advantage, but I didn't due to my abhorrence of publicity. Eventually, the poets and artists came to realize that I was not a showoff or showboat, and once they did, an appropriate fascination possessed them via the passion I displayed for my paucity of serious readers, any readers, actually. I'm not sure why I wanted to interview them, but I did. I guess I felt that they were pretty great.

Then one day serendipity struck. I was out in my backyard raking leaves when a series of acorns attacked my head in rapid fire succession as if someone with a machine gun rigged for firing acorns was high in the oak tree and shooting at me. I have often enjoyed the rat-a-tat-tat ("You, dirty rat…") sound the acorns made bouncing off the yard shed prior to falling asleep. The force of the acorns, or rather the number of them, temporarily dazed me. I turned in a circle, looked up at the tree and took a staggered step backwards. As serendipity would have it, I tripped on the rake and fell to the ground, hitting my head on one of the large rocks that crisscross my yard like a miniature archipelago. I must have been out for a few seconds because in that interval I felt as if my soul had left my body.

This had happened to me once before, many many years ago, when I consented to smoke a pipe of hash with some leaves of DMT (dimethyltryptamine), the Spirit Molecule, sprinkled on it while at a holiday party. On a single hit, my soul shot from my body, taking up a position in a corner of the ceiling, watching the party below progress. I was a completely conscious spirit on the outside of my body and heard everything that was being discussed ("Where the fuck did he go?") as I hovered in the corner of the ceiling like a helium balloon. As a first time immaterial being, I didn't have an agenda and/or flight plan. I don't remember if I was one with everything at the time or not. Looking back on the experience, I don't think I was. It was more like taking a single jump on a trampoline and not coming down. I was free of gravity. If the ceiling hadn't been there, I might have just entered the night sky and from there who knows where I would have gone. But I felt no fear. A young woman held my hands and asked my soulless body to retrieve the soul that had taken flight. I wasn't sure how I pulled it off, but my soul dove back inside my body, leaving me with an intense headache as a side effect of reentry. There was a round of applause for my reanimated body by those only stoned on hash.

This time it was much different. There was no ceiling, but like the Soul 1 Solo

Flight, my soul took advantage of the situation and streamed through an open hatch of my body. I remember a few moments where my soul, perched on an oak branch, argued with two hostile blue jays about their incessant noise and attacks on my cats. My soul then flew off in the direction of twilight and the glimmers of a half moon. However, I distinctly remember staying within the boundaries of the Milky Way Galaxy. There is something quantum about the soul, which reminds me of an article I read recently about the microtubule structures in the billions of neurons in the brain that function as a quantum information and knowledge processing center. The authors of the article proposed that the quantum knowledge processed in these microtubules was equivalent to the soul or spirit, and that upon death, the knowledge accumulated (Know Thy Self etc.) by an individual headed for a more reliable cosmic atmosphere rather than degrading with the newly dead body (Dumbass in Space). I didn't think my head careering off stone killed me or anything, but here I was traveling in the matter/antimatter of space like a loose cannon of estranged particles. The soul was free and becoming quickly addicted to roaming freely through the blast furnaces of stars and everything.

Heavy, man, and it was – until my soul began to sputter and lurch like burned out engines on a jet. It went into a dive. I saw my body coming into view, lying on the ground next to the rock. I saw right through my body and into my brain and mind. *So the brain and mind are different entities than the soul*, I thought? And quite a show was going on inside my brain. All the identities I had accumulated over a lifetime, and up to this moment, were unleashed and were smashing into each other and annihilating each other. It was as if my consciousness and the thoughts and identities composing it were composed of charged and anti-charged particles, going at the business of annihilation like electrons and positrons in the Large Hadron Collider. The entire antimatter portion of my brain and mind was squaring off with the ordinary matter of me. It was like I had a midget universe inside my noodle. By the time my soul squeezed back into its corporeal form (**see poem**), goosebumps surfaced on my arms, legs and the back of my neck.

As I returned to consciousness, a consciousness still dazed and slightly bewildered, the title for my next work appeared in my mind, *Goosebumps of Antimatter*. By the time I got into the bathroom to check the damage to my bald head, I had grasped the entire structure of the book. It would be three books in one. The first book would be a selection of poems and stories (Occupant mail) chosen according to the Periodic Chart of Elements (revealed secret: Hydrogen told me to use the chart during Soul 2 Solo Flight); the second book would be composed by my heteronyms – Duck Martian, Ant McGoogle, Al Pants and Dik Tater; and the third book would be interviews with poets and artists. Besides structuring the book into three books in one, I decided to present what may vaguely resemble chapters as "Pages" and have the "Pages" run consecutively across the three books. For example, Book 1 has 11 Pages and runs more than 160 actual pages. As a carry over from *boink!*, I decided to maintain my love of the spontaneous parenthesis and whatever occurs inside of one is the result of the spontaneity of the text. My work has remained generally unpopular due to "techniques" like that. It exhibits a certain distain for following a structured path or design even when there is one.

So be it. As I washed and bandaged the wound on my head, I conceived that "Goosebumps" as a book, as an entertaining and dangerous read, would function as a dose of antimatter to the reader's consciousness, firing it up with unpredictability and suitable annihilations. It would blow up the brains of critics leaving a drool of unintelligible remarks and threats about my work and life. It would destabilize book shelves in libraries and corporate bookstores. It would guarantee me another five or six readers – readers who would plot to meet me, put my house and writing studio under surveillance or commit to driving me away in a stolen vehicle to a reeducation camp run by the most prestigious MFA writing schools and programs ("Stick to narrative poetry, dumbass.")

One final word: reading *boink!* is not a prerequisite to reading *Goosebumps of Antimatter*. It might be helpful and certainly would extend my readership of that master work, assuming its sequel (this is not a sequel) was released without fanfare as Occupant mail to still more ungrateful neighbors and friends.

For now or to begin: Attention papillae. It's erection time.

*Goosebumps: a roughness of the skin produced by erection of its papillae, especially from cold, fear, or a sudden feeling of excitement. Also goose pimples.
Origin: Goosebumps, 1919 from goose (n) + bump (n). Earlier in the same sense, goose flesh (c 1810) and goose skin (1785).

**Antimatter: In particle physics antimatter is material composed of antiparticles which have the same mass as particles of ordinary matter but opposite charges, as well as other particle properties, such as lepton and baryon numbers and quantum spin.

***boink!: Available from Lavender Ink as a free download. There are a few rare hard copies still in existence and available for purchase. Go to: www.lavenderink.org

****suggested reading: surprised by french fries by Joel Dailey (ugly duckling press, 2011).

(see poem)

Pot Shots

Pain and the body meet
On 50 Million Hand Guns Avenue
It's anytime
And the reason
Is the history of money
Who has it and why
So bang bang
And a bullet
Goes through the head
Of a cab driver
Into the heart of the young girl
By a fence
Who thought it was a good day
To jump rope
And it will find her friends
And grandfather
Having a smoke
At the kitchen table
The teenager running down the hill
The teacher correcting papers
The janitor cleaning lockers
It's a busy sucker
Likes the feel
Of tissue and bone
And searches for us
In malls
On highways
In backyards
Around the rim at the courts
It flies through walls
And doors
Enters with moonlight

Through windows
Like a bat after blood
It loves a good neck
And never looks back
At the design
Left on bed sheets
Or sidewalk
It's a bullet man
And it's in the face
Of the ex-wife
Ex-husband
Ex-children
Every now and then
Skips like a stone
Through a lung
Of a president
A movie star
A singer full of sad notes
It can't be stopped
It's all motion
The apple-pie bullet
The semiautomatic-all-we-plan-to-do
Is-obliterate-some-weekend-ducks-NRA-bullet
And it's available
Free as the market
Because God's in heaven
And still American
And knows about good guys and bad
And we trust in Him
Like a drive-by-shooting
To explain one day
The nature of violence

As He steps through clouds
(Mea culpa
Mea culpa
Mea culpa)
Twirls his six-shooters
In His hands
And takes a couple of pot shots
At us

from *Estuairies* #27 (1995)

(**see poem**)

The Naked Man in the Bathroom on Your Birthday

He's been drinking
with poets
and needs to tell you
Whitman believed
the body is the soul
and this is why
his head pops
around the shower curtain
and his eyes
like priests
on a procession
to a virgin
beneath a tree
with white flowers
smoke like incense
when they see water
swirling off buttocks
down thighs and calves
into the pond
of soap bubbles
around your feet.

He talks of the moon
he followed
on a path of steel clouds
as you lather breasts
whose nipples
brown and erect
curve upward
like morning prayers
to the sun.
It was high and full
and seemed to start

its journey
from somewhere in his head
when he thought
of love
as an ocean
of unknown creatures
who at the blackest depths
appear as flames
inside neon bodies.

The naked man in the bathroom
on your birthday
watches the rotation
of your hand
across abdomen and pubic hair
the slip of soap
past vagina
and remembers the dream
of the child
who grew up thinking
the body
is an act of will.
He recalls
the orbit of mother
when he felt sunlight
not blood
in his veins.
How she roamed the house
disguised as a ghost
with a mouthful
of diamonds.

The naked man in the bathroom
is a lover
willing to mine jewels
on the surface
of your soul
with his tongue
but handing over towel
and ending discussion
on the time it takes
for a present before work.

from *NEBO: A Literary Journal*, (Fall-Spring, 1989-90)

Book 1:
Invent Purpose

Like people, I imagine God dies in a variety of ways. This seems strange and contradictory to what we've been told all of our lives. God(s), goddesses, and the God of Abraham are immortal. Not mortal. Not made of carbon, water and other heavy elements cast to the winds of time by exploding (supernova) stars – stars in their death throes and rattling after billions of years of service burning alone in cold space.

God(s) are immaterial. Not made of material – thus forget about carbon and the other elements in the Periodic Chart of Elements (**see sonnet**). You can also throw in everything you know about quarks (up, down, strange, charm, top and bottom), protons, neutrons, electrons, atoms, molecules and the four known forces binding the whole experience of life and the universe together. The Gods of Olympus, Rome, the Pharaohs, Hindus, Buddhists and Abraham (**see story**) are outside of that. In fact, we've been told (or schooled or indoctrinated) that they created all of that electromagnetic stuff – good stuff, wondrous stuff, awe-inspiring stuff. Stuff – at least some of it – that proceeds dust to dust/star dust to star/dust – what we're made of in the final analysis.

Although, like I said, God dies in a variety of ways; the one immortalized death of God that we've all heard something about (especially Western tradition believers and fanatics) is the death of Jesus Christ (**see sonnet**). The story of His death has been told for over 2000 years and has billions of fans and converts. It's quite popular due to the fact we are mortal and Christ offers resurrection after death – a way not to be mortal (enjoy radical finitude) – a way to be perfect (perfected) – a way to live in harmony and love with God for all eternity – a place or state that denies the arrow of time access to its direction because there is no time, no spacetime fabric (**see Page Four**), and consequently, no Big Chill or Big Crunch (**see sonnet**) as surmised by the brightest minds. Eternity is the hang-out (polis) of souls – eternal souls – happier than clam souls beyond or behind the curtain of being (Maya) – just the other side of the singularity, perhaps – that fuzzy patch of nothing denied to our telescopes and computer probes and models.

But like I said (insist, insistent), God dies in a variety of ways. And even though there is an extensive and varied list of swan songs for us during our time on earth, I can't or won't produce a swan song list for God. Because there isn't one.

(**see sonnet**)

Bobby Socks

The circumstances of elements burden my heart
Last night I took to the sky
and wrote you a letter   not in stars
but in wisps of smoke about how things
enter the mind
We had to balance chemical equations in high school
Once I noticed the silver in your eyes
I understood the phases of moon   or was it mercury
After that we went bowling but didn't realize
the future stalked us from behind   banging garbage can lids
I imagine the Periodic Chart of Elements (**see Page Two**) has astonished
everyone at some point in their lives
We could invoke the moon   now   watch it
pool in our hands before slipping through fingers

(**see story**)

DISASTERLAND

According to insistent, persistent and mostly unreliable reports, the birth of every human being (along with the animals and insects, and debate continues to rage as to whether these beings are divine or not) offers the human being, starting with the stage of brave infancy, a complete and unabridged tour of Disasterland, formerly known as Earth, the third planet from the sun.

The above was in Lloyd's head (bald head, plus additional perks: beer gut, toothpick legs, flat feet, dashing eyes) when he woke up from his afternoon nap. He sat on the edge of his bed for a moment – saw that his room hadn't changed during a brief sojourn through a dreamless state. There were books everywhere, papers stuffed into three wastepaper baskets and paperclips and coins on the floor. Lloyd nodded in agreement to the unchanged status of things in his room. There was a time when he thought the objects in his room engaged in an all-out free-for-all once he donned the apparels of sleep. Convinced that they were no longer goofing on him, he took a second to gaze out the bedroom window. Disasterland was bathed in sunlight. So much so, the light falling on the hemlock trees in Lloyd's backyard seemed like a lover's kiss on the buoyant green needles. Lloyd liked to stand in the stand of those trees even during the coldest months in Disasterland. Trees meant something to Lloyd. At times, Lloyd equated Disasterland with Paradise. With a slight sigh, Lloyd stood up, brushed the crumbs from his white boxer shorts (he had a penchant for Ritz crackers before slipping off into Napperland) and began the search for shoes in the chaos of his room.

There are three major religions – Judaism, Christianity and Islam. Buddhism and Hinduism seem pretty big in terms of world-wide participants. Could there be four or five major religions? What's the Middle East got on Asia and India? Four or five is too damn many. Three is too damn many. There are usually a big three when it comes to basketball teams: Bird, McHale and the Chief; Kareem, Magic and Michael Cooper; Jordan, Pippen and Rodman; Shaq (equals 2) and Kobe; LeBron, Wade and Bosh. This is how the mind works sometimes.

The above was in Lloyd's head (bald head, plus additional perks: beer gut, toothpick legs, flat feet, dashing eyes) during the hunt for his shoes – Nike running sneakers, actually a size too big, due in part to the orthotics and the unproven fact that Lloyd's feet were shrinking. Really, just ask him.

Reader: "Lloyd, are your feet shrinking, and if so, why?"

Lloyd: "They've been shrinking for some time now, along with other critical parts of my body. I'm not sure of the reason. It's not like I have them submerged in water all day, and even if I did, or had an inclination to do so, they, and I'm talking mainly about my toes, don't look like testicles, do they?"

Disasterland is the only subject of the news and what people who own the news want those who don't own the news to know about (excluding those who blog their own reports and rely mostly on the same unreliable and/or slanted evidence on any given event in Disasterland). In other words, even though one's point of view is total bullshit, it most likely represents an overactive and/or underdeveloped imagination, doesn't it, and therefore has some validity, don't it (donut). People – those brave little infants now fully grown, in various parts of the world (including ours) remain committed to killing each other in the name of God and Allah; in the name of property, power and resources; in the name of money (show me...) and past and tragic wrongs: You're a savage (read: other) to me...so that makes you one, correct? *Life is one continuous mistake...History is a nightmare from which I'm trying to awake...*Dogen-zenji/Suzuki and Joyce, respectively. Continue please: the planet shedding layers of ice, new and cagey viruses and death in its motley array of forms; and last but not least, what the hell is going to become of us during the Robot Apocalypse?

The above was in Lloyd's head (bald head, plus additional perks: beer gut, toothpick legs, flat feet, dashing eyes) as he realized searching for his shoes prior to putting on a pair of pants was a dumbass thing to do. Lloyd stood there, shoes in hand. What were his options? He could proceed downstairs in his underwear with his shoes on his feet or in his hands. Would his wife, Lucy Mae,* rebuke him for this? Lloyd had been rebuked before, not by Lucy Mae, but by a member of the audience at a poetry reading. Lloyd had tried poetry for a while during his "bohemian" days.

The rebuke occurred at a community college in upstate New York. There was a bunch of poets jostling for a turn at the "open mic" and Lloyd was one of them. When Lloyd's turn arrived, he read an eleven page poem about a bad sunburn, the effect of amphetamines and cocaine on consciousness and pretty much the destruction of Los Angeles via a nuclear bomb in a suitcase. When he came off the stage, a young man said:

"I rebuke you in the name of my Lord and Savior, Jesus Christ."

"What?" Lloyd said, a bit stunned.

"You heard me," the man said.

"You can't do that," Lloyd said.

"You've been rebuked," the man said, walking away.

Lloyd gave up poetry for good (and his "bohemian" days) after trying out the same poem at a gathering of poets who gathered at a local (somewhat famous) poet's house. Again, all the poets let loose with their poems. After Lloyd read his, the German shepherd in the house bit him. The poet's wife defended the dog (**see poem**), and in a mild fit (ok, rage) told Lloyd to get the hell out of the house.

Lloyd stirred. Suddenly he imagined various world leaders in his room at a makeshift podium, offering up their lies and dotting their i's. As the venomous words spewed from their mouths, Lloyd flung one sneaker then the other in rapid succession at their hydra-like heads. *Mission Accomplished.* Lloyd embarked on the search for a decent pair of pants.

Some think that the planet, formerly known as Earth, has always set the stage for unique and plentiful disasters. Why just the other night, a comedian, trying to be the last comedian standing in a televised contest of raw wits, did a bit on that by noting that Disasterland should be considered in prime (primo) condition when compared to the past. "We're living in the best of times, not the worst," the comedian said, backing up his claim with a cogent review of medieval barber techniques (pinched from Steve Martin). There was no need for a laugh track once a patient's arms were gone and the stumps got infected, I guess. However, drone strikes (even packages delivered by drones) and terrorists getting their hands on nuclear materials offer a counter argument to the groovy times of the present. J. Robert Oppenheimer, the father of the atomic bomb, quoted the *Bhagavad Gita* after witnessing the first atomic blast during the Trinity test (three again) in New Mexico, on July 16, 1945: "Now I am become Death, the destroyer of worlds." He – and most of the other physicists working on the Manhattan Project – thought the unleashed power of nature should be shared with the world to prevent a nuclear arms race. What a bunch of prescient fools they turned out to be.

The above was in Lloyd's head (bald head, plus additional perks: beer gut, toothpick legs, flat feet, dashing eyes) during the hunt for a decent pair of pants. When he found a pair beneath the Shaker rocking chair by the window in the alcove of his room, he executed the proper technique and put them on one leg at a time.

Why is the mind so small in understanding its arrangement with time and space, and at other times, so large? Kant thought time and space were intuitions of the mind. Einstein made a fabric out of them – a pretty difficult one to understand, but a cloth of some type or unity in which all objects had their say in bending space and slowing down time, depending on their speed. At light speed my toenails would not grow so fast, which would please Lucy Mae, if I'm getting the gist of the theory.

The above was in Lloyd's head (bald head, plus additional perks: beer gut, toothpick legs, flat feet, dashing eyes) as he opened the door and proceeded downstairs. At the bottom of the stairs, Lucy Mae greeted him with a warm and toned smile.

"Not bad, honey," she said. "At least, you've got your pants on this time."

*(Full-bodied brew of womanhood)

from *Buffoons in the Gene Pool* (Lavender Ink/Fell Swoop, 2016)

(**see sonnet**)

Rearview Mirror

Hawking gives the universe 30 billion years
to morph into Crunch or Chill
Atomic clouds used to drift through my neighborhood
I'm no Prufrock
Uncertainty plays poker with the boys on Thursday night
Late in life Kant was unaware of his accomplishments
Word play asunder
What are dirty pennies made of
We can open a can of sunlight
or holler all we want about moneychangers
inside the temple
I've spent an adequate amount of time
under the sea   Though planets formed in the doorknob
grasped to slam the door

(see sonnet)

VIBES

Recent scholarship on Jesus asserts
the Romans seldom stripped a crucified man from the cross
Those familiar with the Tao understand the shortcomings
In the Theory of Everything   (burger/bagel)
Sugar Smacks was my favorite cereal during childhood
I also ate a lot of white bread and TV dinners
What is your favorite fact about food
I saw the Mick and Roger Maris hit back to back homeruns at the Stadium
Yesterday's word festival was a huge success
for those with diaphanous wings   or thesaurus handy
Blue Velvet was my Confirmation name
Don't chase balls into the street
Don't step out between parked cars
I have nothing against the woodpecker in a tree

from *Techniques in the Neighborhood of Sleep* (Spuyten Duyvil, 2016)

(see poem)

Dog Walk

Here's a reason
Here's a really important fact

It's mosquito season and blueprint night
Invades sleep

Dig
And we did

Now see the tunnels
We all must pass through

It's because our brains
Are so damn full of meaning

Plus TV
And that sociology to contend with

Romantic hands convert it
To Paradise

Chaos off the leash
Tunes its ears to birds

from *Techniques in the Neighborhood of Sleep* (Spuyten Duyvil, 2016)

(see poem)

Free Immanuel Kant

Objects defy perception
Over the right shoulder the politics of privilege maintains
  1. the notion of privilege
  2. limited government
  3. enough global gas to clog an avalanche
Bus exhaust and green energy refuse to mate in front of polarized cameras
Words are political
Spacetime is an intuition of the mind
                                        Get over it
The "I" of tomorrow assumes the position SOS say   or a bottle afloat in a
cosmic sea
It will find the shore – at least close enough   to proclaim
                              Alien Universe
That's right
Alienation is still the theme
       The parade of existentialists marching in avant-garde commercials for T-Mobil
       has texted despair (ladder of)
Release the prisoner or *HELP*   *I need somebody*
Thanks to the Beatles
You decide

from *Techniques in the Neighborhood of Sleep* (Spuyten Duyvil, 2016)

Periodic Table of Elements
(according to atomic number and including discovery date)
as a list (**see poem**)

	Element	Year	
1.	Hydrogen	1776	
2.	Helium	1895	
3.	Lithium	1817	
4.	Beryllium	1797	
5.	Boron	1808	
6.	Carbon	ancient	
7.	Nitrogen	1772	
8.	Oxygen	1774	
9.	Fluorine	1886	
10.	Neon	1898	
11.	Sodium	1807	
12.	Magnesium	1755	
13.	Aluminum	1825	(**see story**)
14.	Silicon	1824	
15.	Phosphorus	1669	
16.	Sulfur	ancient	
17.	Chlorine	1774	
18.	Argon	1894	
19.	Potassium	1807	
20.	Calcium	1808	
21.	Scandium	1879	
22.	Titanium	1791	
23.	Vanadium	1830	
24.	Chromium	1774	
25.	Manganese	1774	
26.	Iron	ancient	(**see poem**)
27.	Cobalt	1735	
28.	Nickel	1751	(**see poem**)
29.	Copper	ancient	
30.	Zinc	ancient	

31.	Gallium	1875	
32.	Germanium	1886	
33.	Arsenic	ancient	
34.	Selenium	1807	
35.	Bromine	1826	
36.	Krypton	1898	
37.	Rubidium	1861	
38.	Strontium	1790	(see poem)
39.	Yttrium	1994	
40.	Zirconium	1789	
41.	Niobium	1801	
42.	Molybdenum	1781	
43.	Technetium	1937	
44.	Ruthenium	1844	
45.	Rhodium	1803	
46.	Palladium	1803	
47.	Silver	ancient	(see story)
48.	Cadmium	1817	
49.	Indium	1863	
50.	Tin	ancient	
51.	Antimony	ancient	
52.	Tellurium	1783	
53.	Iodine	1811	
54.	Xenon	1898	
55.	Cesium	1860	
56.	Barium	1808	
57.	Lanthanum	1839	
58.	Cerium	1803	
59.	Praseodymium	1185	
60.	Neodymium	1885	
61.	Promethium	1945	
62.	Samarium	1879	
63.	Europium	1901	
64.	Gadolinium	1880	
65.	Terbium	1843	
66.	Dysprosium	1886	
67.	Holmium	1867	

68.	Erbium	1842	
69.	Thulium	1879	
70.	Ytterbium	1878	
71.	Lutetium	1902	
72.	Hafnium	1923	
73.	Tantalum	1802	
74.	Tungsten	1783	
75.	Rhenium	1925	
76.	Osmium	1803	
77.	Iridium	1803	
78.	Platinum	1735	
79.	Gold	ancient	**(see poem)**
80.	Mercury	ancient	**(see poem)**
81.	Thallium	1861	
82.	Lead	ancient	
83.	Bismuth	ancient	
84.	Polonium	1898	
85.	Astatine	1940	
86.	Radon	1900	
87.	Francium	1939	
88.	Radium	1898	
89.	Actinium	1899	
90.	Thorium	1829	
91.	Protactinium	1913	
92.	Uranium	1789	**(see poem)**
93.	Neptunium	1940	
94.	Plutonium	1940	
95.	Americium	1944	
96.	Curium	1944	
97.	Berkelium	1949	
98.	Californium	1950	
99.	Einsteinium	1952	**(see story)**
100.	Fermium	1952	
101.	Mendelevium	1955	
102.	Nobelium	1958	
103.	Lawrencium	1961	
104.	Rutherfordium	1964	

105. Dubnium	1967
106. Seaborgium	1974
107. Bohrium	1981
108. Hassium	1989
109. Meitnerium	1982
110. Darmstadtium	1994
111. Roentgenium	1994
112. Copernicium	1996
113. Ununtrium	2004
114. Flerovium	1998
115. Ununpentium	2004
116. Livermorium	2000
117. Ununseptium	2010
118. Ununoctium	2006

(see poem)

Postmodern Attention Span as a List

1. A collapsed bridge in the desolate light of yesterday.

2. Listen to this Sal: *I was in a bar/scratch that/restaurant/with my imagination on fire.*
  Then…

3. News on
  Background music on
  Fear of government –
  Stuff like that.

4. Marge and Harry joined a Laughter Club. "Laughter clubs are great," Marge chuckled.
  "Laughter Clubs are boss," Harry guffawed.

5. Romanticism like a kidney stone in Modernism like a kidney stone in Postmodernism.

6. Hesitation Ellipsis Hiatus Caveat (The gang's all here).

7. Composed of talk the known universe remains unknown.

8. A phalanx of mystics and critics bask in the relaxation of rules.

9. RULE.

10.

- Fingers
- Accurate wine pour
- Doubt
- Complete vibration
- Spanish guitars
- False or lost duende

- Hair replacement therapy
- UFOs
- Sports Psychologist
- Love

from *Techniques in the Neighborhood of Sleep* (Spuyten Duyvil, 2016)

(13. **see story**)

No More Mrs. Nice Guy

Cranked-out Sally insisted that Divine-Right-Kind-of-Guy* exit her bedroom post haste. Cranked-out Sally (from this point on referred to as C.O. Sally or just plain CO) had had a rough day at the office. Divine-Right-Kind-of-Guy **(from this point on referred to as D.R.K.G. {please move to the next available asterisk} or just plain DRKG***) didn't understand what a rough day meant or could mean for C.O. Sally. Lacking empathy, he chose not to inquire about her day and felt quite comfortable in the knowledge that a DRKG**** didn't need empathy to remain a favorite of his subjects.

"I'm not a subject or a subject of your subjectivity," CO said to D.R.K.G. {please move to the next available asterisk} on numerous occasions.

When piqued, she lamented:

"We're married, asshole!"

DRKG***** witnessed and recorded (in a small and stately notebook) a definite uptick in C.O. Sally's "pique" sessions after she had turned fifty years old and now deep into her fifties had turned this "you're no longer a part of any meaningful demographic" decade into an epiphanous mandate to lower the boom on those who crossed her path or who found themselves at cross purposes from hers.

As CO conveyed to D.R.K.G. {please move to the next available asterisk} via a small sauce pan to the back of his head one morning:

"I've had enough of being nice. I've been nice, really nice. And what comes back from being Miss Cherry Two Too – nothing but a kick in the shins, a kick in the head, a kick in the pantsuit and failed business models. That's it as far as I can tell."

DRKG****** didn't like that kind of talk or noggin bruise. In fact, he feared it. Was she referring to him or a whole battery of folks that pissed her off? Or both?

It couldn't just be me, D.R.K.G. {please move to the next available asterisk} often thought while on his throne (of what can be done about it or anything).

It hadn't always been that way between CO and DRKG*******. They had gone through the normal process of a relationship. Generationally outside the lure of Match.com, Cupid.com, Farmer's.com, Christiansaints.com, and the host of other dating services now available to lonely singles, CO and DRKG******** met at a singles mixer while in college (Hoboken Community College). CO was cute in the classical sense: body by Aphrodite, size by Amazon, eyes mined in

Ireland. D.R.K.G. {please move to the next available asterisk} could hold his own with .001 of Charles Atlas (shrugged or not) and the rest of the muscle men he read about or saw in the back of comic books or cheap magazines. Pheromones on the loose, they got drunk, romantically inclined, spawned kids and found success in their various vocations – in the case of CO, entrepreneur, and no vocation to speak of for DRKG********* (though he had some ideas: Brain Surgeon, TV Personality, Art Critic, Horse Trainer or Whisperer, Grants Administrator or Postmodern Bandit, Politician or Postmodern Bandit).

As known, entrepreneurship is not that easy unless you're a bank too big to fail. At first, a number of CO's business ventures flopped. Her line of fan pants (Tilted Windmills) – pants for men with tiny plastic fans sewn into the crotch area to keep the "boys" from overheating never took off with manly (mansplaining) menswear. And her single coffee cup maker for luxury vehicles didn't generate any profits – only lawsuits.

But then she hit on the idea of a monstrous-size cupcake – a cake four times the size of the regular size cupcake and decorated with anything the customer wanted: the bust a of former president or head of state, a replica of a marriage license or divorce degree, and totem animals of children, former lovers and Olympic heroes. You name it; CO could create it out of cream and butter fat. And she did and got everyone fat – Super Fat (not fly)! – until the whole nation (talkin' US of A) became one giant Land of Lard or, more specifically, lard-heads.

Also captured in the appellations: Fatheads or Fat Asses, whichever you prefer.

Forbes Magazine, in an exclusive article, "Dirigible Hips for Hipsters," detailed how CO's business model flamed from her garage to a small shop in the neighborhood, to multiple shops in multiple neighborhoods, to a line in local supermarkets, to cross-country distribution. The Ubiquitous Super-Size Cupcake Company had landed in the fatty tissues of the populace.

CO rolled in the dough (pun intended) and thought of taking her company public.

But good things (delicious things) don't often last. The days of riding around in cars without seat belts, shimmying up monkey bars with concrete landing areas and smoking at work or even in bars or even outside of bars were long gone. The Greatest Generation got to do these things but not subsequent ones. Freedom tempered by knowledge and 24/7 surveillance were the new freedoms. And the surveillance cameras conclusively showed what was happening:

Americans were fat and getting fatter.

Almost overnight, an Anti-Obese Crusade occupied (not Wall Street) the airways, and it wasn't long before global warming, terrorism and Wall Street thievery found the backseat of the news. The whole country was getting fatter by the minute, and it was CO's fault and those like her. We were supposed to be One Thin Nation under God, damn it (and screw body types – ecto, endo and meso). Laws were enacted that made it a crime to eat a giant cupcake, drink a giant soda, consume a tub of popcorn, munch on a burger (3 times the normal head size) filled with cheese and deep fried and nibble on supersize candy bars and other assorted treats – laws that prevented citizens from gorging themselves on foods that tickled their desire to consume foods and drinks that tickled their desire to eat more foods and drinks that tickled their desire…ad infinitum – foods chemically (salt, sugar, fat) created to hit the sweet spot in the brain and turn the neurons into saps that sent a single message: MORE! MORE! MORE!

Punishments for breaking the EATING LAWS ranged from being tasered on the street by a zealous cop for slurping a giant Slurpee to DVD lectures sent to your home by mayors and TV personalities in various cities – *The Obesity Tapes*, as they came to be called. The offenders had to watch them, write essays on why the DVDs were good for them and then sign up for Jenny Craig or Weight Watchers.

Some of the fat manufacturers went underground and a black market came into being. For a price, one could procure a giant-size bag of Doritos or gulp in an alleyway a King Kong soda.

CO stayed above ground and watched as her business went in the proverbial "shitter."

Who could blame her for being irritated with DRKG**********?

When she tried to talk to him about the culpability of the Big Telecommunications Companies (10. Softbank, 9. Deutsche Telecom, 8. Nippon Telegraph & Tel, 7. Telstra, 6.Telefonica, 5. America Movil, 4. Vodafone, 3. Verizon, 2. AT&T, 1. China Mobil) and Informational Technology Companies (1. Samsung, 2. Apple, 3. HP, 4. Foxconn, 5 IBM, 6. Panasonic, 7. Microsoft, 8. Dell, 9. Amazon.com, 10. Fujitsu) – about how they had a whole nation on their butts in front of computer screens and video games, let alone the state of neighborhoods, and how kids couldn't go out and play anymore, even if they knew how to play anymore – did he listen?

No. He simply mimed Chauncey Gardiner:

"I like to watch."

"But my business DRKG*********** is going out of business fast," CO said. "Then what will we do?"

"A man's home is his castle," DRKG************ said, before forking over the frying pan to his incensed mate.

*Jean Bodin (1530-1596), a French jurist and political philosopher. His writings helped to codify that wonderful medieval idea that God bestowed earthly power on kings – a power that was absolute in both political and spiritual authority.

**The divine right craze had a pretty good run during the reigns of James I of England (1603-1625) and Louis XIV of France (1638-1781).

***The divine right hoopla took a major hit via the American and French revolutions.

****What about the Pope?

*****The "popes" had a nice run before Jean Bodin, and it may be possible that JB got the divine right thing going on in his head from the Pope's direct link to God. Of course, this is pure speculation.

******Speculation is a powerful pastime for me. Say the church had fallen under the influence of St. Paul. Would there be any need of popes?

*******DRKG was not always a DRKG. Something had to have happened. Come on, it's the 21st century.

********Let's return to St. Paul for a moment. He was on his way to Damascus from Jerusalem to persecute some more Christians when a blinding light appeared in the sky and told him in no uncertain terms to knock the persecution crap off. St. Paul was stunned, and it took him some time to fully recover. However, the event changed his life – ideas, ideals and behavior. No one at the time told him that the intense light and voice that he had heard may have been the result of sunstroke, seizure, temporal lobe epilepsy, psychogenic blindness or mood disorders associated with psychotic spectrum symptoms. Demonic convulsion was the only other alternative at the time.

*********The blinding light for DRKG came in the form of a bolt of lightning – not a direct hit, but beneath his feet, a quick and painful zap after the bolt hit a tree in his yard while he was weeding in a patch of weeds.

**********DRKG's Road to Damascus came in the following clichéd epiphany: *A man's home is his castle.*

***********But is it….*when the phone's tapped anyway/orders from the DA* (Dylan)

************Le Creuset® Stainless Steel Nonstick 12.5" Frypan.13.5"Wx23.3"Dx3"H Tri-ply stainless steel construction: Full **aluminum** core Hard-anodized nonstick interior Brushed magnetic stainless steel exterior Ergonomic double-riveted stainless steel handles For use with traditional gas and electric, induction and ceramic cooktops Use with silicone, heat-resistant plastic or wooden utensils Dishwasher-broiler-and oven-safe to 500 degrees Made in China.

(26. **see poem**)

3

It's not a question of intelligence
Flowers fold into themselves
During thunderstorms
Knowing when to pause

The point of not coming to the point
Has to do with the rearrangement
Of what we perceive in front of us
Like a bus

The melting point of **iron** in the mother dust cloud
Was low enough to establish a core
Line by line
Language tolerates the mind's confusion

We are here
Grain accretions of temporality
& because it's summer the ice cream truck
Trundles through the neighborhood

from *Strip Meditation* (Igneus Press, 2009)

(28. **see poem**)

Rocks

The blue **nickel** of fate rolls

In the gutter of time

I was never indigenous or lived in a tent of gods

As magnificent as the sky

I arrived in a polar vortex of wind

Staked flag in precious rock and wept

It was Saturday

The internal clock of earth ticked green

And wild

We are all screwed up

Buddha said: All is suffering

And went supernova

Each day the light from old or dead stars

Faints in consciousness

We want to play

We're children

Clouds are kites without strings

In our tiny hands

It's not enough to offer maps

And clues of existence

Buried in light

Words improvise

 Accelerate and soar

Syllables sky dive in and out of identity

Not oblivion

Language hoards the instant

Like a precious rock

(38. **see poem**)

Reverie in a Shaft of Light

Forget consciousness
I'm in the declarative mode
Sometimes a line a phrase a melody
Enters the mind as part of the evaporation cycle
There is a story to tell
The time the weather whisked you away
To a cabin in the woods
The hunger you felt in the lips kissing yours
The way the History Channel missed your life completely
Why it's pouring outside
Puddles as a smashing success

As a child I played *Capture the Flag*
Threw eggs at passing cars
Dad worked his job
Mother…her neurosis
Strontium 90 ensconced in clouds
Rained on the neighborhood
I was safe under a wooden desk
Or when making the sign of the cross
Now I pack heat
Attend the opera
Admire the art thief next door

Contradiction molds us
Into the personalities of light
The mind is a black hole
The body plays on a silver screen
To a packed audience
Celebrities of the ungraspable
We choose quotidian sides
Language is our home –
The nerve center of philosophy
A preliterate moon reflects what we name
In the drift of stars

(47. **see story**)

BLING IN THE NURSING HOME

At the ripe old age of 60 (60 is the new 50), George "Georgie Boy" Hammer bought a pair of exquisitely priced dark brown Arrowhead II Kiltie Tassel loafers from an exclusive men's shoe store – Extravagant Feet – located in the heart of Smog City and nestled between the outrageously popular Bling Factory Outlet and the monstrously engaging (and commercially related) Bling Factory Outlet's Outlet. These beloved jewelry and accoutrement stores catered to the young and hip (hop), which "Georgie Boy" – despite recent clandestine hair plug work and chin-chin-chinny tucks along with starburst white, laboratory-enhanced teeth {pling – remember that sound, as in heavy sexual (though retro-commercial) overtones from the lost 80's (say Ultra Bright toothpaste) prior to ubiquitous dissolving whitening strips and advanced laser polishing by disinterested dental hygienists} – was not.

"Gerogie Boy" had missed the hip bus and the hip hop bus too (by golly) from the very moment of his conception and/or reincarnation. In fact, he came into his planetary existence a prisoner (at the very least a victim) of staid and conventional dress (outfit-challenged). Although he would never be accused of looking like a cadet in the Red Army of Mao Se Tung, he did come across as an entrenched resident of Drabsville, and was duly christened by highly critical family members (the whole clan of them: parents, siblings, aunts, uncles and cousins) with the moniker *The Man Without Style*, before the first sex pheromones sashayed (wafted) through the pubescent atmosphere of (in his case) his late teenage years.

For example, during the wild and whacky period of bell-bottom jeans (circa late 60's – 70's), "Georgie Boy" did not only shun the pealing denim (including those adored with peace and astrological signs), but also conventional wranglers, preferring instead to stick with khaki slacks and a pressed short-sleeve madras shirt. Interestingly (if you're a style buff {00N}), he seemed to hold up quite well, even as he was dismissed by one young lady after another (during a time when it was quite permissible {circa late 60's - early 70's} and even encouraged {collective wish fulfillment}for young men and women to participate fully and freely in the blissful moments of love suddenly throwing a "wrench" in the ordinary sense of planetary time – the inexorable and implacable march of centuries to some unknown teleological end {known in more erudite circles as the inevitable and relentless operation (implementation) of the second law of thermodynamics) as a regrettable, lamentable and entropic oddball.

"Nope," "Georgie Boy" would say. "If I can't get any because of the way I dress, then I shall remain a Bachelor in the Universe of Things, a single-minded Columbus on the fourth-dimensional timeline of my tiny sea."

Of course, nobody in his family (the whole clan of them – parents, siblings, aunts, uncles and cousins) knew what the hell he was talking about.

"He's a freaking nincompoop," his brother, Pete, exhorted during the ever popular Disco Period (circa mid to late 70's), when everyone, who was anyone, danced beneath shining crystal balls to a relentless four-on-the-floor beat laced with reverberated vocals in rhinestone-studded leisure suits and see-thru sheer red dresses on the very edges of platform shoes and spiked heels, respectively.

"That's for...for sure," his sister Matilda stuttered during a glitch in time (text time) which mysteriously supported (via the misguided or misused elliptic gap) her penchant for dreadlocks and smoking splefs in the back of luxury sedans while cruising the beach scenes in coastal cites around the globe (circa anytime).

"Style ain't for everyone," "Georgie Boy" told himself, actually repeated it like a mantra of OM, if you will, while every screen (computer, movie, television, cell phone) in the Western World flashed the following subliminal message: *Style is Substance*, varying it on occasion to burrow into the brain (along with an irresistible craving for popcorn and Coke) as *Substance is Dead*.

Still, time in its bugle-weariness marched on (hut, two, three, four) while Georgie Boy shuddered in his lonely kingdom (secretly plotting a hair plug revolution) of conservative (compassionate) blue suits, muted ties, and ancient wing-tips – a connect-the-dot trajectory from the short-sleeve white shirts and clip-on tie from his boyhood days (and sadly, dear reader, the following semi-intrusive "Georgie Boy" diary entry comes from those bleak days: *Dear Diary, Today, mom made sure my shirt was tucked in and she matted my cowlick with mom spit. She also made me wear black rubbers over my new combat boots with the cool army guys with their bayonets. Of course, I got beat up by the other kids. What kind of choice did they have?* {Author's Note: "Georgie Boy" Hammer could never hear the phrase *Your mother wears combat boots* without recalling this humiliating episode from his early life. More than likely, incidents like this {or maybe just this one} propelled him to change his name from *Smith* to *Hammer.* He would have preferred *Hammered*, but the folks at the *Office of Fictional Names and False Identities* (OFNFI) were opposed to verbs as valid, fake names.}) to his present work (and attire) as an actuary in the firm of Grey, Grey & Sons.

The purchase of tassel loafers at *Extravagant Feet* signaled something was up (the revolution will not be televised), some rift or split in the "Georgie Boy's" planetary experience was underway. By the time he left the store, the rift had widened and a transformation (transfiguration) of his senses was in full-tilt boogie, enabling him as he hit the street to hear a sound (and ideophone actually): *bling* and/or the music composed by a ray of light striking a diamond. He stood in hushed awe in the middle of Smog City, with cars, buses, trucks and the *herd* all around him. *Bling bling* rang again and "Georgie-Boy" picked up the sound like the perked ears of dogs snaring silent whistles (Hear, fella). He wasn't sure if the sound came from The Bling Factory Outlet or The Bling Factory Outlet's Outlet. It didn't matter. The sound had an electromagnetism to it and pulled him to the right until he found himself gazing at the shining objects in the display window of The Bling Factory Outlet. In a trance, he peered at the glistening objects as he read the store's merchandise guarantee, rendered in flashy atomic-orange neon upper case letters: *OUR JEWELRY (OTHER THAN OUR DIAMONDS) IS MADE FROM THE HIGHEST QUALITY AUSTRIAN CRYSTALS WITH THE BEST SILVER PLATING POSSIBLE!*

"Georgie Boy" entered the store with the music of the spheres cruising through his body like the exhilaration of a first kiss.

"I'm ready," he said, approaching the first jewelry case and the young woman behind it, radiant as Isis in a golden storm of light, and looking phat in her black V-neck Goddess Top with foil and studs, white Janelle shorts and Baby Phat Ellen sandals, highlighted by just a single accessory, a Diamond Half Moon Pendant Choker gracing her slender neck.

"You're ready for what, sir," the young women politely asked.

"Bling-bling me," "Georgie-Boy" said.

"Don't you mean IcedOutFromHeadToToe?" the young woman laughed.

"Proceed," George-Boy said, with a wide and wild smile on his face.

The next day, when "Georgie Boy" showed up at his sister Matilda's house in the exclusive suburbs of Smog-by-the Sea, glowing like a supernova in his conservation (compassionate) blue suit iced out with a 10K White Gold Men's Rope Hip Hop Chain, a **Silver** Batman Bling Watch, a solid White Leather Belt, a Thug Fashion Five Strand Diamond CZ Hip Hop Bracelet, along with the Arrowhead II Kiltie Tassel loafers on his feet, and bearing a set of Black Glass Pimp Cups for her and her family, she knew something had to be done and done quickly. Mental health clinic or assisted living, she thought, shielding her eyes with her hands from the bling-glare, before pouring herself and "Georgie Boy" a stiff one into the pimp cups.

"Jesus, "Georgie Boy," she said, gulping bourbon and trying to calm herself. "That's quite a look. I think I should call Pete."

"Bling-bling," "Georgie Boy" said, sipping from his pimp cup.

After conferring with her brother Pete over the phone (whose only response was: What a freaking nincompoop!) over "Georgie Boy's" new and sudden style shifts (including the aforementioned hair plugs, chin-chin-chinny tucks and starburst white laboratory-enhanced teeth), it seemed plausible (and preferable) to place (register) him (60 is the new 80) in The Sunshine and Darkness Nursing Home and Independent Living Complex for the Young at Heart, a well-known (and fairly expensive) facility for the elderly, semi-elderly and want-to-be elderly in Smog City.

"Georgie Boy" enthralled and dazzled by his sparkling new personality seemed to care less where he lived (forced retirement and all) until he saw the sign (upper case letters in fuchsia script) posted on the front door of his new abode upon his arrival the following week with his stressed siblings: BLING IN THE NURSING HOME IS STRICTLY FORBIDDEN (and in small print near the bottom of the sign: *for insurance reasons and the deleterious effect of ideophones on the aged*).

Then the fight was on.

from *Altercations in the Quiet Car* (Lavender Ink/Fell Swoop, 2010)

(79. **see poem**)

Rubric

4

Four blondes smoking cigarettes under a fall lamp
Syntax is complex
Superheated coffee cups imitating dawn
Style unique & appropriate to purpose
A bouquet of high-heels on brick sidewalks
Stays focused on topic
Eyes shift into red cabs
Use of high frequency words
Full of office products buildings linger without tasks
Details fit where they belong
Zero in on rivers
Tone appropriate & controlled
Copper leaves snap in a stiff wind
Awareness of audience
Palms of **gold**

3

Three brunettes smoking cigarettes by a small lamp
Syntax is fairly complex
Heated coffee cups imitating dawn
Style unique & fits purpose
A bouquet of pumps on brick sidewalks
Focused on topic
Eyes follow red cabs
Use of high frequency words
Full of office products buildings languish without tasks
Details fit where they belong
Zero in on tributaries
Tone appropriate & monitored
Russet leaves drift in the wind
Awareness of audience
Palms of gold

2

Two redheads smoking cigarettes with a flashlight
Syntax is nearly complex
Warm coffee cups imitate dawn
Style stolen & feigns purpose
A bouquet of saddle shoes on brick sidewalks
Unfocused topic
Eyes hop into red cabs
Use of swear words
Full of office products buildings vanish into tasks
Details flit where they belong
Zero in on creeks
Tone brash & free
Leaves drift in the wind
Awareness of audience
Palms of gold

1

One black-haired beauty smoking a cigarette
Syntax is recklessly simple
Coffee cup imitates dawn
Style without purpose
A bouquet of slippers on brick sidewalks
Unknown topic
Eyes like red cabs
Use of erotic words
Full of office products buildings crumble
Details slip where they belong
Zero in on raindrops
Tone whispered into ear
Drift in the wind
Awareness
Gold

from *Modulations* (Asylum Arts, 1998)

(80. **see poem**)

Precipice of Hope

I open the cage of regret
to free the cries of birds at sea
They're not lost I repeat

to myself in prayer
The sky is a blanket of waves
a language in motion

I used to sell poems like this one
on street corners
until the ice cream due home

melted
This is the daddy long-legs of time
The metaphysics of the present narrative

plummeted via gravity's mandate
thus, the expression *Don a Disguise* became popular
in the lexicon of saints and addicts

I wish I had stolen the hot air balloon
from Murray's Car Emporium
instead of the '57 **Mercury** Turnpike Cruiser

Synonyms for "flabbergasted" peal
in the dictionary of yesterday's mistakes
I said you were gorgeous and disarmed

by the sophistication of trees
Who knew they would lecture us
on their blossoms

Sometimes in the minds of materialists
waves of disorder pound
the shores of logic

(92. **see poem**)

BALMY LIPS

Who could have predicted the perfect mall
a place where all of us would go
to buy and sell
the bits of language still left on our tongues:
blue sky
child
warm day
for December

***

Kiss me honey
you make me hot

***

Look at the world twirling like a fish
in a cameraman's eyes
O the spin of image and fact
the tacky jargon posted on the refrigerator:
Check out OS2 Warp
Oz is Dead
Pentium chips and mugs
of your favorite right-wing fat mouth
on sale
in time for Christmas

***

I licked your breasts
during the Pledge of Allegiance

***

Transmissions come and go
it's part of an alien culture
pill of paranoia
the reward for being a good citizen
Let's not strain here
pull groin or stomach muscle
to show
the page is a business of space and signs

***

The money I make
is for your
sexual wardrobe

***

It's not like I never met a philosopher
I've known plenty of them
dirt under nails
holes in pants and shoes
always up for a shot and a beer
addicted to horizon and chance
the play of clocks
in the lovely eyes of lost women
the constant jokes and blubber of reputation
I
wash and wax my car
collage my mind with sprinklers and bad debt
so you know
I know what's going on

***

O bend me twist me
lilt of legs
hem of dress

***

The prison of fettered conversation
"There's so little to celebrate today."
Something about Worcestershire sauce.
Talk about heavy duty!"
Saying we can't help ourselves.
In this case.
"That's a different case."
Joy of living.
"I'm sorry – not crazy enough."
Reminded every day not to let the bastards get you.
"That's what you're saying?
They tell me you look great."
Lots of time. We can't. We try to wake up and say hmmm.
"That's the way he looked at things."
I can remember one time – shortly such a – the only time – there is.
"She's in that department?"
Big girl. Joy of the morning.
"I noticed your secretary …"
Too bad …
"One hand …"
Happiness is …
"That's right …"
At some point …
"Kind of …"
That way you have to appreciate what you've got.
"Not a very friendly man."
57 when he died.

***

She poured out of her sex outfit
she was a flood of flesh

***

It was a time in which famous people were shot and killed
a time of great environmental catastrophes
skies darkened by reactor mishaps
young children wandering streets on **uranium** legs
Debates … on and on
A cold war came and went
A time that smelled of oil and cigarettes
of nameless politicians
who lived in a white space
surrounded by fire
and death
who told the poor to get off
their butts
to control sexual organs
who screamed like preachers
about family
and work
in their rat-lever techno-industries

***

Kiss me
over and over again

from *Modulations* (Asylum Arts, 1998)

(99. **see story**)

Permission

1.   This story begins with your permission.

     As you may recall, I sent you an email on Tuesday asking for your permission to begin the story, and if not, would this be a suitable second sentence to present to my readers while I waited for your response. I have taken the license in the third sentence to answer for you in the fourth. I'm just not sure that it is and would like to get started anyway.

2.   This story begins with your permission or not.

I know that we're in agreement that nothing much is being said today except for the standard stuff. The talk shows keep busy with those who keep a close eye on the society and the state of the world. I think *keeping an eye on* is important use of the cliché (but I'm not sure why).

3.   This story begins with your permission or doesn't it?

Recently, I read a short history of the Inquisition, entitled *A Short History of the Inquisition*, and discovered that it came in a variety of timeframes and growth spurts, i.e., the Medieval Inquisition, the Spanish Inquisition, and the Roman Inquisition. It is clear that many people died for their heretical beliefs, and that each phase of the Inquisition (medieval, Spanish, Roman) became more efficient via record-keeping, ongoing training on how to interrogate, and if necessary, torture someone, and the development of a class of techno-bureaucrats who went to work every day in the Office of Inquisition. The Roman Inquisition went on until 1907 until it morphed into The Congregation of the Doctrine of Faith – a watch group still in session and formerly headed by Pope Benedict XVI (now retired).

1.   This story begins with your permission.

Faith is a complex subject, wouldn't you agree? The human brain reaches a certain stage of development after eons of interstellar antics and collisions, and eventually arrives or comes to an awareness of death. That what is going on will not one day be going on. It takes considerable grey matter to perceive that fact and considerable more to accept and understand it. Faith allows us to bridge the gap in what we understand or don't. There are, after all, gaps in what we think we understand. For an example, we used to understand (or believe) that the earth was at the center of celestial motion – the sun orbiting it etc., with dear Galileo spending his life under house arrest for knowing this was not the case. I wrote a sonnet recently that makes it quite clear we have bridged that previous misunderstanding with a more appropriate knowledge of the heavens. I present it now for your enjoyment:

Costume Jewelry

Now the ocean comes in from its grey depression
sits on flowers   marries a cute meteorologist
and it's 30 degrees Fahrenheit/-1.11111 degrees Celsius
as your hand shivers in mine
What if I said the brain is a frozen tundra   or yogurt
Would I be banned from the Summer Olympics
be forced to take a course on the necessity of geography
Not once in the history of our immaculate conception
have I felt disconnected   We fell in love with the street
before it fell in love with us   According to the most reliable pollsters
25% of the American people believe the sun orbits the earth
I used to be a fact checker for the New Yorker
O those facts were bastards
in disguise

2.   This story begins with your permission or not.

I believe Kierkegaard wondered if faith is commensurate or incommensurate with reality.

3.   This story begins with your permission or doesn't it?

The story I've been commissioned to write has to do with your inability and/or lack of desire to grasp the inevitability of death (correct?). The question is why?

1.   This story begins with your permission.

Why is a ponderous and noble word, don't you think? Back in my undergraduate days, before I met Judy, (which ultimately led to a series of absurd consequences that I hope to reveal to you, if what I write decides to plummet in that direction), I read Martin Heidegger's *Introduction to Metaphysics*. Martin chose the following sentence as the opening sentence of his book: *Why is there something rather nothing?* I wish I knew, don't you?

2.   This story begins with your permission or not.

Plummet is also a fascinating word. Didn't Chicken Little think the sky was falling? **Einstein (ium)** worked out the details on gravity. The Fall of Man is an interesting story to hear or be told prior to one's kindergarten years. Nothing… no thing… as opposed to something…some thing. However, there has been intense fascination and speculation on the part of some physicists lately about the possibility of the universe, you and me, also) coming into existence out of nothing. This should alleviate some of the questions about what are we doing here and what the end game might be. Permit me one more sonnet. Here goes:

Oops

We need to know we're no longer here
before proceeding   (bitching about where we went)
Buses and other forms of transportation have synced
their schedules and timetables to this knowledge
It is so quiet from a human perspective
birds can hear themselves chirp   Think
birdbrain if you must   but don't leave your virtual chair
The television is on   The news is all good
Carbon dioxide levels in the atmosphere have subsided
Ocean levels are receding and beach front property
has re-emerged in the brilliant light
The earth remains a blue pearl in a cosmic sea
Let's get on with it   now
that we're not here

from *Techniques in the Neighborhood of Sleep* (Spuyten Duyvil, 2016)

3.   This story begins with your permission or doesn't it?

Let's get back to the Cold War, considering the recent activity of Russia in the Ukraine. Raise your hand if you ever hid under a wooden desk waiting for a nuclear blast. Did you feel safe doing that after brushing up on the arms race? I heard on television the other night that Eisenhower bluffed the Russians into thinking that he might use nuclear weapons but had no intention of ever doing such a thing. He had seen war. He had been the Supreme Commander of the Allied Forces during World War 2. He knew destruction and didn't want that for anyone. Bobby Kennedy, however, asked his kids if they wanted to move from Washington, DC, to out west, thinking that a nuclear showdown was possible with Russia via the Cuban missile crisis.

Closer to today's date (August 2, 2014), I caught John Oliver on his show, *Last Week Tonight*, last night. John had a few things to say about our nuclear weapons apathy and the overall safety of them (see him on YouTube for the laughs). Recently, a House Committee meeting on nuclear weapon safety registered an audience, according to John, equivalent to a weekday crowd at an open mic poetry slam. Hundreds of thousands turned out in Central Park to protest for nuclear disarmament in the eighties. As for safety, here's one to consider: a Major General and a Vice-Admiral were relieved of their direct access to launch procedures for odd and disreputable behavior. The Major General lost his privileges due to intoxicated behavior while in Russia, which included getting into a fight in a Mexican restaurant. There was a Russian Beatles tribute band on stage at the restaurant and the Major General got into fisticuffs with a band member (or patron) over his desire to play the guitar. The Vice-Admiral got caught using counterfeit chips in a Vegas casino. Of course, military officers suspended for cheating on nuclear weapons proficiency tests has also been in the news of late.

1.   This story begins with your permission. I've always wanted to meet Bob Dylan (*A Hard Rain's a-Gonna Fall*). As for Judy, she was a successful thief, a person who more or less owned Wall Street the day I met her. She gave me permission to write her story, which went something like this one, if I could only find it and send it to you for your approval.

2. This story begins with your permission or not.

    I understand that I sort of "promised" to disclose the absurd
    consequences of my affair and/or entanglement with Judy. The
    best and most efficient way for me to accomplish

this is to ask you to bear a final sonnet. Thus:

NORTH BY NORTHWEST

The dream I'm running down a narrow tunnel
into the next visual a tow truck careening down a street
clogged with snow the man in the truck says "Hop in."
He takes me to his house he wants to borrow money
I look in my wallet a ten and two ones not enough I think
I need the money for the subway There's another man
in the house dark shades grey suit black tie shuffling
and organizing papers I run from the house the neighborhood
echoes Secrets are after him I can't be certain I take my seat
on the subway it's traveling south how can that be
the title is *North by Northwest* Judy Judy Judy I'm Gary Grant
foreign spies are after me tow truck guy and his friend think
I'm a government agent My daughter calls me on the cell
"Dad where are you," she says. "What are you doing?"

3. This story begins with your permission or doesn't it?

PAGE THREE

This morning I wrote Page One upon waking up from a pretty good night's sleep (**see poem**). Pretty much all the sentences in Page One were aligned in my mind as I got out of bed, around 6:30 A.M. No dream hangover (**see poem**) – a fragment of one, maybe. I was on a train with some other guys and we were all packing heat. One of the guys looked like Hitler. We were about to shoot at each other but didn't. No reason. The dream disappeared into a tunnel, along with the train.

I wrote Page One with pen and paper before my first cup of coffee. No big deal. The same goes for the fact that it happens to be Thursday, July 24, 2014. I'm not an advocate of dating writing, a bit of a superstition, I guess. I don't consider mentioning the date that Page One was written as an act of dating this piece of writing. It just happens to be Thursday, July 24, 2014. Later today, I have to go to Tufts Medical Center in downtown (Chinatown) Boston to have a patch of squamous cell cancer removed from my chest. Again, no big deal, I've been dealing with dermatologists (**see story**) for a long time. If you're interested, you can check out how my bouts with skin cancer got started by reading my second book of poetry, *White Man Appears on Southern California Beach*. I think Abe.com has some copies for sale. I would also be happy to send you a copy for free plus shipping and handling. Five bucks will cover that and as a bonus I will include my well-received CD, *Improvised Trees*. So slip a Lincoln (**see story**) in the mail addressed to: Richard Martin, 40 Searle Rd, West Roxbury, MA 02132.

(**see poem**)

TECHNIQUES IN THE NEIGHBORHOOD OF SLEEP

for Rich Blevins

1

Sleep ticked
in the bright
handcuffs

I was out
of rubies and
mouthwash

The sun
in a pocket
of tenebrosity

I had spent
the day
writing synonyms

for fatigue
on a wordless
blackboard

Lethargy
Lassitude
Listlessness

It was the
image of your
body

in a procession
of metaphors that
secured night

2

Electric slang available when cooing
To pigeons or addressing concepts

Alive to concepts
Ones that flutter through my mind

Pigeons were once Renaissance artists
Concept here is invention

Addressing with paint & fortitude
The ceilings of heaven

Maybe reincarnation (a bouquet
Of it) or karma –

Some kind of humor lodged
In the mechanism of eternal sleep

That the sky explodes into beginning re-
Arrangement & words is more of an idea

Projection uncertainty of mind & hand
As they foment digression & white space

While my neck bobs
In an aesthetic of tempo & grease

On streets with brushes &
The alarm of competent assistants

3

I went to sleep in a haystack of thought
Time was a needle   concept   word
Morning expected to dawn
In a storm of false accusations

The weather report was all over me
I would turn cold at first
Become blue crystals of air   then
Set the neighborhood on fire with heat

Methodology came under attack
I had no formal education
In the interpretation of dreams
Placed in a poetic context

Night chased into a marriage
License of palm trees and boisterous
Waves fell apart in token   line
Breaks Clouds extinguished flames

I remembered the scent of a lost lover
Neighbors located their handguns
Hoisted flags of cultural heroes
The right to bear arms

I was target practice –
On my way to the store for basic supplies
(Pins and time for hands and feet) –
And survived in a firefight   of pillows

4

Of course I was in a chair or some underwater contraption

with hammerhead sharks and egg salad sandwiches

floating around me

I was a bit of a morsel in a rough time

It seemed sleep deprivation was bumped from a two credit

course to a four credit one at the local university due

to a drop in the GNP In addition the tectonic

slippage of one century into or under another had

turned the progress of ideas into a National Security

State Go figure But like I have indicated I had my own

immediate situation to deal with

I   mean   and   now   I   am   addressing   you   as   if
you   were

        me   Don't   I   remember   or   is   that   you   in
the   haze

of   recollection   remembering   the   halcyon   days   of   love   or
is

        that   a   revision   in   our   judgment   as   if
errors were

an   Olympic   sport   Tell   me   why   memory   reconfigures
the

        death   of   relationship   into   what   was   impossible in the
possible

Are   we   just   ephemeral   beings yes   or   no   guests
on   a

        disappearing   cosmic stage   yes   or   no   and   wide   awake

or   asleep yes   or   no   with   enviable   and   unanswerable
questions

5

During the latest migration into the bowels of sleep the windows of
the house were open and it was snowing outside – a long and painful
snow of thundering white and wind. I opened the windows before
retiring in case I had forgotten to do something:

1. Go to the store
2. Shimmy down a drainpipe to your room
3. Watch you sleep
4. Pretend I was a ghost
5. Sleep researcher
6. Ex-l(over), new l(over), your l(over)

My dad was a sleepwalker
always carried a BB gun with him
      on trips into shadows
enjoyed taking random shots at night birds
      and cohorts
from the roof of his house.

I'm not asleep now.
The windows remain open.
I'm not sure if there is a connection between the activities of sleep and
the activities of death.
It's hard to meditate on nothing – a nothing fully alive and productive.
I remember now how our bodies touched in restless sleep and melted
darkness.

6

Sometimes I sleep in a ménage of catcalls and weasels
With a hurricane outside the bedroom window
Politicians with gums debate politicians without gums
The molecule of what really is
Has finally been defined

At the very least
I grew up within the boundary lines of the semi-
Conscious
Dreams like apples fell from the sky
My skin soaked through with clouds
I wandered the wayward path
To kiss into life the memory
Of the unknown

Thus my fight with school books came
To the tragic end
Of a new beginning
I clamored for roads made of peaches and dust
Released misery from its contract
Campaigned for the right of unsolved mysteries
Wrote essays on the joys of somnambulant objects

I know
I hesitated in the arms of beauty
Went to the mat in a sweat of love
The past etched its demands in my forehead

There are tunnels of sleep
Moments I drift awake in raucous shouts
And gurgling
I'm home
Traced across the map I am

7

I took the sleeping pill according to the instructions on the amber vial and the ghosts arrived. Some traveled with chilled bottles of French champagne and hair dye – encouraged celebration and a flexible identity in the milieu of vortex. Others camped with neurons set on stun. The task was straightforward: drop a word – rosebud, banana, shoelace, tiger – into a bottomless well, entertainment during the trek across the hemispheres of the brain.

It was a gorgeous night. The usual symbols for the universe sparkled, raced and decayed. New worlds were and weren't. Wars were specks – blemishes on the sidereal screen. I traveled through sight and sound, learned the alphabet of jazz, tasted honey on sweet lips. It was all part of a package deal. The vial mentioned strange and unusual dreams. The ghosts spoke of the outer edge and the beginning of time. I felt timelessness in my bones. My nose sniffed the rocky terrains of earth for clues. I was mountain and valley. I may have barked.

I used to be afraid of ghosts. They came in so many shades of thought. There were the Holy Ghost and ghost particles in the gold mines and tunnels under the ocean and in the ice of Antarctic. The materiality of the immaterial came to mind as my options to visit the past, present or future became the topic of conversation. Was I asleep or not when I called out your name in the morning chill?

8

Words muttered under the influence of sleep:

Angelic

Oubliette

Bosky

Pomegranate

Froufrou

Augury

Vendetta

Recusant

Feckless

Iconoclast

Countermand

Mephitic

Mad

Hatter

Higgs

9

Now sleep is rolled into tight curls
And hungers for space
Forgive me   if it is   morning   noon   or night
I have journeyed this   far
Into the language of silence   Not really
I saw you standing in a skiff
On a stranded ocean – seagulls in full
Conversation above your head   some-
Thing about the sky signaled a sly smile
Like me you were headed some place
Outside the polis of dreams
This is the "line"   no the next after the next
To present the rhetorical questions

Where is that? Have we been there before?

Seen a replica
Perhaps on television
          A subliminal moment
After the blond buried in potato chips
The universe works microwave radiation
Into a map of lost galaxies – those
That disappeared over a horizon we thought
Was there   but wasn't
It's not my job to make sense
I'm asleep   tucked inside a fetal vision
When it's time for me to walk on waves
          I'll bring flowers

I have tracked the sun in footfalls of sleep Understood the mind   as
rays   of   color
Remember the bouquet of yellow tulips   left at your vanishing
door
As for a wardrobe   red and violet dresses on display in
the   middle of the night
Your penchant for indigo lips on blue highways Green and orange flags of conflict
Time is a companion of light
has already been to where   we're going and back   Consider the message
in the memory of my body next to yours I was alone in a thousand rooms without
you
Out of cigarettes   beer   picaresque novels
How romantic can loneliness become
Does it sing like a bird in a barren tree Recite Shelley from memory
"I arise from dreams of thee in the first sweet sleep of night…"
Abandon the mask at a Masquerade Ball Does it sleep   under a bridge
Hear the moon drain into the river Follow a current of fish into turbulent silence
Quiet   fulfilled   devoid of questions

11

Principles of Sleep

1. I absolutely love the planet
2. Feel its mute turning inside of me
3. Its joy of placement
4. In a constructed, perfectly
5. Inflated space
6. As consciousness ascends & descends
7. Into kingdoms & caverns
8. Of volatile knowledge
9. Sleep is not sand, Mr. Sandman
10. But a grain of it
11. Possesses Imagination
12. The be all of being
13. Here
14. As if I could remember that
15. While awake
16. (Roethke wrote: "I wake to sleep, and take my waking slow.")
17. Walking through and beneath
18. The grey skies of neighborhoods
19. & wondering if extra pillows
20. Could help
21. Change the plane – the IQ of sleep

12

The rain in sleep has the blues
with no mention
of the beloved
in a town of whispered

memories

There is extensive territory
to cover
as the mind drops
off the

clock

Look at the lathered horses
How they've waited
for sunset
to elope with credentialed

stars

Suppose we were divine
Before "logic" convinced otherwise
showered us in edicts
of muscle time and

smoke

claimed we had lost
our infinite identity
in gun battles unrecorded
in the storied history of

energy

To whom am I
addressing these suppositions
divinations outside
shadows cast by nacreous

night

I hear the rain
the violated beat
as if clouds eschewed
sleeping aids and

potions

to bank above
pools of
thought forming
in the drizzle of

reflection

13

Error prone & perfect
I sleep in a heaven of mistakes
The mind opens & shuts windows
in the walls of night
Snowy Owl   Snow Leopard   Snowy Egret   Snow Goose
A bat in the attic of thought
Who am I in the charade
of caricatures &
wind currents
Dream is essential

I'm walking down the street
to a movie house in a pre-historic landscape
Rocks converse
Plants wither into violent storms
Is it a question of former lives –
the existence of wild rivers
& heartache
Would popcorn help –
a date with a madam from the 5th century
who digs me

In deft acts of levitation
sleep alters the height and speed
of the body
The night sky of the brain shrinks
Words break the sound barrier
Consciousness reverts to musical notation

I'm a tune –
a melody of celestial voices
I'm not sure what I hear
In the rustle of sheets

Who's there I ask
half-awake

14

Faucet
Leaks
House
Creaks

Mail delivery
Between synapses
Slows
Then stops

The roar of the world
Succumbs to quiet
Night purrs
Panther enters sleep

The animal in me sees me
Have I said my prayers
Loved enough humans
Hunted for something denied

Sleep opens cages
Panther crouches
Sees something I can't
Decides to investigate

15

Something froze in the township of sleep
I was busy
(with detours   false trails   an avalanche of loopholes   and popsicles)
                              not exactly in a coma
There were plenty of well-maintained clay tennis courts
mirrors thrown into the act of conception
even the Office of Records
                              had something to say
I was born on a steamship in a valley of ice
was no longer taking calls
                              from aging starlets
according to a file of poisonous flowers
I remember specifically asking the Chancellor of Someone
                              for the correct
                              space and time of things
when a tiny bureaucrat squeezed my toes
                              told me to go home
                              to beat it
                       before the cops arrived
                    with their elixirs of silence
For a while I jimmied locks
                       sallied with clouds
                    through an horizon of doors with homeopathic portals
        "The other side of what," I clamored in a thick fog of pots and pans
                    Choice was limited
I practiced the language of evasion
                       fell at times into a fit of words
                       rehearsed icicles into song
                 to counter the vanguard of theories
                    pelting me with hailstones

16

Sleep enters the arena of words
With a whip and a stash
Tonight the clouds are high
Pregnant with sentences
Of what could be
You're enamored with me –
Have taken out loans on my behalf

We'll fix the roof –
Hammer the sky into a feasible shape
Ask
Ponder
Why our bodies are so quiet
In their lonely pursuits

Rain would comfort
Leaves force a smile
Russet
Rustic
What's the difference

In the contagious acceleration of being
What are the latitude and longitude
Of lips during sleep
Are they rinsed –
Reddened with sunset
Or enflamed birds

Sleep scores my back
With absence
If I turned on the light
Where are you

17

1

It's not that blue skies are unavailable
To sleep
Or the *Book of Day* refuses to turn
The page
On the elevator ride to the
Tar pits
Sleep is a state of
Varied states
"What chapter would you like if you
Were me?"
Sleep says in a voice more anthropomorphic
Than one might suppose
Sleep is dark in the fiery darkness of planets
And stars
It is a sea of seasick shadows
Cast on waves

2

Page 6 in the *Book of Day* records day and night exist
In sleep
So it's a fact the mind continues to orbit the sun when sleep descends
         And seals the eyes'
Portals

3

I remember reading entire novels under the nightlight
Of sleep
Characters exhorting flowers to open and close on a whim of light or
Sudden darkness
Sleep is
(Unregrettably arbitrary)

A woman

A man a dog a cat a crackling fire the slippery slope of slippers padding
        from one security checkpoint

Into the bathroom

The siren song

Of sleep

Frequency of it in our veins

We feel to admire

18

Sleep burrows into the self
The time my father chased me across a roof of sky
Wet with clouds
I parachuted into the city of love   too romantic
I wrapped myself in a shower curtain
& accepted the beating deserved   neither
Later
I walked into your body without map or exit strategy –
Love with streets of no direction
Meanwhile
Life occurred at regular intervals
We owned a car
We didn't
The kids grew up
I became a captain of industry
Viewed drinking as a sport
Wrote an essay on the ontological structure of death
Said something about stars –
How they collapse into endless cycles of being

                                        Went kalpa
                                        Got quanta
Took the mound on the ball field   of mind
Sure there were ridicule & rules in the peanut gallery –
Moments when I understood the paralysis of a kiss
The concupiscence of rain inside the heart
I worked with language to restore & create the world
Gained access to birds with & without names
To study
Became flight
Landed in soft grass
Ran into the twilight of the park

                                        I knew
                                        Waited

In the tall trees of tomorrow
For headlights to pass by
Fear gone
As the staccato rhapsody of a woodpecker
Exposed dawn

19

I'm in a

> downward
> spiral
> of sleep
> wind shear
> of REM

I have

> acknowledged
> my protagonists
> my antagonists
> washed my face
> in a baptismal font

I'm not

> sure where the past
> lives
> hangs out
> with time
> not there

I can

> spell
> "hippocampus"
> that's about it

I've seen

> the brain
> advertised on TV
> its commercials
> metaphors
> love &
> tragedy

I know

           there's a rock formation
           with my name on it
           beaches
           littered with stones
           moon glitter
           pottery
           archetypes

I'm a shelf

           of selves (unvarnished)
           sleep understands
           evokes
           eternity
           forms of it
           pervade the night
           elements in the act
           of rebirth
           roll the dice

20

Sleep is a ventriloquist
and I'm its dummy

"Talk to the forest inside of you, Dummy," Sleep says.
"Imitate the birds singing in the trees if you would."
Sleep manufactures facts
My head is made of wood
My thoughts are branches without leaves
A jigsaw cut my heart into being
I don't care for polka dot ties
baggy pants
the supersize of my shoes
My eyes could use more paint
"What did you expect?" Sleep asks.
"I've squeezed night into tiny boxes just for you."
Sleep is control freak
My lacquered lips open and close
in a rhythm of words and silence
The audience of dreams loves us –
promises to tell neighbors to come and see
Sleep and Dummy perform
Sleep is a play
Roses
pet food
unsigned pre-nuptials
litter the stage
Dreamers throw what they can afford

21

This is not an essay on sleep by a gifted somnambulist. It will not offer tips on cooking while asleep or the appropriate attire to don for outings in a neighbor's backyard. It will not record the passage of time. Time, as we have come to suspect, is a sweatshop. In the case of the present and perilous situation, it simply wears a pair of dark socks. I didn't realize, until quite recently, it had a fashion sense.

Sleep mocks the logic of remaining in bed. Say I found the line – *To impress you, I've walked on waters of dissonance* – I had been chasing across a page of memories inside a jade locket. What would it mean, if I were on a street corner in flashy pajamas with a drone about my head? Could I say I know your lips, describe them as a vase of words, convince others of a garden of souls? How far down the street has the mind sauntered? Who's gathering information on me now?

Sleep affords options for timeless explorations and excavations – provides shovels and miner hats to reach ancient sites and read their walls under the glare of words. The word "conniption" just popped into my head like an estranged subatomic particle. Where did I just go? Did you see me when I asked myself that question?

Sleep wanders from one polis to the next. Remember, I packed a lunch of symbols for our trip to the lake. What kind of symbols? Could you use a cross, an owl in flight in the cavern of sleep or something that tastes like licorice? I am the legacy of what blossoms at night. Cacti or moon is anyone's pick.

22

No boundaries!
Sleep crawls out
Of a hole
In my mind
To argue
It has a mind –
Remembers where
We first uttered
Prayers of love
Assures me

During the wanton
Night
We were beneath
The kitchen table
In your family's house
No saints or guards
On duty
We could feel
The foul play
Of flowers

In our bodies – decided
Rain without clothes
Was a better option
Hit the yard
While a sheltered moon
Paroled the sky
Without the slightest notion
Of daylight
Or birds dead asleep
In the trees

Poplars weren't they
With a faint breeze
Attentive to the slumber
Of leaves
How our words
(Invocations
Imprecations
Supplications
And
Litanies)
Transformed
Into a twist of bodies
In a sea of erotic grass
Mystified the Father
Of Metamorphosis
(Guess)
In the turn
And shifting shapes
Of sheets
I witness in the mind

Of sleep
The fractured looking glass
Of who I am
There is an ant
Vociferous in its silence
Trekking across
One of your breasts
Without either one
Of our bodies
Being present

23

Sleep is a drug lord – ignores
                the intercession of saints and penalties
of logic During nights of fear
it likes to gamble   play the horses
twist the world   into balloons
and funny hats
of addiction   Stay high

Sleep hallucinates: a ladder with an inverted task
a series of words lowered into darkness   without a flashlight
Sleep takes a hit   blows smoke into my face
      "How far down would you like to go?" it inquires.
"What treasure do you seek – boon
              of what exactly
in the sea of bioluminescent creatures?"

24

I wake up
>under stars
>of nothingness
>to dream the morning
>of sleep
>Clocks release the prisoners
>of my soul

An ark
>of amorous animals
>debarks
>into the streets
>Whoever wants
>to dance
>may do so

Mirrors
>of clouds
>wash
>to shore
>like gossamer shells
>of memory

I was an infant
>in a nursery
>of breasts

a boy
>on a bike
>without pedals

Manhood struck the moment I fell
>under a spell
>of lips –

those days you kissed me
>into consciousness

each memory complete
>with the sound
>of ocean

voyages
        under full sail
        in the perfect night
What is dark vanishes
Light commands
There is a great harangue
        of differences –
words abandoned
        in the tenses
        of time
Earth
        in ephemeral garments
        of mountains
        meadows
        everlasting sky
and sea
is free
approaches
        speaks:
"I am
        in you
now.
The whirlwind
        of things
        to love
is in you."

25

My condition has passed into the now of not yet
There are place settings for animals
and exotic medicinal remedies
Time looks defeated from a war it didn't wage
If the stars are out   they give no notice
I may be ripe for birth
or a card game bogged
in numbers

Last night I drank wine with others –
gave love a second chance
Some thought I could play second base
for an undefeated team
Work for a newspaper in an online collapse
Grow hair back on a head
relapsed into shadow
Move nimbly through an alphabet of names

I heard you get up to walk the dog
Positive the moon was full – had shed tinges of orange
from its earlier life in the sky
We were in the car with the radio blaring
Remember there were waves of snow –
an ocean of flakes each one as silent
as the next   something
we imagined in surround sound

Should we inspect fragments of sleep
That woman in the blue sofa chair   is not you
The man at the podium without a microphone – face
like a pocket size travel map   is not me
They appear to be talking in code
Others paddle into the scene of a lavish room

adorned in aquamarine jewels
Sunlight presents the day – calm messenger

 from *Techniques in the Neighborhood of Sleep* (Spuyten Duyvil, 2016)

(**see poem**)

In This Corner

The hangover arrives
in clodhoppers
and boxing gloves
it uppercuts the head
and stomps groin

below the belt, ref
what's the matter – you blind
hey, I had your mother last night

The hangover pounds
the body
works it good
then back to the face
take that pretty boy

what an animal

again and again
it attacks
a cut opens near the eye

man, this guy is a bleeder
hangs on the ropes
The hangover lands
punch after punch

what technique
what skills

there's a shot
to the back of the head
the groin again

who said kicking was allowed
and what about the bell
the fucking bell

from *Modulations* (Asylum Arts, 1998)

(**see story**)

That Is the Question

Everyone has the potential to be or become a bum, William thought, sipping a pinot noir (vintage yesterday), flipping through his financial portfolio – was it or wasn't it aggressive enough to do the retirement trick for him, after being completely rejected by his offspring (as in...*No way Pops, we got our troubles now and lack the adequate coin etc. etc. to support your regrettable habit of being an old, nasty geezer with little on his mind except the little on the mind that accompanies the geezer stage, i.e. unlimited (vintage yesterday) red wine and/or shuffleboard and/or both wrapped in some quasi-religious significance like the antiquated imperative, Honor thy Father and Mother*), and eventually checking his Blackberry for his next appointment and/or series of rat-a-tat appointments with his **dermatologists**. William had a team of dermatologists – his "Spate" as he called them – working impatiently and nearly 24/7 on a host of regrettable but fortunately non-contagious skin ailments that plagued him and drove him into the "Special Cream Section" of your common, corporate – we got a Big Heart... local convenient...gas station and bank too on the premises – pharmacies.

Enough said, William thought, like he had taken a minor in Interior Monologue at No Exit Community College, while mired in his Dog Grooming major. When, in fact, "Enough said" was the curt expression he picked up from his wife Lily (quite a looker in her hey day – Twiggy with some pounds) who had survived and even prospered in her relationship with him by knowing exactly when to cut him off from one of his interminable explanations, especially those concerning his various skin disorders which he cataloged and would gladly expound upon like any epic poet or chronicler of events who felt compelled to list the rations and various supplies brought along on a trip to nowhere and back.

It was possible that WEE Willie was on a trip to nowhere and back, and that his trip, odyssey, peregrination, or flight into the nowhere of nowhere was the primary cause or at least the coordinates of his need for him to explain his various (and let's be honest, documented skin ailments and other maladies [which text time and space will not permit the sharing of]) "problemas de la epidermis" posted like (remember?) virtual Burma Shave signs on his integumentary highway.

Had enough? Sure you have, just like Lily when she applied "Enough said" like an aural eyeliner to his floppy ears and eager brain at the moment he launched, or was about to, into a tedious definition of dry skin (it has other names you know, which he often threatened to disclose to close associates) and the history of his bushy eyebrows and their culpability in the production of said skin due to the lack of the fundamental, genetic moisture or rainwater needed on a daily basis.

Get thee to genealogy O waifs and unbelievers, as the religiously wrathful often say, and/or at least to the reasonable explanation in the next paragraph to fully understand Willie and his clan.

It was known (at least among some semi-conscious family members) that Willie's paternal grandfather, Uncle Knuckles, had big bushy eyebrows – eyebrows that some say (who the hell knows – whom? slash/who, we {as in me} are referring to) stimulated a pronounced and somewhat uncomfortable literary response, in that, they caused more than just a few of the familial hostages caught in the playing field of Uncle Knuckles to recall and sometimes to relive certain passages in classic Russian novels.

Take Turgenev (Ivan Sergeyevich) for example. Surely, there was a main character in one of his stories in which small birds and other winged things had taken refuge/residence in the poor slob's beard while he wrestled with the existence of God, the cruelty of czars, and the fact that his man servant, for Christ sakes, was an arrogant lush and tormenter, who did torment the tormented soul of his master (the fate of main characters) by failing on a preordained (the genetics of being a lush) cosmological cue to heat the samovar for a decent cup of tea. And if such a passage were even remotely referred to in the presence of Uncle Knuckles, in making a point about the landscape crew that would be required to do something about his "bushes" and the aviary guests tweeting and bickering inside of them, well then, Uncle Knuckles brought (didn't he) his nickname to bear on the head of the literary snob, relative or not. Without a doubt!

Willie knew about such passages via his own excursion into Russian Literature (genetics again?), and even dropped a first wife along the way, due to his penchant for reading Russian novels (particularly, Dostoyevsky; specifically, *The Brothers Karamazov*) while flat on his back on the cat-clawed coach in his trailer park home, instead of looking for work. "I've got brain fever," he used to say to his young wife when she returned from a day at the meat processing plant.

Oh, the game of that was then and this is now is always contingent on the realization of whether the "then" is really gone or whether it's just a "now" caught somewhere (snagged) in the garment (some say, fabric) of space-time. As if the space-time fabric (some say, garment) were an enormous (without saying infinite) spider web (dressed to the nines) populated by a hefty (without saying endless) number of nows – which beckon for analysis in and of themselves, but again due to text time and space must drift unfortunately into etc. and non-italicized text stating that Willie was a locked treasure chest of Uncle Knuckles stories (WEE Willie as metaphor), which kind of (well, actually did) pop open during his momentary reflections (WEE Will not as metaphor) on bum-hood, pressing financial need, and/or the lack of a cheap red wine (vintage yesterday).

"Look, Lily," he said, "Who knows how far back into the annals of genealogy this problem with dry patches of skin under bushy eyebrows extends in my family. Sure it may skip a generation or two. My dad escaped, but not my granddaddy, Uncle Knuckles."

Because it was vacuum-the-floor-day, Lily had just retrieved the vacuum cleaner from the hallway closet and without the opportunity to plug it, imbibed, to her almost terminal regret, Willie's query from his lazyboy chair (post) in the living room. Entering the room, she studied her husband for a moment. He was overweight, bald, tattooed by various red marks and splotches – some with geographical significance (Tiny Greenland, for example) and some without – generally more amoeba-like or simply bumps. A man that time had removed from the cover of GQ for obvious reasons.

"William, please," she said. "No more Uncle Knuckles stories. Enough said, OK?

"Well, I was just thinking of that Christmas morning when Uncle Knuckles started shaking his head so violently after receiving a holiday package of cream or jell that the room filled with…"

However (as in saved by the bell, and to Lily's unfathomable delight), the motor of her plugged in Hoover Upright absorbed his words like a simile of dust particles in a bag sealed with super glue. *Thank God*, Lily thought, leaving the Hoover to idle, as she raced to the kitchen for the cache of household cleaners in the cupboard beneath the sink. She chose one of her favorites, Lemon Pledge, by Johnson Diversey (formerly Johnson & Johnson, which sounds a hell of a lot better). *Lemon Pledge is a most excellent choice* (Unique blend of rich natural waxes cleans and brightens dull furniture without waxy build-up. Dustblock formula repels dust. Excellent on wood furniture, cabinets, paneling, vinyl and leather. For computers, TV's, VCR's and stereos, try anti-static formula PLEDGE® For Electronics. PLEDGE® Wood Cleaner's advanced formula gently cleans and conditions wood surfaces and more with no sticky residue and a fresh citrus scent) *and will put Uncle Knuckles back where he belongs*, she thought, as she raced back into the living room and the electric whirr of her lovely machine.

Willy (totally paranoid and deadly afraid of household cleaners) never had a chance.

"Enough said!" Lily screamed, squirting a single shot of the toxic (20% hydrotreated Heavy Naphtha (petroleum); 20% propane: 20% butane etc.) Lemon Pledge mist into his face.

"Oh, you got me," Willy lamented, slumping deep into his lazyboy chair (post), while fumbling for his Blackberry, and observing without comment, the motor-crunched, ellipsis wasted-words of his Uncle Knuckles memory zip and dart through the lingering particles of mist like a flock of tiny, homeless birds in a scaly snowstorm.

I'm no bum, William thought, waiting for a member of his "Spate" to answer the damn phone and to offer advice on what to do about a new burning sensation.

from *Altercations in the Quiet Car* (Lavender Ink/Fell Swoop, 2010)

(**see story**)

Neurotransmitter Waltz

In high school, Rat flunked Earth Science, Biology, Chemistry and Physics in that order. Earth Science bored him; Biology scared him; Chemistry freaked him out; and Physics plagued him with the notion that physical objects were composed of nothingness to the highest degree of reliability. He had a shot at passing Physics until he nodded off during an extemporaneous speech (tirade) on Abraham Lincoln by his physics teacher, Dusty O'Jameson. Dusty admired Lincoln but hated the self-indulgent boys at Maniac Prep, especially ones like Rat (as his friends called him) who took off to the dreamland of inattention (pre-Attention Deficit Syndrome) during, say, a F equals MA demonstration with a ball bearing and sundry inclined planes with defined slopes. It wasn't beyond Dusty to wing a ball bearing at one of these little brats in front of him to reestablish their focus. However, when the paying attention infractions attained critical mass, Dusty aborted the demonstration and retrieved one of his treasured biographies on **Lincoln** from the creaky bookcase near his desk.

Lincoln freed the slaves. Lincoln preserved the Union. Lincoln suffered from depression and melancholy. Lincoln knew how to write and inspire the nation with immortal lines. Lincoln played politics like everyone else. Lincoln was ahead of his time. Lincoln came from humble beginnings. Lincoln was a hard worker. Lincoln was a hero and pretty much the opposite of these little bastards in front of him – the pampered offspring of the rich enrolled in Maniac Prep for the sole reason of keeping the lineage line of connections so highly prized in a rigged world.

Yeah, high school, Rat thought, sitting at the bar of the Plank & Grill, sipping chilled Pinot Grigio, staring vacantly at a college basketball game (Old Rover vs. New Dog Tech) on the HD Plasma TV and intermittently (like windshield wipers) biting into his Chicken Caesar wrap. *That was like eons ago when time still ticked or at least seemed to – as in the shuffle of days and seasons. How different is all of that now – now that I've stepped out of time into timelessness.*

Swallowing a lump of Chicken Caesar, he looked down the bar, furtively (to the right side first, then left), to see if any of the other Saturday afternoon drinkers (gee, not a single one with a Pinot Grigio in front of them) had picked up on a timeless guy in their presence.

Nope, it was all small talk –

- politics
- sports
- women
- gambling –

with intermittent assaults (like fierce rain showers on a sunny day) on their thick steaks and mounds of pub fries with gleaming ketchup.

Timelessness had struck Rat quickly like a new disease suddenly on the horizon (and evening news) after years of being below the horizon with other nascent viruses and microbes. And timelessness had decisively knocked Rat out (ten-count) and off the game of time, wiping out his relevant past and squeezing what was left of his future in the mysterious fingers of the Static Now.

So be it, Rat thought, admiring the translucent gold of his wine while thumbing through the local rag – *The Dirty Scoop* – Gag, the bartender, had tossed his way once he had settled on his stool.

Certainly, there was a peculiar timelessness to the news: stress, unrest and distress various headlines proclaimed before Rat came across a piece in the Entertainment Section – "Love in a Time of Neurotransmitters."

The title had a familiar ring to it, and after a quick hit of his wine, Marquez's *Love in a Time of Cholera* surfaced in Rat's mind. Unfortunately, due to incurable literary amnesia, Rat didn't recall anything about the book. But somehow by focusing on the shape of his wine glass, he did recall an article in *Playboy* about the great South American writer. It seems Mr. Marquez's grandmother played a role in the author's penchant for magic realism via frequent night visits to young Gabriel's bedroom to gently nudge him from sleep into the magnificent awareness of her kitchen filling with the blue butterflies from her mind.

And then, there was the time with the woman on the train, Rat thought in mid-Caesar mastication. *Yeah, she was reading One Hundred Years of Solitude and I tried to pick her up with a witty exchange:*

"I can't help noticing that you're into Marquez," I said

"I'm a lesbian," she said.

"I'm an ex-Catholic," I said.

It was all gravy after that – drinks in the bar car, cards and that burning kiss she planted on my cheek when she got off in Atlanta.

So much for unrequited reverie, Rat thought, turning his attention back to the article.

According to it, there were a number of neurotransmitters involved in the dance of love and also that certain personality types (Rat inside the parenthesis thinking thusly: *Plato came up with four didn't he? Think, Rat. What did Professor Flatbelly call them in Philo 101? Oh, yeah, Artisan, Guardian, Idealist and Rational. God, I hated this kind of stuff even back then*) were actually fueled by these various chemicals (including the hormones estrogen and testosterone), which basically allowed one nerve cell to receive the impulse from another nerve cell (via synaptic leap) that the "babe" or "hunk" in front of one was hot.

Damn, Rat thought, trying to suppress a squall of anxiety passing through him (re: chemical reaction to his long-suffering aversion to Chemistry, in particular, to balancing chemical equations in eleventh grade, which he sucked at, resulting in the creation of mutant water molecules, sweet salt, bitter sugar and detention slips), *I wonder if these neurotransmitters play a role in a sense of timelessness. Love is timeless, isn't it? And what's an extra suffix in the grand scheme of it all?*

Reading on produced no such luck. Sure, at one time in his life, Rat had been a dopamine-riddled Explorer (first personality type) rushing from one novelty act to the next as ordained by the dictates of the neurotransmitter. That's why marriage and employment were so tough on him – for once the infatuation for these states subsided, so did he. But give him some credit, for although he tried his luck with other dopamine freaks, he did move on to estrogen-verbose Negotiators (second personality type) and testosterone-jacked-rational-minded Directors (third personality type).

It was Jackie the Director, his third wife, who convinced him to return to his father's Law Office – Rat, Rat & Rat – through a series of mind-numbing Aristotelian syllogisms on immaturity and sloth, along with her threat of ordering a straitjacket for him from an online supplier of black market psychiatric accoutrements.

Ash Can City, he thought, as he approached the end of the article while polishing off his wine.

But then B I N G O – the Builder (fourth personality type) – the serotonin-driven people-oriented Builder came into view in the final paragraph. The Builder had a knack of working with others and without fear would touch and hug friends and foes. And once the precious fingers of the Builder touched someone, the body produced the neurotransmitter oxytocin in the touched individual, which in turned produced the desire to touch and be touched.

No way, Rat thought, thinking of the years spent in touch-free homes and zones.

After a "timeless second" in the lonely years of those days, he thought of his estranged wife, Sally (#4). How she loved and treated people – almost dog-like in her enthusiasm for others. How she loved to dance. How she had purchased ballroom dancing lessons for them as a Valentine's Day gift. *How many years ago?* How he balked and grumbled and would not go even after she said:

"They will transport you, Rat."

"Transport?"

"Yes, to a timeless reality of motion and a bond of joy never to be broken," she said.

"No asunder, asunder?" he asked.

"No asunder, asunder," she said.

Man, he thought, as Gag passed by in a whirlwind of bills, drinks and food before stopping on a slippery dime to inquire:

"Another one?"

"No," Rat said, reaching for the cell phone in his shirt pocket, "I'm way overdue for my appointment with a builder."

from *Buffoon in the Gene Pool* (Lavender Ink/Fell Swoop, 2016)

Page Four

Spacetime is a bitch. It has revoked my attractive man status and posited me in the unattractive status category. I used to be able to say to friends and close associates that I am a handsome man. Not anymore. Ever since spacetime worked its magic, I've been stripped into a male specimen who lacks hair on his head, entertains floaters the size of mutant mosquitoes in his eyes, suffers from poor hearing and low sexual drive and output. Once baby soft and pliant, my skin is now like an old shoe – tight and cracked – found in some alleyway. And let's not forget the barnacle-like encrustations strategically placed on my face to affect a seafaring journey through spacetime. Wisdom spots, my ass; spacetime has a dire sense of humor.

I'm not depressed or in despair over the physical changes to my makeup. Yes, mirrors hate me and I'm no Ishmael. I know there are pills and wonderful surgeries to alleviate the playful effects of spacetime on my constitution, but to the dismay of those closest to me, I abhor them all.

I'm stuck in the now of being who I am. Granted, being is a phenomenal state to be in and complaints about being part of the fabric of being, or I suppose spacetime, should be kept to a low roar – something akin to tinnitus, which I'm happy to report that I have.

A long time ago, back in the days (or day) when I was a good looking but an inept philosophy student, I knew very little about spacetime. I was cool with the four dimensions of it after smoking a joint with friends and thought that there may be a few more dimensions other than four, after the first time my body climbed aboard its astral soul for a psychedelic ride. White rabbits galore in the passing lane or being transfixed by a dewdrop on the tip of a flower petal, and nothing else for hours on end, has to be some kind of a dimension.

I just picked the wrong major and department during college to be initiated into the cunning tricks of spacetime. My philosophy professors didn't talk or lecture on spacetime. Though I learned what Plato, Aristotle, Descartes, Kant and Hume (**see poem**) were thinking about, I can't remember Einstein's name being mentioned. I needed to figure out what a 'self' was and what a 'thing' was and appreciate the limits of mind and language in coming to terms with so called "objective" reality. Spacetime eating away at my manhood didn't arise.

I heard on the car radio, the other day, a physicist talking about recent speculations about spacetime. According to him, spacetime, the entirety (**see**

Page Five) of it, rolled out at the moment of the Big Bang, and thus concepts of the past, present and future were nothing more than a slice or a particular angle of spacetime. To help the listener, the physicist instructed us to stop texting and imagine spacetime as a loaf of bread (**see story**). Wheat, white, or rye would do. The present were the slices occupying the middle; the past were the slices positioned near the end, the future were the slices near the front, closest to the twist wire. What was cool about a spacetime loaf of bread was that one's life was simultaneously occurring across the multiple slices in a loaf of spacetime and that literally nothing disappeared or died (or even got moldy). I may be wrong here, but I believe the physicist maintained the timeframe of anyone one's life (past, present, future) was simply the function of the position of an observer and his/her rate of speed. It gave me great comfort to know that thanks to a spacetime loaf of bread, I am still a baby in the crib, a handsome man and an old fuck who considers spacetime a bitch. How wrong can a handsome man get?

(**see poem**)

WITNESS

Mind pervades everything is a sentence with clout
Uncertainty is a principle
Cogito ergo sum and the double helix
remain hot news items
We polished off a bottle of Pouilly Fuisse
enjoying the play of mythical children from frosted steps
Are butterflies reincarnated philosophers
Do trees deny the wheel of birth and death
What's your present velocity and location
I've shot pool like David Hume
(*Send the paparazzi to the front(s)*
Send the presidents the monarchs the dictators
The millionaires and the religious leaders too)
It's more than getting one's paperwork in order
or forging the moon's blood work
to obtain the Mind's birth certificate
Great history shakes with the awareness of what has been lost
Pure reflection did explode
See Internet See Spot run
Through equations and livid insights
we encode multiple oblivions
Before it started to thunder
we collected raindrops in pearl pails
There were ghost planes in the sky of homeless soldiers
When consciousness slips on a noose of flowers
eye is not so bad or mad a witness

from (*House Organ*, Number 77 Winter 2012)

(see story)

After mailing his sonnet manuscript to Shakespeare & Co. and deliberately checking the size of his abdomen (bust-a-gut 2014; additional features: small head, somnolent body, one brown eye and one blue, sandy hair with monk tonsure) in the bathroom mirror, Mickey spent his first day of retirement working around the house. Under the direction and watchful eye of his wife, Annabelle, he put away the Christmas decorations – bulbs, stockings, ornaments and such – piled on the dining room table, the living room end tables, the deck table and the side porch (including the LED reindeer on their sides in the mulch between the azalea bushes in the front yard). It was July and this annual summer task suited Mickey's understanding of the holidays (the hangover after them) and his tepid awareness that disorder via entropy was the Lord of the Land. Mickey knew thanks to Public Television Funding Drives that what had come together in the form of galaxies and solar systems during the halcyon days of highly ordered systems was inevitably drifting apart into an absolute state of disorder – molecules and stuff blowing around in space without a sub shop or deli in sight. Mickey loved a good submarine sandwich. He was also fond of rolls and bread – ones full of gluten and made from white flour. His mind was impervious to updates on the lack of value in these dough products and at times he realized his mind might be drifting apart.

"Speaking of bread," he said, one day to his wife Annabelle, "guess what I heard last night on the Channel 44 PBS Funding Drive?"

"Mickey, it's 3:00 A. M. in the morning. Can't it wait?" Annabelle asked.

"Wait for what…for whom…Godot"? Mickey asked.

"That's quite a stretch don't you think, Mickey?" Annabelle asked, reaching for her sleeping pills on the bed stand. "But ok, if you can tell me before I intentionally overdose on these pills, fine."

"Well, according to a physicist on the program – *The Game of Nothingness* – the past, the present and the future actually occur simultaneously," Mickey said. "And get this, the guy asked the viewers to imagine the spacetime continuum as a loaf of bread, saying, the pieces in the front of the loaf represent the future, the pieces toward the back represent the past and the middle section is more or less the present. In terms of you and me, we haven't even met yet, oh, yes we have, and what the hell could we possibly be doing tomorrow, which we're already doing without even knowing it. Pretty cool. Of course, this is all dependent on the viewpoint of the observer and, I guess, the speed of light."

Annabelle had a good snore on.

"Annabelle?" Mickey said, shaking her slightly.

No response.

"Oh, well," Mickey said. "We're all there (Dasein) in all tenses inside a volatile loaf of spacetime. And you know how much I love bread."

Besides putting the Christmas stuff into innumerable blue plastic bins, Mickey hauled crap up from the cellar – old rugs, scratching posts, broken rockers, guitars, birdhouses, butterfly tents, dressers, beds, books and things that no longer went by recognizable names – to the curb. Mickey liked birds and butterflies, but he eventually realized they preferred habitats other than a musty cellar.

Beside keeping a fretful eye on her husband, Annabelle was busy, too, on Mickey's first day of retirement. While he fiddled with the decorations and the cellar haul, she worked out on their redwood-stained deck putting together a black plastic box with the dimensions of a wide-body coffin. It was an easy enough box to assemble in the sweltering July heat, with only 64 tiny screws and washers to place in (expletive foreshadowing) tiny holes to complete the construction. Annabelle was not yet of retirement age, but after years of working in the waste management industry with vile men and managers (she drove a recycling truck through the streets of an historic neighborhood in Boston), she could swear (and did) a blue streak when and/or if a Philips head screwdriver stripped the head off a screw. Especially fond of the hashtag and asterisk symbols, her blue streaks floated through neighborhood and shocked the neighbors thusly: ##*****####@@*##**%.

Mickey wasn't handy with tools and had learned over the years not to approach Annabelle when she had a tool in her hand. She was sturdy in build (additional features: an abundance of blond curly hair, remarkable bosom, perfect complexion as white as albino snow, brilliant teeth and small, dainty feet) and had taken charge of fixing everything in the house from plumbing to cranky fire alarms, and could be considered dangerous with a "snake" in the toilet when asked to consider the possibly of a universe in full regalia coming into being out of nothing by an observant Mickey sitting on the edge of the bathtub.

During one clogged toilet episode with Mickey pestering her with the joy of nothingness, Annabelle offered Mickey a ##*****####@@*##**% plumbing alternative, if he persisted with his cosmic mumbo jumbo.

"Honey," she said, "there's no need to go through the rigmarole of going to the hospital for your next colonoscopy. I can take care of it right now. Just pull your ##*****####@@*##**% pants down."

Sure, Mickey thought she was nuts to build a black wide-body coffin in the direct sunlight on a morning already in the 90's. But it was for a good cause: a place to store the new cushions for the deck furniture so they wouldn't get soaked when it rained. And the new deck furniture had been bought in anticipation of a family reunion for adult children and grandchildren on the Fourth of July weekend.

Mickey kept his distance and the morning proceeded without a hitch. He thought of quasars and quarks as he carefully put the red, green, gold and blue ornaments into their boxes in preparation for the plastic bins. Occasionally, his mind drifted to the 40 years he ran Mickey's Convenience Store before selling it to one of the chain convenience stores taking over Boston. There had been considerable robberies and brawls in the parking lot over the years, but overall selling milk, hot dogs, lottery tickets, cigarettes, chips, cat food, soda, boxed doughnuts, mealy fruit, cookies, coffee and newspapers, when combined with Annabelle's waste management job, had provided the money to send three kids through college. At one point during his domestic labors, the start of a new sonnet traipsed through his mind (*Me thinketh thou stinketh…*), a form he had come to and enjoyed during the downtimes of the business day or while munching on a boxed doughnut during a stickup. With a fondness for nothingness, he entitled his manuscript: *I'm Not Here Are You*.

When Annabelle called to him to come and witness the finished box, he had just thrown the last of the threadbare throw rugs onto a pile of them already at the curb.

"Coming, dear," he said.

Walking up the steps of the deck, he saw the finished black box gleaming in the sunlight.

Annabelle sat by it with rivulets of sweat running down her face.

"What do you think?" she asked.

"It looks like a coffin."

"Really, why don't you ##*****####@@*##**% climb into it and try it on for size," Annabelle said.

from *Buffoons in the Gene Pool* (Lavender Ink/Fell Swoop 2015)

Page Five

Out There

the simultaneity of
there
perception becomes phrase
phrase
has meaning
lacks one
which is the
world
by moment
of sunlight
on hybrid
oaks
and the voice
of leaves
to secret
self
as blackbird flies
in blue sky
over trees
and news
about century's
exhaust finds
nervous pedestrian
by window
while the happiness
of dogs
barking at children
persists

from *Modulations* (Asylum Arts, 1998)

(One Gluten-free Slice of Spacetime circa 1965 – approximate speed: Holy Shit!)

Nurse Mumford glares at me with medicinal eyes set in a sternly wrinkled face. Her white uniform, as starched and stiff as a nun's drool bib, protects a nondescript body that passed its prime eons ago. A little white cap sits like a crown upon a mountain of grey hair, held fast by black bobby pins. Her teeth stained from coffee, cigarettes, bacteria and filed for effect into tiny knives as if a weak-kneed orderly was a plausible snack.

"Well, that's your job, Paul", she says, "and if you don't do it I will be forced to call your mother."

"Come on," I say, "pick up the bedpans in that old cart and bring them back to this dungeon. You have to be kidding me."

I am sixteen and standing in Central Supply at St. Mary's Hospital. My mom works in the Emergency Room as the secretary and forced me into this job to make sure my life is hell on the weekends. I have to wear white pants, white shirt and white shoes. I'm a sterilized boy without hope or prospects. My friends in the neighborhood – those who take pleasure in pummeling me with their fists – taunt me on my way to St. Mary's, a few blocks from my house.

"Hey, ghost boy," they shout, chasing me down the street.

I submit to not having my mom come over to Central Supply – a storeroom for all the gross stuff used in hospitals – bedpans, thermometers, scalpels and other medieval barber tools, such as rubber gloves and various IV and distilled water bottles. The orderlies assigned to Central Supply get to pick up and clean the vile stuff used on the various floors in the hospital. As the new recruit in white, I inherit bedpan duty. According to the hierarchy of jobs available to the squad of orderlies working in Central Supply, I will move on to gathering and cleaning rectal thermometers once I master the art of shagging bedpans from around the hospital for processing at Central Supply.

With Nurse Mumford in my face like a virulent strain of protocol, and the threat of mom in my mind, I latch onto the bio-hazardous metal cart, pull it through the supply room door and like a "junkman of filth" head down the hallway to the elevator that will take me to 3 West. Pan pickup starts on 3 West, moves to 3 Central and onto 3 East before dropping down to the next floor, moving east to west during the next round. There are nine floors to cover in the hospital, each with its own brand of disease and illness – cancer wards (**see poem**), geriatrics (**see poem**), psychiatric (**see poem**) ward, intensive care and host of remaining floors that deal with diseases that affect the body. A considerable number of patients have to use to bedpans and urinals. The bedpans as expected are pretty gross. Metal pots with a dull sheen, most have had a cursory rinse by a nurse or floor aide or orderly, but usually a turd or two still clings to the inside or outside of most of them. Rhyme is good even with accidental. Pan rhymes with man, and that's what mom says I will become by working in the hospital – a man.

The only advantage of being a bedpan junkman is some of the other nurses (**see poem**) on the floors. Many are much younger than Mumford and a few burst right through their uniforms to real part-time jobs as sex goddesses. I like that. As a man-child, I could use a sex goddess.

It takes me an hour or so to cover the floors before I return to the supply dungeon with the cart brimming with bedpans, urinals, soap dishes and emesis basins – curved little numbers that patients spit and puke into.

Nurse Mumford is on me like a fly on shit when I yank the cacophonous cart back into the supply room. She scans her watch and says:

"Maybe, we have something here. Not bad to grab all those pans in little over an hour."

Marvin (**see poem**), the other orderly in Central, jumps from behind the door and rubs his hands all over my mouth. He tells me that he just finished cleaning the rectal thermometers. He and Mumford laugh and tell me it's all part of the initiation package.

Once their laughter subsides, Mumford leads me over to the giant tub of a sink to continue my initiation. She points to it and with a bit of spittle at the corners of her mouth, says:

"Now, Paul, dump your load into the tub and wash them."

Lost in a panic over the fecal bacteria on my lips from Marvin's hands, I can only mutter:

"What?"

Nurse Mumford holds "mom" over my head like a guillotine blade, and I realize that my life will never be the same. I began to unload the cart into the tub, turn on the faucets and ask for gloves.

"You won't need gloves," Mumford says. "Stapheen (**see poem**) will kill all the bacteria."

She nudges me, reaches under the tub into the cupboards below and pulls out a giant bottle of the disinfectant, Stapheen. Skull and crossbones are clearly displayed on the bottle. With glee, she pours a long stream of the liquid into the water and immediately the water froths and foams like the dance of piranha at lunchtime in the Amazon.

"Dive in, Paul," she says. "When you're done Marvin will show you how to use the autoclave machine to complete the sterilization process."

I'm left alone with the pans, suds and the occasional turd that floats to the surface and bops and weaves in the messed pants of my life.

Later, I'm not surprised when I get up in the middle of the night to take a piss that all the skin from my elbows to the tips of my fingers has peeled and flaked away like scraped paint. The fact that my fingernails have slid forward in their cuticles alarms me. Stapheen is a bastard. I think about knocking on my mom's bedroom door to show her the results of my first day on the job. I would like to show her that I'm the kind of man that loves initiation rites infused with hostile bacteria and deadly chemicals. But for some reason I don't, and just pick at my skin and attempt to slide my fingernails back in place.

(see poem)

Room 203

He's lost most of his mouth
and throat to cancer,
one lung black as a tire,
the other twilight.
He asks for a smoke.
I light a Marlboro
and stick it
in his tracheotomy hole.
We nod a conversation
then stare out the window;
the sun like an ash
breaks off into night.

(**see poem**)

Mr. Buzz

Mr. Buzz, your brain
is a cowboy today.
At lunch between the spoonfuls
of Jell-O I put on your tongue
and the weak tea rushing
from the corners your mouth,
your recall the days of the Old West.
You were a stagecoach driver,
once took an arrow in the chest,
but then your mother called you
for lunch and you survived
by eating a bologna sandwich
and drinking a glass of milk.

But you move to more serious concerns
after lunch; you tell me
they've got the wrong desperado
locked in this jailhouse,
that you'll give a sawbuck
if I'll help you escape
from them fancy-legged sheriffs.
All I have to do is let you know
when the coast is clear;
the rest you'll do.

I ask where you'll go.
"Who knows things like that anymore,"
you reply.

(see poem)

MARIE

Since she was nine
your mother dreamed of Hollywood
and stardom.
At eighteen she was
knocked up with you;
she had a new dream.

When you came to the Towers
you were sixteen,
had played a whore
in a fairly successful movie.
After a private showing
there was a bottle and a half
of Librium to take.

Your mother tells the nurse
if she hadn't found you in time,
the dream of stardom
could have vanished.
"As it is her eyes will look like
a stuffed bird's for at least a year."

(see poem)

L.P.N.

She offers me
her legs and breasts
for after work.
She calls it chicken dinner;
she's cooked it many times.

It's the hospital –
it's the legs, breasts,
penises, faces
she has to deal with
that got her talking
like this.

Before nursing she had
a little girl's soul,
performing acts of kindness,
saving, smelling
nice afterwards.

But now she has to wash
rejected tube feedings
from her hair
and rinse urine from her skin
after saving.

There's more to love than she imagined.

(see poem)

Marvin

Marvin is forty-one,
studying to be a Baptist minister.
Eight hungry kids kept him
from preaching hell fire
earlier in life, so he says.
He has Duty One:
cleaning blood, hair, and skin
off instruments.
He's supposed to leave room
on the autoclave cart
for my pans and basins,
but doesn't.

Marvin told me the other day
the Bible is the only truth.
I asked about clay figurines
and God-breath up nostrils.
"It's true!" he said,
showing me a replica
given to him by his oldest son.

Later that day
he sang "Rock of Ages"
as mountains crumbled
in his febrile brain.

(see poem)

Staphene Fingernails

The first day of pan assignment
I washed forty sets.
The Staphene felt warm
on my hands,
like Ben Gay.
It kept my mind off
occasional pieces of shit
and vomit
that floated on the water
like rubber ducks.
That night when I washed my hands,
all my fingernails fell
into the sink.
Mumford said,
"Staphene is worse than acid; wear gloves."

(from *Dream of Long Headdresses* (**see poem**): *Poems from a Thousand Hospitals*, Signpost Press, 1988)

(**see poem**)

DOCTORS

Gods, they repair death.
At night they drive to brick houses
In long silver cars,
drink, check the wife's breasts
for lumps,
look down the kids' throats,
sit back
and dream
of long headdresses,
masks,
drum music,
charms,
moon potions,
deer hearts
to stop the suffering.

Page Seven

Soon after a gypsy from California stole my first wife, I left Rochester, New York, and returned to my hometown of Binghamton with an NEA in Poetry (**see Page Eleven**) in my pocket and my two children in tow. My Uncle Filibuster rented me a second floor apartment in one of the houses he owned on St. John Ave., on the west side of the city. I was broke and living on a set of canceled credit cards without much success. Things picked up when I found work as a reading coordinator at BOCES (Board of Occupational and Education Services). It was around this time (1982) that I founded the Big Horror Poetry Series (*boink!* Free download from Lavender Ink Press contains information about the series; also Rare Collections at SUNY Binghamton houses a complete set of DVDS of the series, thanks to Bern Mulligan: **see Appendix D: Preservation Act: Digitizing a Literary Reading Series**) after failing to get into the MA Creative Writing program at SUNY at Binghamton. This kicked off my long feud with the university and my disgust for academic poetry and MFA programs in general (**see Page Eight**). A cult lived on the first floor below my kids and me (**see poem**).

Our apartment was not too far from St. Patrick's Church. I had gone to St. Patrick's Academy during my elementary school days, and from that experience, I wrote the story *Christian Soldier Academy* (again, see *boink!*), part of my failed and incomplete novel *Mounds*, which I just tossed into the recycle bin after sheltering it in dust in my cellar for the last 32 years.

As I remember it, I wrote the story in the St. John Avenue apartment. A rather gangly wasp toured the room and flew past me (actually over my head) pretty much at the exact moment I set pen to paper. This freaked me out. I'm bee-phobic and my mind danced off to visit Dante's Inferno in that instant. Was the wasp an omen or a coincidence? I wasn't too sure but proceeded with the task of writing about my first grade experience at St. Patrick's Academy.

Upon completion of my horrific tale, I sent it to *ACM* (Another Chicago Magazine), a magazine that had published a few of my poems. They rejected it (**see story**) – a bit too much and over the top for their tastes and sensibilities. I knew it was pretty out there but I wrote it out of an excited and terrified kid's imagination. And that was just it, according to my mom, the frightening and gruesome events recounted in the story were all imagined and never happened to me (again, I refer you to *boink!*) She told friends and family more than once that what I talked and wrote about never really happened. "It's all in his head," she said, slightly alarmed.

Bullshit! Intimation and fear mongering were rampant in Catholic schools during my tenure in them during the fifties and then again in the mid-sixties. Faces slapped, heads jammed into lockers and tales of horror and retribution were common during those heydays (all the way back to the Dark Ages (**see sonnet**) – let alone the documented cases of sexual abuse that have surfaced in recent years. Why just the other day while vacationing on Cape Cod (**see poem**) with my family, a woman and her tribe vacationing near us recalled a gem from her Catholic folklore. According to Babs, an aunt of hers, while a youngster in a Catholic penitentiary, had to climb on top of the "punishing" stool in the corner of the classroom and grab ahold of the hot pipes exposed near the ceiling in order to grasp the severity of her second grade crime – talking while the nun took the class on an imaginary tour of the Vatican. Of course, this never happened!

Celine once said the job of the writer is to record the crummy things human beings do to each other before rolling over into the grave. God dies every day in the various religions promoting His existence (**see Page One**). You just can't intimidate, control through fear, maim, and kill in the name of God and Allah and expect these omniscient Beings to survive the mayhem. You also can't forget – star dust to star dust, baby. Think, star dust!

(**see poem**)

THE CULT DOWNSTAIRS

The cult downstairs loves Band-Aids.
There's one stuck on the mailbox
with their name etched into the soft pad.
It reminds the mailman of his wounds
of hundreds of dogs plagued
by wild visions and the desire
for fresh flesh. He sprays the box
with mace before leaving them letters
with fine scratches across their bodies.
The cult downstairs worships wounds.
At midnight they extinguish small candles
and shield their eyes from seams of starlight
with Band-Aids designed for the deep gash.
They move around, stubbing toes on furniture
bumping into walls and windows.
Their screams muffled by layers of gauze
soaked in the memories of old blood
and pressed against their lips.
When it is time to sacrifice unblemished skin
they drop large preconceived parcels on the floor.
At fifteen-minute intervals they slam
fingers in the outside door.
Then they crawl up the stairs to see who's home.

from *Fell Swoop: The All Bohemian Revue, #9*

(**see story**)

Rejection Slip

Clive retrieved his mail from the front porch mailbox – one of three unadorned black boxes tacked to the downstairs apartment wall – in his white cotton "boxers" and without the support of his pearl handle cane. It was a hot and oppressive day – an August day … a dog day – and Clive with some irritation (say a tooth extraction) hurled the obvious bills for phone and electricity etc. – keeping two actual letters in hand, one from his brother, Paul, and the other stamped From the Literary Offices of Last Chance Press – into the pile of trash (of significant height, say a mutant gumdrop) on the scrawny front lawn, obviously the default designated area for bills and junk mail addressed to the other occupants of the apartment house.

Clive lived on the third floor of a triple-decker apartment house (just off Washington Street in Urban City) with his wife, Peg, a hot manicurist, his demon cat, Alexander the First and a giant, irascible parrot named Invisible. The three flights of stairs to his place were a bitch to go up and down without his cane, and he cursed himself (%^&*$#@) and Invisible (%^&$#@), the likely culprit in his cane's disappearance, as he hobbled back up the stairs into the steamy apartment with his mail. Since Clive sustained an incurable knee injury, resulting from his attendance at a rowdy poetry reading a number of years ago, Invisible had become a real pain in the ass. For some reason, the giant bird took umbrage to Clive's disability, perhaps thinking Clive was faking his limp and/or simply didn't buy that poetry was that rough. Whatever the case, Clive's pearl handle cane was often missing or lost when he needed it most. And without the cane, Clive was vulnerable to Invisible's attacks, one of which Invisible unleashed the moment Clive reentered the apartment with his mail by dive bombing his head.

"Goddamn it, Invisible," Clive shouted, protecting his face and head with his arms, "there will come a day when I'll see into invisibility and wring your feathers good."

"Nancy-boy, Nancy-boy," Invisible mocked, returning to his perch on top of a bookcase to preen his invisible feathers.

Assault time over, Clive stood for a moment, caught in a blank stare of momentarily forgetting the next sequence of events. As blank stares go, this one was fairly effective in capturing the contents of Clive's (and Peg's) modest living room, i.e., couch, coffee table, end tables, lamps, bookcase, boom box,

13 inch broken color TV, throw rug with a worn-out glimpse of Atlantis, spider plants hanging in the corners, unruly ferns in front of the windows, Alexander the First (with a gleam in his demonic eyes) ripping the couch apart with his claws, numerous Bud beer cans (some stacked in mock imitation of the Leaning Tower of Pisa), half-filled ash trays, a few dust balls and some empty boxes of various cracker brands, most notably Cheez-It boxes.

Snap! Clive returned to sequence:

1. He hissed at Alexander the First and Alexander the First hissed back.
2. He set the letter from his brother Paul on an end table near the bookcase.
3. He limped into the kitchen and liberated a Bud from the refrigerator.
4. He limped back from the kitchen and out onto the front porch.
5. He sat down in a beach chair with his Bud and the Last Chance letter.

The porch – little more than a shaky platform with a railing – was the favorite room in the apartment for both Clive and Peg, due, in part, to the stately American Elm over hanging the porch, which provided shade and cover from the heat and noise of Urban City.

"Sultry weather with a breeze is not so hard to take," Clive had said just the other day to Peg, as she buffed a black sheen into his fingernails.

"Certainly true, honey," Peg responded, finishing her work with a sirocco of breath on his nails and a quick rub of her body against his.

"God, you're hot." Clive said

"In so many ways," Peg said. "Want a beer?"

Clive simply loved the little porch (and black fingernails), considering it his sanctuary after hours at the typewriter (battling tempestuous metaphors, establishing open-field high-energy data grids and processing mysterious dictations), and often went there to cool off his "literary heat" with a six-pack of Bud, if and when necessary. Clive would do anything to protect his sanctuary. And in fact, he had saved the elm from extinction by convincing the plumbing business next door (owner of the apartment) not to cut it down to increase the parking space for its fleet of trucks. The owner was a little more than bewildered over Clive's attachment to the tree.

"I had no idea that you felt so deeply about the tree," the owner said, during a conversation about its destruction with Clive.

To which Clive replied:

"Take a freaking whiff of Urban City will you, the whole place is nothing but exhaust!"

"Well, yeah," the owner said, scratching his bald head with a piece of copper tubing.

For a moment, Clive just sat in the beach chair looking at the letter as if it were a portal to a better universe or a diamond of rare opportunity. He read it again, saying out loud, From the Literary Offices of Last Chance Press. He knew what this could mean. He had submitted a manuscript, *Ducks in the Dawn of Self-Awareness*, to Last Chance Press months ago, and according to an editor friend at "Language Trash Review," Last Chance worked in this manner, i.e., a letter in the mail after a set of interminable months, and without a returned manuscript, nearly guaranteed publication by Last Chance.

Clive took a big burning swig of Bud, and as he slid his finger under the sealed flap, Jamal from the "decker" across the street came out on his porch to rap, *Some Day I'm Going to Kick Your White Ass*. Timing, Clive thought, acknowledging Jamal with a quick "thumbs up" as Jamal's dad grabbed his son by the throat and hauled his ass out of sight.

Clive turned his attention to the letter and read:

Dear Clive Mesmermeat,

Without a doubt, you are the kind of poet Last Chance Press loves to bring to the public's attention through publication. I found your poems, and most specifically the lines composing them, crackling with raw energy, insights, and may I go so far to say, a literary originality and freshness I've not witnessed in most submissions over the years (we get 16,000 manuscripts of verse a year, publishing only four).

Unfortunately, Mr.Mesmermeat, Last Chance Press is not just about a startling, original poet with a voice for the ages. It is also about the poems from different poets "talking" with each other, establishing via this "talk" resonances and associations unique to the collaboration. And although Ducks in the Dawn of Self-Awareness made it into the final six manuscripts under consideration (with four as I mentioned to be published), it stalled, and may I go so far to say, petered out in the collaboration requirement so highly valued at Last Chance Press.

Still my appreciation for your work remains incredibly strong and I have sent "Ducks" (I hope you don't mind) to a new press – This Is It Press – recently started and under the sure hand and editorial fire of Mr. Scott Dibbleworth, a former editor here at Last Chance. I'm sure Scott will be interested in it. In the meantime, I look forward to entertaining another manuscript from you within a year or so. Take care!

My very best,

Connor M. Puddlehouse
Publisher, Last Chance Press

Clive reread the rejection slip a number of times (may I go so far as to say, 25 times) before folding it into a paper airplane and setting it to sail in the pungent air currents of Urban City. Then he executed the following sequence:

1. He got up from the beach chair and went back into the house.
2. He evaded another attack by Invisible.
3. He hissed at Alexander the First and got a claw in his foot as a gift.
4. He liberated another Bud from the refrigerator.
5. He sat down at his typewriter and wrote a note to Connor M. Puddlehouse.

Dear Connor M. Puddlehouse,

That was one hell of a rejection slip. Unfortunately, I'm a volatile and a disturbed individual, and I sent your kind rejection slip into the environs of a toxic breeze in my stunted neighborhood. I look forward to hosting a convention of splinters in my ass as months pass to the suggested submission period and/or hearing from This Is It Press. But I don't give a fuck!

Sincerely,

Clive Mesmermeat

Six months later (During which time

1. Peg left Clive for a fiction writer.
2. Invisible became more invisible and aggressive before his untimely demise.
3. Alexander the First started attacking Clive during his sleep like he was the couch.
4. Jamal and his buddies "keyed" his old VW bug.)

Clive received a letter from This Is It Press (again without a returned manuscript).

Dear Clive Mesmermeat,

*In all seriousness, **Ducks in the Dawn of Self-Awareness** is a master work and would (I say "would") go well with the first two publications from This Is It Press: **Don't Shout Closure While Jumping from a Cliff** by D.F. Tankfaith and **Metaphysics or Attack Dogs** by T. Susan Fetisher. However, my wife (and co-editor) finds "Ducks" alarmingly self-absorbed (and slightly unfair to ducks) and I've been forced to recycle it (I hope you don't' mind) or go without sex in my life for the next 12 months. Good luck with finding the right publisher. You're magnificent, bro.*

Cheers,

Scott Dibbleworth
Publisher, This Is It Press

What to do now? Clive thought, fetching his pearl-handle cane to kill the unnecessary lighting in his apartment before entering a snow white night.

from *Buffoons in the Gene Pool* (Lavender Ink/Fell Swoop, 2015)

(**see sonnet**)

BLACK GOWNS & BRIARS

for Wm. Blake

The green rain comforts salamanders in the park
My room swivels like a chair through presence and absence
Lessons from my Dark Age were written in white chalk
Not pastels – no stickers or glitter   either
Who knew the light filtering through the blinds
was a rainbow of various forms of sight
Who was in charge of gerrymandering the soul
There in that clump of grass (where)   religious groups
bicker ferociously with each other
God is a divine atom blasted into quarks & quirks
What's the frequency, Kenneth
Or the day we surfed across a purple wave
I'm on holiday now   remembering your Camaro
on narrow streets of lust and passion

from *Techniques in the Neighborhood of Sleep* (Spuyten Duyvil, 2016)

(**see poem**)

Present Risk

Change is the anthem of existence
Prior to the dream I walked along the beach
Tuned to black syllables of sea
The shaved head of the moon rose in the eastern sky
Children danced in a shower of sparklers
Scorpio stung silence

Juxtaposition creates energy
The curve of lips in tainted mirrors
Engages memory
Nietzsche predicted the "herd" would graze
On cheese doodles and use social media
To locate itself in space

The contours of youth haunt me
The wasteland is hacked on a need to know basis
The sea is one of many cosmic hearts
Civilizations bicker into dust
War and religion
Do not advance divinity

An allergy to prayer deforms me
When it's my time to leave
I'll harness ambivalence
To a weathered mind
As the sun steers a seagull
Across a stone sky

from *Techniques in the Neighborhood of Sleep* (Spuyten Duyvil, 2016)

Page Eight

In Defense of the MFA and Exotic (Vacationland) Writing Workshops

-Is mos non cohere-

I never had the time to pursue a "terminal" MFA degree or attend an exotic (Vacationland) Writing Workshop and many (list favorite poets here) have written (threatened) me to state (in unequivocal free verse and/or iambic neo-formalist pentameter (**see sonnet**) that this might be the sole (soul) – undoubtedly is – reason for my banal existence and total (well-deserved, buster) obscurity in the obscure world of competitive poetry.

This type of lambasting by recognized poets in the obscure world of competitive poetry is hard to stomach, since it's known (document this) that I've banged out damn good verse since my preschool days – just ask my Aunt T. S. Eliot (i.e., Theresa Suzanne – reach her at: *Stickyourtongueout.com* for confirmation), and she'll tell you that she read me Mother Goose rhymes during toilet training sessions with her. Sure, Auntie Eliot's knuckles on the crown of my head for plunging one or the other of my legs into the toilet on more than one occasion helped to spark the Muse inside of me; however, I have to high five the Goose for its part. After all, the cow jumped over the moon and the moon was a heavy (man) influence on my early poetry. Once during an episode of Episodic TV, the moon played *Peeping Tom* through the living room picture window with my young wife and me. My wife was a good looker, and I remember (as a bad looker) how excited we were about the event. Soon after, I started to howl at the damn orb and wrote the following poem after a night of shooting pool with the locals and migrant workers in a dive bar, in a small town, south of Rochester, New York, that we called home:

Man and the Moon

When he first started
seeing the moon
it was like a demolition ball
cracking the night
into large chips

rolling back laughing
dangling like a plumb line.

After that they drank
quite often together.
He would sing his wolf tunes;
the moon would imitate
his drunken walk
and try to pick up ladies.

This was fine
until townspeople grew uneasy
of girls with moon
on their breath
like mouthwash.

from *White Man Appears on Southern California Beach*
(Bottom Fish Press, 1991)

A literary journal called *Modern Poetry Studies* published the poem in its Winter 1976, Volume VII., Number 3 issue. At the time, I was a grade four elementary school teacher and unsure of how to celebrate my success (got Aberration); I chose to do nothing at all.

I'm not sure how many MFA programs there are today and/or the number of Exotic (Vacationland) Writing Workshops that are available to budding poets and writers. In regard to the MFA programs, the multiplication of the loaves parable from the New Testament seems to apply. There's a lot of hunger out there. As for Exotic (Vacationland) Writing Workshops, the rule appears to be the more the merrier. I've seen many advertised in *Poets and Writers Magazine* – some very enticing, offering from a week to ten days at tempting locales, such as, The Gulag Archipelago or at Pound's old pad in Spoleto, Italy. And once the eager participants pay for flight, food, room, and tour bus "trips" to the most memorable sights in a specific locale (it's a cultural experience for Chrissakes), they get their poems "workshopped" (not a word according to Billy Gates' Microsoft spell check; his choices include – "work shopped," "works hopped," "worshipped") by a Craft Master.

Pardon the Interruption (popular sports commentary show on ESPN) but in this case an influx of information. According to the Poets and Writers database there are 264 MFA programs. Now, considering an average of 50 students in each program who will eventually offer their own Exotic (Vacationland) Writing Workshop as soon as they exit a given program, some interesting options come into play, as in, 13,200 Exotic (Vacationland Writing Workshops) for those who didn't attend and/ or get into MFA programs to choose from to learn the craft during any given year. (not responsible for math calculations)

My life has been pretty bleak in terms of contact with Craft Masters. But back – prior to the loaves bit (and the information bit) – when there were only a few MFA programs available, I did get jumped by two graduates from the Iowa Writers' Workshop. According to them, I didn't know a damn thing about poetry and the painful fact that I received an NEA fellowship for writing about my experiences as a hospital orderly was nothing more than monkey-type lottery luck, and I should accept their *ass-whuppin'* in atonement for my good fortune.

OK, I'll admit to the fact that for a short time (ten years) I washed bedpans for a living in an assortment of hospitals prior to my gig as a teacher (**see Page Six**). I did other things other than "pans" while working in hospitals, such as the manual labor required of an orderly on geriatric and psychiatric units, which in turn led to poems like the following:

Mr. Cliff's Pee

"Hell, what's a little pain?
It's this damn forgetting
of where to pee that's
the pain in the ass.
That's why them ungrateful
kids brought me here,
because I peed all
over the house.
Why, all the damn times
I cleaned up their goddamn
pee, hell, the wife and I
never complained or brought

them to a hospital. But
they got their own lives
and feared their kids'd
get strange impressions
seeing their grandpa
pee in the closet.
Before the wife went I
always peed in the right place.
A great woman she was;
sure she'd be mad if I peed
on the rug, but she wouldn't
get rid of me like a fucking
dog."

from *Poems from a Thousand Hospitals: Dreams of Long Headdresses*
(Signpost Press, 1988)

As monkey-type lottery luck ordained, poems from my hospital days scored the NEA on my first try with the federal government (not counting previous audits for making under 10,000 during the Reagan Administration) which meant $12,500 in cash without restrictions (in 1982, the money came without a required oath not to buy drugs and/or do something despicable with the cash, as has been the case in subsequent years). At the time of the fellowship, I was up to my eyeballs in regret at being an elementary school teacher and a participant in a failing marriage, and I decided to temporarily flee to LA with the dough.

LA was delirious with sun and bums that enjoyed a free drink on the government, and with my willingness to fund drinking sprees, and my stupidity of leaving my Irish "white bread" skin in the sun for long intervals, I gathered enough literary experiences to write *White Man Appears on Southern California Beach*, my second volume of poetry, which was published by Bottom Fish Press in 1991.

Time Out

1. It's funny what comes to mind when writing an attack piece (in the form of a defense) on MFA programs and Exotic (Vacationland) Writing Workshops. For instance, I'm a big fan and admirer of Diego Rivera's work, and I just remembered reading somewhere or someone telling me how Diego was an inveterate liar when it came to representing the details of his life. So, assume that I have been lying about things so far:

Prevaricate When Possible

I eat my soup
Light
Clam
Chowder
& drink my wine
Pale
Golden
Pinot Grigio
& feel no envy
In the lies
I tell & tell
Myself
Like
All my friends
Have become
Distinguished
Professors of poetry
Or physics
At universities
I couldn't & can't
Get in to
& so what
Is not a cure
In the present
Condition

Of the world
Which was today
Like running
Off at the mouth –
A mouth full of molecules
& metaphors

So just suppose I was –
Because I don't have to be
In part 2 of this poem –
At a bookstore
Before soup
With Wittgenstein's
Tractatus Logico-Philosophicus
In my hands
& had stumbled on that
Via a tome on God
By an ex-nun –
Who spoke of Hell (fifties style)
In the preface
But knew how neither it
Nor God (as abstract being)
Really existed
That somehow God was an act of creative
Imagination
Which Blake knew
& Einstein too
In his dis of knowledge
& likewise di Prima in one
Revolutionary letter
Which counseled on the
War
The ongoing
Everyday war
In almost all walks
Of life
(Especially political)

Against the imagination –

& a new one – *Sifting through the madness for the*
Word, the line, the way –
By Buk
Telling in his posthumous, ethereal voice
Not his drunken, real one
Wannabe writers to scatter
Back to wives and girlfriends
& forget the task of words
On the very first page
Of the very first poem
Before Ludwig (in other words)
Got in his shots
That the world is composed of facts
& language gains its
Purity – its beauty (logical, OK, logical beauty & perfection)
Like the girl we both used to
To know & want –
From them

Which ain't no lie

from *Big Hammer #12*

2. And even though this piece is an attack (in the form of a defense) on MFA programs and Exotic (Vacationland) Writing Workshops (often advertised in *Poets and Writers Magazine*), it will in very short order consider and/or at least allude to the "indeterminacy of text."

3. I'm not bitter (foreshadowing).

Time In

I remember how excited Tom Haines (the publisher of Bottom Fish Press) and I were when the Federal Express truck showed up at his rural castle on Ingraham Road in Binghamton, New York, with boxes of the *White Man*. We sprinted to the truck with such an intensity the flummoxed driver asked: "What do we got here, boys, pornography?" Oh, the trials of manhood associated with bringing this work to light. Tom restores buildings for a living (in addition to being a great artist) and re-painted the largest building in town to fund the project. Since 1991, he has not published another book, but may soon do so, by the renegade landscape artist and poet, Peter Kidd. Kidd, by the way, read and mentally reviewed the *White Man* while barreling down a New Hampshire highway in one of his company's trucks. His written review of it appeared in *The Bellingham Review*, Vol. 15. No. 2, Fall 1992.

It's pretty easy to infer at this point that my lack of admission to an MFA program or attendance at an Exotic (Vacationland) Writing Workshop has had _____and led to_____ for me.

(This is the required <u>Audience Participation Section</u> of the "essay" and the start of an extremely long and taxing parenthetical comment with the possibility of parenthetical closure not even an option…So, please turn-n-talk, call, email, or text someone and fill in the blanks above before continuing with **In Defense of the MFA and Exotic (Vacationland) Writing Workshops**.

Resume Reading {parenthesis continued}

and now that you have filled in the blanks or considered doing so, let me point out that after I came back busted from LA, and with two little ones to raise, I did try to get into SUNY Binghamton's MA in Creative Writing program in order to garner the stipend (3,000 grand or so) to live on but was met with outright hostility by the Program Director. {Let me just say in brackets, that I have a real problem with Program Directors and Program Coordinators. I nearly got banned from elementary school teaching by the Program Coordinator of Teachers at SUC Geneseo. Without going too far into it, he thought I was an asshole and unfit to teach in any public school in New York State. Without challenging the notion of the utilization of brackets within a long and closure-free parenthesis, I jumped over the desk separating us during his harangue about unfit status etc, grabbed him by the tie and wrestled him to the floor, which led to a security escort off the campus and eventual placement in the Campus School – one rigged with a two-way mirror for spying on prospective teachers. Though I gave the finger to those behind the mirror while working with second graders on choral poems, nothing much ever came of my protest signal to the – you guessed it – Program Director} Stay with me now, I'm back inside the parenthesis [but obviously not for long with the handy square bracket available during this claustrophobic sojourn inside a parenthesis.

OK, back when I was a sophomore at SUNY Binghamton, I took an introductory poetry course for the hell of it. I still have the volume we used – *Open Poetry* – where I first read folks like Creeley, Ginsberg, Merwin, and a guy name Mezey whom I really liked. I had no poet in me at that time but I gave it a shot and started to compose depressing poems about my shitty love-life. I got up the courage to show one to the graduate student in charge of the seminar component, but he shook his head in total discouragement about my woeful understanding of poetry and how to write it. He was kind enough to share a poem written on a piece of scrap paper by the most promising student with me and recently turned into him:

> since feeling is first*
>
> since feeling is first
> who pays any attention
> to the syntax of things
> will never wholly kiss you:
> wholly to be a fool
> while Spring is in the world
>
> my blood approves,
> and kisses are a better fate
> than wisdom
> lady I swear by all flowers. Don't cry
> -the best gesture of my brain is less
> than your eyelids' flutter which says

we are for each other: then
laugh, leaning back in my arms
for life's not a paragraph

And death I think is no parenthesis

Pete Rabbit

"See," the graduate student beamed, "see what this student wrote, handing me the soiled scrap of paper. Now that's poetry." What could I say? He was completely right. I loved the piece immediately and couldn't wait to buy the kid a beer the next day. It took me years to use the words *paragraph* and/or *parenthesis* in a poem, but I became an instantaneous life-long admirer of Pete Rabbit's poetry due to that encounter.

assignment on waking

for peter rabbit (aka e.e. cummings)

the argument of painted shoes
rejects the jargon of the master

bells ring

the **paragraph (see story)** walks on stage
the litany begins

soft monsters fold flowers into balls
the solar system coughs
on cue the future shines
on the alphabet highway

all rise

the judge disrobes
and judgments haunt

the stalled philosopher of manners

roll over enjambments
trick the dead line into life

so this is consciousness of the dance
whirlwind of tiny kisses transmitted
by a savior of mild confusion

off goes the editing button

the child of busted alarms
resists the punishment

TOO

a hurricane of numbers forged on syntactical darkness

just when you think connections
bounce off the shoulders

of giants
the phone rings
the stew in the pot grows cold

Hurry up honey, the rambling typist
promised the interview committee
a session of colons by dawn

consistency is the verdict of small minds

aphorisms grow shutters
when windows relinquish
the meaning of light

caught in the rhythm of dissonance
the revised stare enhanced

shadow

empty institutions flitter away

rules of mind ease up

from *against news*, Fell Swoop #83

Time Out

Dylan hiatus: *"And my best friend, my doctor/Won't even say what it is I've got"*
          (Just Like Tom Thumb's Blues)

Indeterminacy: "A term drawn from poststructuralist crit. which suggests the
          impossibility of stabilizing a text's (or word's) meaning."
          (The New Princeton Encyclopedia of Poetry and Poetics)

Once the text left, heaven it has been wandering in a wilderness of signs.
(I said that)

TIME IN
RESUME READING

      Title

      Whether "faith" or
      Not
      Is part of
      The religious experience

      A satchel of rivers
      A satchel of river
      Poems

      Stone steps
      The wisdom tree

Shouting omnipresence
Into a crowd

The number of interpretations
Possible
Meaning cowering in fear

Momentary wait
Rereading the event
Of words

Who's guiding the unknown hand
The sex of it
Deep in the bones

All those flowers
And kids
The upright walk
Attributed
To the clown of happiness

Splash some art
On it
Unfurl magic commandments

Consider the
Act of construction
The stapler
On the desk
Arrangement of scattered
Pens
And pencils

Postcards of
Encouragement
Surround you
Say nothing

(In the
Parenthesis)

Romantic train
Whistles
In the distance])

from *Under the Sky of No Complaint* (Lavender Ink/Fell Swoop, 2013)

    Sorry, I need to bail from the parenthesis/braces/bracket fixation for the sake of sanity, so please pardon any floating fragments and/or disconnections in the "essay" up to this point – call it the indeterminacy of text (see above – I know I have the jitters), which in Unofficial Verse Culture is as popular as The Indeterminacy (uncertainty) Principle is for today's physicist, which I've attempted to address in the two poems below:

Choo-Choo

My brain's crushed by sunlight.
I could have said mayonnaise or darkness.
I have that much control
Over the objects of prepositions.

It's actually a very cerulean day.
My textual shoes fit and though
My fellow pedestrians dart between cars
None of them have been hit.

*

So so so so so
I'm at a bar full of smoke, conversation,
Music, TVs without sound, and we're all
Waiting for the train to take us home.

I could have said *Messiah* -
Once again finding my words
And sense of control
In the presence of a preposition.

*

Let me be forthright here:
I've been feeling tense today.
I'm on hold.
Cerulean is a better adjective than nice.

I'm not looking for things to come in threes.
I've been introduced to the *Trinity*
And the three-point line.
Numerology is not my number.

*

In fact, I'm lost in space.
Suppose (for instance) each line
Of a poem behaved like a single electron
In an empty box.

What is the position of a given line?
Does its velocity increase
As the mind collapses around it?
So where is it after all?

*

You know what I mean.
Someone actually coined the term:
Quantum foam or was it *froth?*
We know where *quark* came from.

But I'm pushing here –
Not drugs or knowledge
But a day at the office
In America, choo – choo!

from *Marks* (Asylum Arts, 2002)

SLOW LIGHT

1

When you chill a clump of sodium atoms
To a millionth of a degree above absolute zero
Light slows upon entering the clump.
Now a muon has acted up inside a technical doughnut.
Let's fire the paperboy!

2

Now for the news:
What a pitiful saying in times of trouble.
But it snowed today – a
Wet and heavy snow destined
For hemlock branch and children.

3

Whacked by imagery the stellar noodle
Gained the lamppost's respect.
So the highway turned past dawn
And the charm of brilliant teeth
Broke the prairie quiet.

4

No thoughts rehearsed.
But where the hell did my heel inserts
Disappear to?
You know the kind: Scholl's.
I thought about becoming a doctor once

5

Then took to walking past blank cities –
Hitchhiking afternoons
Into every evening I could think of.
Twilight was always a number for me.
I knew that much about the geography of stars.

from *Marks* (Asylum Arts, 2002)

OK, I know crap about modern physics and poststructuralist criticism, but I'm moving at a certain speed now and my location (maybe even position on things or in these words) can't be known. Of course, I didn't get into the damn MFA program in Binghamton. A divorced guy with two young children (sympathy vote) with a fresh NEA fellowship for writing about bedpans didn't cut it with the PROGRAM DIRECTOR. He said something about other talented students and would let me in without any dough to pursue further studies. I can't remember if I gave him the finger or not, but I left his office with a profound distaste for creative writing programs and workshops. *Don't Take It Personal* has always been my motto. (prevaricate when possible)

Right after that I founded the Big Horror Poetry Series, which ran for fourteen years in downtown Binghamton. A crew of friends – poets and musicians – managed and supported the series (**all noted in boink! – free download of my anti-memoir at lavenderink.org**) The series catered to poets and writers from the *multi-un-i-verse* of poetry. No school. No school of thought. ETC. ETC – just quality, difference, and variety. Even MFA graduates and workshop freaks were accepted and incorporated into the series.

A few years ago, I tried to resurrect the *multi-un-i-verse* idea in Boston. For a year, I ran a diverse series in the neighborhood I live in. I brought in Fanny Howe, Bill Corbett, Robert Mooney, Dave Kelly, Joel Dailey and others. The crowd badgered me for Robert Frost and no music please with the poetry. And one guest author even offered his best wishes to me on a *multi-un-i-verse* of verse, while noting university poets at one university don't attend readings by university poets at another university and vice versa throughout glorious Academia, and by extension most, if not all, university poets wouldn't waste their time with poets from the street (kick in a vice versa here also). Poets are busy people and necessarily stuck (by choice) in their neat little categories happily teaching hordes of duped students (**see poem**) how to maintain insularity from each other and all the others out there who scattered into the proverbial hills upon hearing sweet Poesy's name.

Of course, I'm bitter.* The bile spills out of me like oil from a breached tanker. But I hope a little cantankerousness didn't interfere (indeterminacy of text or not) with my livid and progressive defense for MFA programs and Exotic (Vacationland) Writing Workshops.

*Please follow the * to see how to escape my bitterness jag.

```
**********************************************************
**********************************************************
**********************************************************
**********************************************************
**********************************************************
**********************************************************
**********************************************************
**********************************************************
**********************************************************
**********************************************************
**********************************************************
**********************************************************
**********************************************************
**********************************************************
**************************************************
```

Bitterness Tanked

*T*here has to be a connection between a dip in serotonin and testosterone levels and a lack of bitterness toward others, Peabody thought. Of course not everyone would agree or buy that random thought moving through Peabody's head like a derailed locomotive. Why should they? Who the hell did he think he was, anyway?

The Rhetorical Society of America and Gun Club was aghast, scandalized … (and minus an and) pissed off. In fact, Riordan McDuffy, executive secretary of the RSAGC, and vaguely in charge of monitoring random thoughts in members' heads and the relationship to the overproduction of rhetorical questions in typical and atypical conversational events, dashed off a quick missive to Peabody. Something in the neighborhood of:

Date Etc.

Dearest Peabody,

We at the society are aghast, scandalized…(and minus an and) pissed off.

Locked and Loaded,

R. McDuffy

PS. Remember we are also a gun club.

Hmm, Peabody thought. *I'm not even a member.* On the other hoot (which could be "hand" if Peabody was even slightly ambidextrous), Thelma, his wife of thirty-five years, thought the old bastard had finally lost his mind. Peabody (and she knew this better than anyone) had always been quite bitter toward others. And why not (*too duck or not to duck?*), Peabody's mom (it had to start somewhere) had informed him through a series of short, 8 millimeter home movies (one of them shows little Peabody without a tear in his eyes as his mother presents a series of flash cards [SWEETIE PIE   CUTIE   WHAT A BEAUTIFUL DAY   HELP ME   STOP IT YOU'RE KILLING ME] representing her emotional highs and lows associated with raising an insensitive log) that he had been born with a wooden heart. It's a fact (just Google woodenheart. org) that wooden hearts and those born with them lack the spectrum of robust feelings that define "heart" and generally default to the frozen zone of bitterness as a safe haven response to the travails and trivialities of life. So, a sudden lack of bitterness, even within the milieu of a random thought off the rails like *the engine that could,* seemed and had to be deemed suspect.

In addition, Peabody was not an exceptionally bright bulb (i.e., that he had thoughts or the capacity to think was under review, had to be, if you know what I mean, don't you think at this point? If, indeed, you are a thinking reader, or minimally Cartesian?). To the point, he flunked the alphabet in elementary school, and during his middle school years he wore plastic bags over his feet while showering after gym class due to the crop of plantar warts on the bottoms of his feet. Peabody went to West Junior High School where the mantra there was nothing less than the catchy phrase, *let's play sports in the nude (see poem and toot my own critical comment)*, which unfortunately for Peabody introduced him to his first problem and encounter (sort of like with aliens) with testosterone. For some reason, possibly genetic and/or manipulated and plotted by a host of fun-loving gods and goddesses (Peabody had at least heard of Mount Olympus), old Peabody, as young Peabody, was not given and/or could not produce the recommended dose of testosterone that would have enabled him to project some indication of true manhood in his early teenage years. And if facts be told, just like they should be, the actual laughter from cruel middle school mates had nothing to do with the baggies on his freaking feet, but rather the howls and belly-gut guffaws had everything to do with the size of Peabody's pecker, a terribly little and restricted wiener, no bigger than a cocktail hot dog – the kind served swarming in ketchup sauce at the exquisite soirees in the banquet halls of roadside truck stops. (Peabody's Uncle Milhouse also loved the little doggies and enjoyed the haute cuisine of mixing the *barkers* with tiny, Swedish meatballs in a grand crystal bowl to celebrate certain holidays and family traditions like *Scratch Off Ticket Day Winner* and *The Ponies Came In Day*, but that's another story as they say [who again] in the parenthesis business).

O, poor Peabody of the wooden heart and tiny pecker, Peabody used to say to himself during his young adult years when many a fine-looking and young lassie left him standing in the rain, after dumping his ass for being such a stupid shit (bulb redux) when it came to knowing what a young woman really wanted from a potential mate and/or in a long-term beau. Peabody's stock phrases from his bitterness library – *the world sucks; we're all doomed; how the hell did we end up in such a place under such circumstances; has the universe tricked us; is this truly the best of all possible places* – didn't exactly prime Cupid's arrow. Nor did his regrettable stories of his total embarrassment of shivering his naked butt off by the edge of the middle school's chlorinated pool – while the coach taunted him to jump into the maelstrom of this particular form of matter (which he feared like the plague or at least tooth decay) as his classmates beaned him with water polo balls – play to or affect a young lady's decision to abandon him like the proverbial, possibly pre-ontological, hot potato to the raindrops and downpours that echoed her rhythmic tone of self-righteous disdain for the real and emerging Peabody.

Serotonin, of course, was another issue, and to say that Peabody grew depressed over time with the vagaries of his lugubrious experiences due to the lack of this neurotransmitter is a tough call. Certainly, the lack of this cranial elixir impacted (some say – those people again – quelled) his knee-jerk and hair-trigger urge to call others around him real assholes and contributed to the days he spent staring out the dirty windows of his abode, thrumming his lips like a common idiot, while his wife, Thelma, shouted in his waxy ears: "Get a job you lout before I leave you, too!"

True (as noted), Peabody was left and/or abandoned by others and for years responded to the indignity of it all with a catalog (small notebook) of wrongs he carried in his back pocket like a revolver. A sampling from the notebook includes: 1. Never breast fed; 2. Never breast fed. Stupid stuff like that which he laid on friends, loved ones, and even strangers when the bitterness he felt, no matter how ineffective or inane, took over like the failed brakes of a runaway truck on the interstate.

Then one day the bitterness was gone from his soul. It just burst into nothingness like the mighty sun laying waste to a recalcitrant and mammoth rain cloud. Peabody had ripened, moving through the years of moderate testosterone availability (tiny wiener and all, he did crank out ten ungrateful brats with Thelma) into a paucity or drought (or even a return to his earlier years) of the he-man substance, and with the concomitant, slow, but continued decline in serotonin levels in his noodle, a kind of resignation (a Dane might feel) came over him, not depression really, just a resignation that the world and its inhabitants – from dogwood trees in blossom, to ants in his cats' dishes, to the individuals and loved ones that still enjoyed sticking their tongues out at him – were nothing less than beautiful.

from *Fell Swoop #82*

(see sonnet)

(THE) DE/DUM 5

14 lines can be broken into four sections 3 quatrains and a couplet
Rhyme scheme: AB/AB CD/CD EF/EF/ GG or ABAB CC
10 beats per line alternating unstressed and stressed syllables
Three quatrains contain four lines the couplet just two lines both rhyme
First quatrain establishes theme/idea (my lover is a knock-out
and doth torture me) 4 lines AB/AB
Second quatrain develops theme/idea (my lover thy wickedness
is hot because….) 4 lines CD/CD or AB/AB
Third quatrain rounds off theme/idea, i.e. possible consequences (my lover
doth see me in a new light and requires certain behaviors methinks
I'm unfamiliar with) 4 lines EF/EF or AB/AB
Couplet summarizes theme/idea or introduces a fresh look at the theme/idea (my lover
thou hast changed thine locks on doors and no longer respond to entreaties
via text messages) 2 lines GG or CC

from *The Year I Wanted to Be on Television, Fell Swoop #132.7*

(**see story**)

Seething with Range

Mitch read Kierkegaard by the age of ten, jumped from the roof of his house into sparse grass with his dad in heated pursuit, disliked vegetables, got lost in high school, flunked out of college, tackled the Matterhorn on acid, evaded the service, wore glasses, married young, divorced young, raised kids in the State of Transportation, lost many jobs, married older, sailed the seas, took a test and discovered he was a pathological liar, swam into the sea as far as he could without a rope around his waist (H. Miller's advice), refused therapy and self-help books, wrote self-help books, argued incessantly with himself and others about the STATE OF SELF, got mad, got angry, broke some stuff, loved clouds and music, read Sartre when he was eleven, defied sequence, told others he had never taken a test and discovered that he was a pathological liar, loved his parents, had siblings, suspected chronology of foul play, bailed on being, enjoyed commas, fought nothingness, went bald, loved croquet, got mad, got angry, broke some stuff, drank fine wine, read Schopenhauer the moment he turned twelve, got arrested, went bankrupt, felt rejected, failed to study the classics, failed a pass/fail course on Martin Heidegger, cried often, wept sometimes, loved anthropology, got mad, got angry, broke some stuff, bathed in starlight, had an affair, begged forgiveness, stayed married, got bored, rejuvenated at last, ate vegetables and would never qualify for early retirement.

It seemed to Mitch, and Mitch knew a lot about seeming, that by the time he had entered the second **paragraph** of his life, which he called NOW, he was seething with range. It felt good to him like a finely tailored suit or a bunch of similes out on the town for some fun and games to have such range, though those caught in his entourage of forgiveness, the by-product of such range, were not so sure.

Take Mabel, his first wife, for instance. She was uncomfortable with Mitch's notion of entourage and her election into it and didn't hesitate to phone one of his wayward siblings. Mitch had a boatload of them, though his intense fixation on philosophy at such an early age kept him from forming any meaningful bonds with them. Thus, while Mitch was testing the rungs on the "ladder of despair," they were out in the neighborhood climbing trees, playing capture the flag, forming crushes and drinking beer in the shadows of school parking lots.

So imagine, if you will (*Veronderstel zo, als u zal; Imaginez ainsi, si vous; So vorstellen, wenn man wil)*, the strange discomfort Mitch's oldest brother felt when Mabel's call came at the exact moment (suspect chronology) he had taken a black and white composition notebook out of a plastic CVS bag in order to finally write down some of his unexpressed feelings about his younger brother – with the first sentence to his own chagrin: *Mitch was a boy genius and a bastard* – who had never connected with him etc. due to an intense fixation on philosophy and a proclivity (as duly documented in paragraph one of Mitch's life) for pathological lying. Setting down his pen, he picked up the walk-around phone and pressed the connection button. "Damn, I think I had something going there," he muttered to himself, as Mabel's voice blew into his ear like a small plane crashing in a hemlock forest.

"Ralphie, is that you?" she screeched in a voice of pure green flames.

"Huh?" Ralphie said, distracted by the crackling on the line. "Who is this?"

"Who? Why me, that's who," Mabel cried, pulling herself from the wreck of her own voice.

"I think you have the wrong number, lady," Ralphie said.

"The hell I….do," Mabel said, momentarily detained by a coughing fit spurred by the ingestion of a smoky lozenge. "I married your idiot brother, didn't I?"

"Mabel?" Ralphie said, incredulously.

"Yeah, it's me," she said, with sooty hesitation before continuing with the bluster of a campfire girl sparking flames with flint and sticks. "Now don't go all weird on me and start asking about why I'm calling you after all these years etc. etc., 'cause that's just a bunch of bullshit."

The tonal quality of this last phrase transported Ralphie into the haze of memories he had retained about his brother's unfortunate first marriage. From this haze, Mabel appeared along with Mitch. She had him in an impressive headlock, on the ground, and screaming into his ear: "I don't give two shits about phenomenological reduction. You got that!" According to the memory, he was sitting in their kitchen and had just popped the top on a can of Bud when the altercation took place. The memory started to degrade after that, but not before Mabel's Amazon sensuality glimmered like a radioactive ghost in his startled, retroactive eyes. She was quite a babe!

"OK," Ralphie said. "What can I do for you, Mabel?"

"Have you been in touch with him or has he been in touch with you?" she inquired like a smoke ring coming out of an elephant's mouth. "Has he written or sent an email to you or anything?"

"Mabel, I don't even know where Mitch is. One of my sisters sent me an email saying she had received an almost totally illiterate note from him saying he had entered the second paragraph of his life or something. There was no return address on the envelope. It appears he may be out in LA."

"Anything else?" Mabel inquired, cooling down to a pond of marshmallow embers.

"No," Ralphie said.

"Well, I got the same note with the second paragraph of his life bullshit that also mentioned in a nearly indecipherable manner that he had some transformative vision and/or had gone through a transmogrified incident like the main character in Kafka's bug story and via – yes, VIA – one of these, I don't know which, thanks to his chicken scrawl, that he's no longer seething with *rage* but with *range*," she said, reheating like a new spark nestled in the needles of a forest floor. "The dope adds one freaking letter to one freaking word like he's the master of Japanese errors, and thinks, after all the chaos he has caused, that he has entered a new and essentially different part of his stupid narrative, oddly characterized as paragraph two. Plus, the bastard has the gall to tell me that I'm now part of his entourage of forgiveness."

Ralphie fell into the flames of her words like a deflated weather balloon into a desert storm of Ohio Blue Tip Matches. *Bastard,* he thought. *That's my term for genius boy.*

Mabel continued like a lick on an enraged guitar: "I'll tell you right now, Ralphie boy, you can tell that dolt of a brother of yours, I will never be a part of his entourage of forgiveness!"

The hard click in his ear told Ralphie to hit the end button on his phone and place it back in its holder. Then he sat back down at his desk, picked up his pen, thought for a moment about the number of members in his brother's entourage of forgiveness and began to write the next sentence in his account of his unexpressed feelings about his brother – a sentence full of warmth as if the sun were cooled by just the right amount of ice cubes by an exquisite, mathematical equation. Something Mitch would understand.

from *Altercations in the Quiet Car* (Lavender Ink/Fell Swoop, 2010)

(see poem)

AFTER PROSODY CLASS

I'm a connoisseur of weather balloons
Sorghum is my favorite
Followed by metaphysics and St. Paul
Sometimes things go awry
In a line of poetry
A tornado hits
Instead of the speed of light
Or a peach cast from a branch
Of thin air

Silence reigns
The ocean is a velveteen quilt
A band member with a broken guitar string
The mailbox suffers an empty stomach of sound
It's time to wait at a red light
For a basket of groceries
Missionaries at the front door
With pamphlets on Presence
Read absent lips

If the past intrudes
Father was a grand mal gangster
Mom played the piano for pleasure
Are lines to scan
Of course there are gaps to consider –
Nights of stressed and unstressed lovers
With hummingbird tattoos
The pattern of grease from a bicycle chain
On a pair of hands

The poem is always about something else
It has a history –
Was a track star at Mineola Prep
Sold electromagnetic fields

Door to door
As well as insurance
Maybe it's the Declaration of Independence
Or the United States Constitution
It detests the strip search

Eventually there is a tower of rocks
In the backyard
Without a metaphor in sight
A visiting archaeologist produces notepad and spade
There is work to be done –
Artifacts and archetypes to plunder
"Watch for gas lines," I shout
Before blue jays in the hemlocks
Steal breakfast

from *Under the Sky of No Complaint* (Lavender Ink/Fell Swoop, 2013)

(see poem and toot my own horn critical comment)

GREENHORNS

Mom makes sandwiches with butter
and without.
I take the ones without.

The President is shot
and a student runs down the hall
smiling and screaming:
"The President has been shot!"

"Aren't you going to watch it
on TV?
It's on TV," my sister says.

I bounce my basketball up the street.
I'm thinking about the dance
And Kathy's tits.

Is it wrong?

They make us swim in the nude in gym class.
They make fun of those
who are afraid of the water.
In the shower my balls shrivel into atoms.

They call us greenhorns
and knock the books from our arms.
A punk picks me up and throws me
headfirst into a snowbank.

When the girl next to me
gets her period
during English class
the teacher locks us in the room
and calls us animals
through a small window in the door.

Dad drives a Bonneville.
The country mourns.

I want to be a gym teacher.

from *Modulations* (Asylum Arts, 1998)

"I've read your *Modulations* with real pleasure, liking the energy of your wit and invention. Everything resonates, and there's one verbal surprise after another. "Greenhorns" is tremendous in the way it eludes expectations line by line. What's valuable in these poems is your escaping the all-too-usual triteness of the ametrical free-form poem that everybody writes nowadays (and reads in an adenoidal whine with fierce seriousness)."
  – Guy Davenport

-DIATRIBE MEUM VEL TUUM-

Th-th-th-that's all folks!

– Porky Pig

Fell Swoop #122

* *since feeling is first* is from **Is 5** by e.e.cummings, edited by George James Firmage (Liveright, 1985, p. 93)

The universe's intentions (or non-intentions) transcend language and scientific inquiry although both of these are useful in disclosing the existence of the universe itself. Mind is needed to jumpstart the project of being.

I just had a turkey club with potato salad and a glass of Pinot Grigio at the Corrib Pub.

The sentence is a beautiful thing (**see poem**) – full of range and mundanity.

I started writing this genre-less writing event and compilation in July (2014) and it is still July. Humid today: trees in a mantra of deep green; joggers, kids in strollers on their way to the park, old men in chairs in front of kept lawns, blue sky and cumulus clouds. Things of summer and the world.

The mind is part of the world and resides in many places. Mind is equivalent to soul. Past souls or minds are fully present in present minds and souls when the mind or soul opts for such a condition.

The soul lives a full life in the future without necessarily conveying that to the mind of the past and present.

I don't understand quantum mechanics but I wished that I did. It seems at times to me to be the "subconscious" infrastructure of the everyday world we live in. Residents of the everyday world expect (wish) and admire predictability and security. The facts that the earth spins at a rate of a 1000 miles per hour and the entire Milky Way galaxy hurls through space at a rate of 1.3 million miles per hour don't often grab our attention or unsettle us. I live on this street and so do you etc. However, our "subconscious" partner of quarks un-united pursues a different path – one of probability, chance and/or random occurrence. And despite (and here's a quantum leap) the proliferation of online dating services, love (**see poem**) is a random occurrence – a set of quarks and quirks waiting to bop into being, become manifested/there in the Greek sense of being.

Sometimes I find myself lost in a reverie (**see poem**) about the equivalence between matter and energy via Einstein's famous equation $E = mc2$. It seems weird that the matter composing our bodies (quarks and friends) could be converted into energy upon the square of the speed of light and that that energy is essentially already part of the grand energy that reigns supreme (dark and otherwise) and quite frankly is stored in empty space, which more or less blows the lid off nothingness, edging in doing so toward a recurring eternity of possibilities, and yet we feel the beat of finitude within us or as Rilke offers in his incomparable Ninth Duino Elegy:

> *"Once* for each thing. Just once; no more. And we too,
> just once. And never again. But to have been
> this once, completely, even if only once:
> to have been at one with the earth, seems beyond undoing."

(Rilke from The Selected Poetry of Rainer Maria Rilke,
Edited and Translated by Stephen Mitchell, Vintage Books, p. 199)

But even with a combo of scientific knowledge and poetic insight, suffering and mayhem persist in the world. Would being eternal suffice? Beyond undoing? And are these questions shaped by the spontaneity of language in the mind?

Voltaire got it right in *Candide*. Without a doubt the world (creation) is a stupendous and mind-boggling achievement. Who wouldn't choose being or over nonbeing? But in response to Pangloss' (Leibniz?) optimism that the present world is the best of all possible worlds because God is all perfect and powerful and thus a world created by God would have to be the best of all possible worlds, Voltaire shares a horrific odyssey of suffering souls. (**see poem**) Imperfections, mistakes and evil perceived by us are simply the result of our inability to perceive God's grand plan. Forget the abstractions, Voltaire counsels, and plant and work a real garden. (**see poem**)

(**see poem**)

Surreal Heartache

1

I've sued icons and figurines
      for imagined regret

before the world was here
      starkly infinite

with football
      and talent shows

2

Language is a habit
      like the mirth of flowers

when the wind requires
      the mind

To exchange thought
      for moonlight

3

The sentence is beautiful
      isn't we say

as snow falls and forms
      a lake of light

as brilliant as the sun
      and mostly divine

4

We pray
　　　　or play

and no one is too plain
　　　　or to blame

as the planet turns
　　　　into a night of mirrors

(see poem)

THE POSSIBILITIES OF LOVE

There is no final ideogram
Or harmonium in my head
Air rain and clouds
Attract the naïve body
We're here
Games between our favorite teams
Forgo cultural exegesis
Extinction demands an audience –
A pope with rings and celestial nightmares
Love filters the present
Botox lips elude sonnets

Words compete for the soul of transparency
Consciousness plays solitaire
In the light of day
It's hard to respect the intrusion of weather
Enough illusionary time has passed
To acknowledge the senseless slaughter
Is narrative dead in the water
Has the white fungus on the nose of brown bats
Been posted on Facebook

The mind plays capsized boat
Without provisions
The mating ritual of sunlight and silence
Spawns boisterous waves
Glacial
Apocalyptic
Precipitous
Fast
Collapsed stars succumb

To encrypted signs
In the name of a recalcitrant universe
I'm lost in the possibilities of love

from *BURP #6*

(see poem)

Reverie on a Park Bench

The gold mirror of imagination has broken in two
It was not a clean break –
Shards in a haphazard pattern cast a rainbow
On a sliver of apostasy

The other day I picked up a book about the universe
The first line claimed that everything is the universe
Or the universe is everything
Including the book the first sentence and the reader

It rained during the night with serious thunder and lightning
Ice cubes – well actually tiny pieces of ice and water droplets
On occasion rub against each other inside clouds like they're lonely
And presto! electrified dreams of the beautiful other

Sequence matters
On mute the universe mimics a dog taking a nap on a bus
No barking allowed
No driver either

Once I strolled down the paved streets of the mind
All the trees were fantastic structures
With leaves like orange doilies or bowling balls
The past slipped into the present and birds took flight

The word is out
Poetry has been eliminated from school curriculums
It's high time high kids learned to write a damn essay
On the history of software and its founders

I heard on the news the next Apocalypse could arrive any day now
Supposedly it was spotted by someone on a snowy summit
With a good set of binoculars and a penchant for coordinates
On a grid of rigged elusiveness

The happiness meter could use a few coins
Which I have in my pocket –
Rare ones like the Statue of Liberty and Mount Rushmore
On play the universe goofs around

from *Techniques in the Neighborhood of Sleep* (Spuyten Duyvil, 2016)

(**see poem**)

Sadness Competition

All those dropped on their heads
punched in the mouth
deprived of food
and clothing
hit by plates
and flying objects

line up over here

Those kicked from homes
had their land stolen
been relocated
incarcerated
tortured
made to disappear

stand over here

Rape
incest
abuse

here

Those injured or maimed in wars
police actions
on the streets

this line

Famine victims
survivors of holocausts
political prisoners
hostages

biological
chemical
fallout guinea pigs

to the right

Alone
sick
forgotten
addicted
from broken homes
outcasts
disadvantaged
to the left

Have we missed anyone?

The dead?

anywhere

OK the object
is to disclose
fathom cause
mobilize

Our judge today is Time

Everyone wins

from *Modulations* (Asylum Arts, 1998)

(see poem)

The Garden of Upside-Down Trees

So brave your heart
Running from the authorities suited you
Past memory and the full contact gear of the present
Who sings sweetly to me now

I've done the math
The archaic maestro of abstruse conversation
Stuck his tongue out at me
Trumpets bent their notes

Mental equations for childhood didn't work
The time to invoke a phenomenological reduction
On the contrite beauty of raindrops
Had passed

Given the status of my green card
It was cold in the barrio without thermostat
Or topological map
I was not the future of the heart's revolution

Granted this was a rough cut
As I recall you crushed a cigarette under foot
Before the chandelier of morning
Crashed to the floor

I thought of that-you thought of that
The mystery of dawn shuddered
After Einstein dropped Newton
Into the maw of gravity

Furiously
I thumbed through fibrous pages of empty space
Until the attack of gumball machines
Entered the fray of neophyte sentences

No kidding my feet itched
But did the holistic therapist need to lower
Cough drops into an imaginary fish tank
When the pilot announced his solo flight

Within range of a thunderclap of lips
The smokestack of ideas collapsed
Into the alphabet soup
Then we drove into a river of moons

I became a dilettante of unrest
Now draw the ellipsis of chance
And waters of neglect to scale
The house band told me

The hysterical addiction of consciousness
To the antics of information fractals
(Like spoiled children in a vat of 3D glasses)
Blew the mind of the JumboTron

Under a hurricane of pissed off street lamps
The parrot in the audio track of dreams
Disclosed the purpose of writing
Once inside a particle accelerator

Meanwhile the Maelstrom of Ceremony
Stole the architectural plans
For a casually caused universe
From the Guru of Indeterminacy

I turned off the light and scrolled through darkness
Outside the wall of doors
The Garden of Upside-Down Trees
Floated by

from *Under the Sky of No Complaint* (Lavender Ink/Fell Swoop, 2013)

The self (**see poem**) is many and takes a considerable (Herculean) effort to keep the many occupied and productive. Over the years, during clashes, seminars and collisions among the various contestants inside my mind, four fairly formed selves or souls have come into being and live alongside my consciousness as poets and writers in their own right (**see Book 2**). Because they're wise and disdain the creepy proliferation of online publications, they have chosen to publish exclusively with *Fell Swoop: The All Bohemian Revue*. The "Swoop" has been around since the early eighties under the tutelage of the brilliant editor and publisher, XJ Dailey, a reclusive SOB whose sole stated purpose in life is to destroy what's left of American poetry. In **Book 3** of this work, I will share my interview with Mr. Dailey and also provide a list of every poet and writer he has published during the course of 150 plus issues. Who's who to you, Horton?

However, I think I made a commitment on **Page Seven** to share on **Page Eleven*** an episode in my life related to receiving an NEA fellowship for Poetry (my only award for poetry** over the course of 40 years and the main reason I have the compulsion to keep mentioning it).

For now let me simply introduce the names of my writing heteronymic buddies (Got Pessoa): Duck Martian, Ant McGoogle, Al Pants, and Dik Tator.

*I was a pretty good high school basketball player and wore #11 as a jersey. I went to Catholic Central High School in Binghamton, New York. In my senior year, my guidance counselor thought I might have a vocation to the priesthood and suggested the seminary as a way to go to college.

A Wonder Bread Slice of Spacetime circa 1967
– approximate speed – *Warp to Forget.*

Father Hogan fixed his green eyes on my soul. I squirmed in my seat before him as if sitting on a jagged rock. His emerald peepers failed to notice that my soul wasn't presently in my body. It was absent and bouncing along the ceiling like a helium balloon searching for open sky. The thought of wasps from Dante's Inferno crawling up a fiery window to find the crack that would release them from Hell buzzed through my mind. I would like to be outside too, either as a balloon or a bee.

Perhaps, there was something wrong with his eyes. As the disciplinarian and guidance counselor at the school, he was heralded for his ability to look right through students to get to the heart of any matter by interrogating their souls. It was tradition and expected that Catholic Central students would weaken under their Kryptonite gaze, cough up their offenses at school and home – cop, in other words, to their copious sins and prepare for punishment. A quick slap across the face. Garbage detail. Painting the porch of the rectory. Things like that.

When it came to advice on what they should do or pursue in their lives, he read their souls like a palm-reader. You were too dumb or too poor to go to college. Be humble. Don't expect much from life. Pray. That my soul was out to lunch, had gone fishing, didn't seem to matter to him. How strange, I thought, staring at his round, pea-shaped head, as my soul played dodge ball with itself about his head.

"So, Marshall," he said, "what does a boy like you intend to do with his life, now that he has almost made it through his senior year?"

As he waited for my response, he picked up a stray pencil on his desk, a purple one, a Crusader pencil with sword and motto: *Crusaders crusade, find yours.* He toyed with the pencil, moving it deftly between middle and index fingers like a tiny baton. When not conducting an imaginary celestial orchestra, he tossed the pencil in the air, caught it, tapped it rapidly on the desk before setting it on top of his Breviary on the right side of his desk, next to the picture of Moses parting the Red Sea.

I didn't answer. Entranced by the movement of the pencil in his hand, I remembered what had happened to my friend, Mick, a couple of years ago in tenth grade – the tale of another pencil in a holy hand.

It was the first day in World History class, and like thirty or so other lucky students, we had been assigned to Sister Margaret Marie's section. Known in the halls as The Body, due to her slight and crooked body frame that even her nun garb couldn't hide, she stood before her classes like a hanger bent into the facsimile of a hooked nose. She demanded absolute silence from her boys and Mick found out quickly what she meant by that.

Standing in front of us with each of her swollen fingers meticulously wrapped in Band-Aids, she explained her classroom rules and policies.

"Boys," she hissed like a snake, a snake made of an exaggerated "s", a snake suffering from tinnitus that slithered into the ears of boys until it made way to the brain's amygdala, curling around the almond-shaped nuclei in support of fear. "There will be "s"ilence…absolute "s"ilence in this classroom. Right, boys?"

I nearly pissed my pants (due to my fear of snakes and the progeny of convents). Mick, who occupied the desk to my left, fiddled with his pencil as the "s" lodged in his brain, lost control of it and gasped slightly as it rolled off his desk into open space. Apollo 11 was a few years away but in some kind of prescient time warp, I saw Neil Armstrong and his mates walking in slow motion toward their spacecraft, as the pencil defied Newton's laws of gravity, opting for its own slow-motion descent to the floor. My eyes were fixed on the countdown. I watched the pencil hit the floor, pink eraser top first, before it toppled and crashed lengthwise on the floor. The Body was all over Mick. She lifted him up by his tie – gallows style, slapped his face and pushed him back in his seat. Like a quantum particle on a heavenly mission, she was back where she stood without having appeared to have left her original position.

"Boys," she said, "S"ilence."

Father Hogan grew impatient. He cleared his throat, drummed his fingers on his desk to regain my attention. There had been other beatings in the school, but so what. Corporal punishment was a featherweight in comparison to the kind of punishment waiting for those who went astray in the temporal zone.

I took a deep breath through my mouth and exhaled through my nose. My soul, tired of balloons, dodge balls and bees decided on new form and hung in the air like a spider on the silk thread of nothingness above the priest's head.

"Well, Marshall," Father Hogan said with some irritation in his voice, "what will you do after you graduate? Your folks don't have any money and the word is out that your father drinks too much."

Dad's drinking problem woke up my ears (**see poem**). A few months ago, after a few too many, he had caught my chin with a good left jab after I gave him the middle finger. No hesitation on his part. I flew across the living room into the wall by the upstairs staircase like a dumbass shot from a circus cannon. The sound my head made bouncing off the wall provoked my mother to speak.

"You've killed him, John," she said, seeing me scrunched into the wall, arms akimbo, a trickle of blood running down my chin. I hit the wall with such force the framed picture of Jesus Christ that hung on it, left its perch and smacked me on the head. Christ had his wounds but the picture that came to rest in my lap revealed as a good-looking white guy with long brown hair, prophet and precursor to the hippies.

"Well, Father," I said. "I'm not sure what I want to be."

Father Hogan grimaced as if possessed by a sudden intestinal cramp – a cramp arriving at the wrong time. His whole pasty face squeezed into the ruins of an overripe fruit, the wrinkled skin of a peach or an apple. I felt some pain too, mostly in my head, as my soul chose that moment to reenter by body. It's well known that a soul leaving the body doesn't cause pain but upon reentry an intense headache may occur for a short time. Biting hard on my lip, the pain transmogrified into the bafflement on the stern padre's face. He picked at a tiny brown wart on the end of nose before saying:

"You understand, Marshall, don't you, that college, at least a good one, is out of the question considering your grades and your family's financial situation."

"Yeah," I said like someone just assigned to a bout of Purgatory.

The priest read the haphazard tone of penance in my voice and perked up as if one of the maids back at the rectory had slipped him a Mickey of caffeine in his morning prune juice. A spry and gallant sun rose in the green seas of eyes. They gleamed, and upon closer inspection, I glimpsed a wee leprechaun (himself) kick up his heels and throw gold coins into the air. It was time for pertinent advice from the guidance counselor. Father Hogan had an idea.

"Look, Marshall," he began, "you're pretty astute when it comes to classes on religion. All the teachers think you might have a gift for metaphysics and advanced religious studies. Did you ever consider that God might be calling you to enter the priesthood, to respond to the vocation He's seeded in your soul?"

"God is dead," I said.

"Don't give me any smart lip, you little son of a bitch," Father Hogan said, "I eat guys like you for lunch."

The disciplinarian side was now on display. He snapped his fingers to indicate that lunch was about to start and bent over the front of his desk to retrieve the "Judge," the hickory switch he used to convert the sinners in his presence with a good old-fashion butt lickin'. His green eyes went radioactive. Edward Teller built a bonfire in them. Some quick thinking saved me.

"Maybe a vocation fits me," I said. "I'm a big fan of the Latin Mass."

Cool water filtered his eyes. He sat back in his seat and ran a hand across his baldhead, stopping in the middle to scratch something, maybe a bite left by my soul when it played the role of a spider.

"Look, son," Father Hogan said, "the seminary is the perfect solution for a guy like you and in your circumstances – a guy without any money, with minimal interest in things, of little accomplishment and no noticeable talents other than a taste for abstruse arguments. Plus the seminary is free. Your parish will pay for it. It's like being on welfare."

It was a lot to take in. I had memorized all the altar boy Latin responses for the mass and had taken to reading the Bible in my room when mom and dad were at each other downstairs. Mom new something was up from the time I was a little kid. Almost every night she snuck into my room and shook Holy Water on me and pinned sacred roses beneath my pillow. I had to wear a scapula and medal beneath my undershirt. For a while I was addicted to lighting votive candles. Father Hogan continued:

"You'll pick up a BA in Liberal Arts at the seminary, and if you decide not to continue for the next four years at the major seminary and become an ordained priest, at least you'll have a four year degree. You can't go wrong with that."

"Sounds pretty good," I said. "I'm not sure if my girlfriend will like it, but it sounds like a good deal. What do I have to do?"

There must be some prize or points accrued when a priest guides another into the priesthood. Who knows, maybe it's a new sleek black sedan to cruise around in or a trip to the Vatican for lunch with the pope. Whatever it may be, it sure made Father Hogan fill with glee. He clapped his hands, said, good, good, and tapped the religious icons on the front edge of his desk with his Crusader pencil. All the religious icons from St. Peter to Mary Magdalene looked pretty happy too about my decision. After digging in his top desk drawer, the happy priest laid the papers for me to sign out in front of me. I executed my John Hancock, shook Father Hogan's hand, and left his office.

The corridors were quiet as usual with students in their classrooms or getting knocked against the walls in their classrooms. *Not bad*, I thought, making my way to my *Why Wait until Marriage* seminar, just a few tense minutes with old frog-eyes, and I'm launched into a paid free college career.

"Dominus Vobiscum," I said, trying out my new language, as my soul leapt from my chest and tore down the hall in front of me to find and inform my girlfriend, Marilyn.

(see poem)

Self

I place my self in the grand tradition of conflict
With the self with others (and their selves)
And nature (and its self)

There is no self
Self-service gasoline is up two bucks

Once I was refused entry into a philosophy course
Entitled *Concept of the Self*

Self-service storage is sometimes referred to as mini-storage

Self contains the word "elf"
The plural of elf is elves
Some claim an individual self is composed of multiple elves
(And selves)

Herman Hesse stated in *Steppenwolf* that approximately
1000 selves comprise an individual self

There is only one SELF
This SELF has many historical and/or astronomical names

Self-service convenient stores are quite popular

Others maintain the SELF is actually all other selves
And just may have forgotten this fact
For some unknown reason

Self precedes the hyphen in numerous hyphenated words
A partial list includes: self-accusatory, self-delusional, and self-deprecatory

Some refer to the self as the ego
(As for etymology self is *suus* in Latin and *sva* in Sanskrit {meaning one's own})
Selfish and egotistic are adjectives

Selfish contains the word "fish"
The self may have or mostly likely evolved from or in water
Self is not necessarily the soul or is it

Selfish is a character trait
Self-cleaning ovens came on the market (patented) in 1963

That the self is alone, distinct, and inside the body
Is a bunch of crap to some thinkers –
Mere propaganda pumped into the self
From the moment of its birth
And reinforced throughout its odyssey of self-discovery
By schools and other social agencies

For many years I took advantage of self-service laundries
Checks payable to self provide ready cash

The *self* is no more alone than the SELF is alone
Scientists are beginning to think of the self (or consciousness/mind)
As the by-product of synaptic activity

Once the self is defined as consciousness it bifurcates into two forms:
Being-for-itself and Being-in-itself
Being-for-itself consciousness is the negating form of consciousness and/or a
Consciousness of lack
It is always consciousness of *something*
Being-in-itself consciousness is earth fire water air

Something contains the word "thing"
Thing or things are objects

Kant established the impossibility of knowing the *thing-in-itself*
Socrates said: *Know thyself*

Therefore if things are unknowable
The self is not a knowable thing

Selfing is not concurrently a recognized verb form
(Or is it as when one takes a selfie of one's self)
Though surfing is

The self loves to surf
As a process (not a thing)
In and out of understanding itself
It may be one…
It may be two…

Of Whom
Or what it is

Fell Swoop # 92

**According to his sonnet "Ordinary Days," Al Pants has garnered the following awards:

The day I was awarded a National Endowment for the Arts Fellowship, Poetry…
The day I was awarded a Guggenheim Fellowship…
The day I was awarded a MacArthur Genius Grant…
The day I was awarded the Pulitzer Prize for Poetry…
The day I was awarded the National Book Award for Poetry…
The day I was awarded the Lenore Marshall Prize for Poetry…
The day I was awarded the Wallace Stevens Award for Poetry…
The day I was awarded the Fellowship of the Academy of American Poets…
The day I was awarded the Dylan Thomas International Poetry Award…
The day I was awarded the Montreal International Poetry Prize…
The day I was awarded the Governor General's Award for English Language Poetry…
The day I was awarded the Nobel Prize in Literature…
The day I was awarded the Howard Nemerov Sonnet Award…
were the ordinary days in my life as a poet

from *The Year I Wanted to be on Television*, Fell Swoop # 132.7

(see poem)

The Bartender Remembers Raising His Son

He gave me the finger so I nailed him
with a left and he flew across the living room
into the wall and his mother ran down from upstairs
screaming: "You've killed him this time!"
Sure, I had had a few.
I was in electronic parts then
working commission
and taking heat from the boss
for telling some asshole with a dick order
where to stick it.
But it wasn't just the job or booze
but the way he looked at me
with defiant eyes.
And don't give me no hormones
cause he was like this
before his first hardon.
Back when I sold cars
his mother'd greet me at the door
with a litany of offenses.
He had a temper – nasty mouth –
and I used the belt on him then.
He was no dummy
but ran and locked himself in the upstairs bathroom
when I got home.
Sometimes I sent my fist into the door.
Oh, I'd give him a warning,
I'd say: "Get out here you little bastard
and face the music like a man."
The time he told me to calm down
I hit the door so fucking hard
a crack like a skull fissure
popped the lock.
When I kicked it open
the prick darted between my legs
into his sister's room

and out a window.
I chased him around the chimney
until he jumped – a good twenty feet –
onto the roof of the porch,
rolled across it, sprung up, and said:
"Jump old man!"
God, I admired his spunk and balls,
and with my hernia
sat down and listened to his laughter
as he skipped down the street.
I remember the stars were coming out
and I gazed at them for a while.

The Bellingham Review (Spring/Fall 1994)

Page Eleven

The Award

Bill glared at me over a mound of canteens on a table near the back of the store.

"It has been hell here, a goddamn war ever since we left Albany," he said.

His blue eyes seemed ready to explode and spurt hot blue blood into the air. His hands shook as he manhandled the canteens –a multi-colored assortment: flamingo pink, yellow, orange, green, red with black racing strips and all mixed together to form a rainbow mountain of water containers.

"What kind of fucking Army & Navy store is this," Bill said. "I want army, man, a typical army canteen to attach to my belt."

He dug into the pile like a dog on amphetamines. He wasn't a fan of boutique Army & Navy stores. Too many goddamn choices. He was trying to escape from LA not land a part in some style-conscious war flick. We had been to a number of WW 3 boutiques already, and with considerable struggle, he had patched together a regular ensemble of G.I. Joe green, black and tan – standard fatigues, boots, floppy camouflage hat, which he wore already (price tag included) and secured on his head with a small acorn-like wooden knob that slipped up two green draw strings until it came to rest on the underside of his chin. But no fucking canteen (his words)!

"Take it easy, will you, Bill," I said. "You're beginning to cause a scene."

A quick survey of the store revealed the eyes of the solitary store clerk fixed on our position. Dressed in yellow and orange camouflage fatigues, with a blue LA Dodgers baseball cap skewed to the left side of his head, he appeared ready and anxious to leave his post at the cash register near the front of the store in order to address Bill's behavior directly. A comment like: "Get the hell out of this store!" floated through my mind. At the moment, there were only a couple of other customers in the store. A skinhead in a faded denim jacket and jeans sat with his head in hands in the boot section near the left front window of the store while a young woman browsed through some camouflage underwear two tables down from us. The manager started to click his pen and turned up the volume of concern in his eyes.

"Bill, take it easy," I said again, when a few canteens fell to the floor from his agitated pawing into Canteen Mountain.

"Take it easy, rich boy," he barked. "I see what I want."

Near the bottom of the canteen pile the standard issue fumbled into his view like a wayward bone.

"Below the belt, Bill," I said. "Fuck you and that rich boy rap!"

"Look, Pete," he growled. "I've had it with you, Amanda, Ray and all of LA. I'm getting out of here tonight. One way or another, I'm out of here."

He unscrewed the cap on the canteen then shook it as if expecting water to come out of it. He screwed the cap back on and sized me up for an attack.

"You get what I mean, Pete. No more shit. No more missed flights. No more cars that breakdown. And no more love triangle bullshit!"

"Sure, Bill," I said. "I suppose Amanda and I are to blame for the flat tire last night on our way to LAX. Believe me Bill; I wanted your ass on that goddamn flight and out of here. ASAP, man. Get it."

Bill flinched and pulled a 12" hunting knife from its sheath and leaned across the table. He flashed the knife before my eyes and then nudged the point under my chin.

"I'm not making some fucking fashion statement here, Pete," he said. "I'm out of here. Out of this war zone, one way or the other, tonight!"

The exposed blade was the catalyst the manager needed. He raced down the aisle as Bill sheathed his weapon. When he reached us, he maintained his cool but showed us the 32 special he kept in his stylish fatigues.

"Enough is enough boys," he said. "Time to pay up and hit the streets."

* * *

Bill was my best friend. When the National Literary Foundation notified me I had been selected to receive a fellowship of $15,000 for a collection of poems about my life as a dishwasher, I gave him a call. The timing of the award couldn't have been better. My marriage had entered the vortex stage – whirlwind of complaints, accusations and cold nights in separate rooms. I knew Bill was having his own troubles with his girlfriend who had not been romantically interested in him since opening her second beauty salon in the Empire State Mall. Bill wrote protest essays and folk songs for a living.

"Think about it, Bill," I said over the phone. "A trip out west: San Francisco, Big Sur, LA. Maybe we could hook up with Ray and his new girlfriend, Amanda."

Ray was a friend from our college days. Up until six months ago, he had been running a small fry literary agency in New York City with a few obscure novelists and poets under contract. But after meeting Amanda in a SoHo (**see poem**) bar on "Margarita Night," he decided to move his operation to LA. She was a weight-lifter who competed in gyms around the Northeast and had just landed a job as the assistant coach of the ULCA's women's weight-lifting team. Bill and I had never met her but according to Ray she was a knockout with biceps and bulging thighs. It was her idea that they drive out to LA on motorcycles.

"Come on Bill," I urged. "I've got the dough. It's an all-expense paid holiday for you. We'll start in Frisco and work our way down the coast."

"I'm not sure," Bill said. "Martha will be pissed at me. I just landed a courier's job. You know running things back and forth for the dumb-fucks in the state assembly."

"Martha's already pissed at you, Bill," I said. "She's been pissed at you since the day you met. Think of the songs and new essays you could write."

"Oh, what the hell. Count me in," Bill said. "A trip might be really good for my music and words. Who knows? I feel pretty stale."

It's settled then," I said. "Horace Greeley we go."

* * *

Things started getting weird after Bill and I left San Francisco. It was a strange feeling having a wad of bills in my pocket. I had always been short by $500, and now after giving my wife enough money to take care of the house and kids for a couple of months, I was up $10,000. Buying Bill's airplane ticket and the camping equipment we needed for our trip down the coast was just a drop in the foundation's dough. We had decided to thumb for rides and camp in state parks along our way down the coast before our rendezvous with Ray and Amanda. Spotting Bill some pocket money each day didn't set off any alarms at first. But then I started to worry. Things popped into my head. What if I decided to leave my wife for good and travel to Mexico to find a cheap place to write? That's a valid concern, I thought. It's probably something the Foundation expects from a college-educated dishwasher and poet. And with Bill into my wad would I have enough bread for that after our trip? The money in my pocket tightened. It grew into fungus and mousetraps each time I dug into my pockets for the cash to pay a bar tab or buy new batteries for a flashlight.

Bill understood.

"I knew this would happen," he said. "Money fucks up everything and everybody, especially poets. No one should ever give a poet a fucking dime."

We were in the backseat of a yellow Camaro at the time, catching a ride from Half-Moon Bay to Carmel. A German shepherd in the passenger seat kept his hungry eyes focused on us. The driver, a man in his early thirties, like us, joined in on the conversation. He looked into the rearview mirror when speaking.

"Money is everything to a real American," he said. "Everything and that's final.

Take me for instance. Sure, I spent my twenties getting wasted on the gorgeous beaches around here. Wasting away, man, with thoughts of oneness pounding my brain like the sea. Not to mention the babes and their take on being one with things, if you catch my drift?"

His eyes stained the rearview mirror with jitters as they panned across us. He petted his companion's head, mentioned that it would rip our throats out if we tried anything, and continued:

"But I got my shit together now. And the bucks...the bucks are flying into my coffers."

He told us he was a computer specialist currently with the War College in Washington, DC and that he was on his way to the US Naval Base in Monterey. He wore an expensive light-colored linen suit, had a rough, good-looking face and a shock of bleached-out blond hair combed back from his forehead and moussed.

"There's going to be some ass-kicking World War III simulations at the naval base," he said. "And the next big one will run by computer. You'll see."

Bill had enough and fell asleep. We were both Cold War babies and nursed on nuclear holocaust. Ronnie Ray-gun was Pres. and Mutually Assured Destruction (MAD) (**see poem**) kept us safe in our beds at night. Annihilation as savior. I kept one eye on the shepherd and let the other frolic in a landscape of cliffs and sea. Seeing our attention to his message wane, our driver flicked on the radio. Top 40. It was April, 1982. Who wouldn't think of T. S. Elliot?

* * *

Money meant nothing to me, and I decided to show Bill that I hadn't transformed into a tightwad capitalist as a result of receiving dough for poems soaked in Dawn. When we arrived in Carmel, I invited Sandy (our driver) into a bar with Bill and me for a drink. It didn't take long before I told the cute barmaid to put a round for the house on my tab. A crowd of admirers gathered around us.

"More drinks for these good folks," I shouted out more than once.

When the tab ran to $200, the barmaid asked to see some money. I fished three one hundred dollar bills out of my pants and told her to keep $50 of it for herself. She blew me a kiss and poured me another Jameson whiskey.

"See, Bill," I said, taking the change and handing it to a stranger behind me. Money means nothing to me."

"You're an asshole," Bill said.

By the time we left the bar, two drifters plus Sandy composed the free drinks entourage. One of them was a kid barely out of his teens. He was thin, with a face of freckles and pimples, and dressed in a leather jacket and jeans. He said "cool man" too often. The other guy was a fat slob dressed in Hawaiian shirt and khaki pants whose left-eye twitched like a banjo string.

They said they were poets.

"Why don't you guys fuck-off," Bill said to them, as we entered an Italian restaurant, *Mama's Pasta Factory* (**see story**), across the street from the bar. "The guy flashing all this cash is nuts. He's spending his kids' inheritance."

The meal at the restaurant slid off the fork fast. Half-way through it, Bill passed out with a mouthful of pasta oozing from his mouth, banging his head on the edge of the table before crashing to the floor. The waitress rushed over and brought Bill back to life by dipping his napkin into his glass of ice water and pressing it to his eyes. It worked well after repeated applications on the groaning Bill, and with Sandy's help, the waitress got Bill back into his chair. Regaining some composure, he ignored the strands of spaghetti on his chin and lunged across the table for my throat. I pushed back him back into his chair and studied the new fire in his eyes.

"I've had it with you, Pete!" he screamed. "Money has corrupted you."

Then he took whatever was left of his pocket money allowance and flung it in my face.

"So long chump," he said, stumbling from the table and out of the restaurant.

I followed him out onto the street in a weave of my own alcohol-induced steps.

"Where do you think you're going without any money?" I demanded. "You're drunk. We can patch this. Hell, I'm drunk, too."

"Don't worry about me, asshole!" he yelled. "I'll find my way to LA without you and your coin."

I watched him as he disappeared up the street and into the night before heading back into the restaurant.

"He's gone?" Sandy asked when I reentered the restaurant.

I didn't answer but just peeled off some bills for the dinner and thanked him for the ride. "Cool man," the pimpled poet said as I left the place.

* * *

With Bill gone, I decided to spend a couple of nights on the top floor, in turret-like room, in a small hotel in Carmel. Though trendy and cute, I liked the feel of Carmel. A little of that California paradise feeling pulsed through my veins. I had some initial trouble booking into the hotel with a backpack and unshaven face, but once I flashed by billfold, and said I was a close friend of Dirty Harry's the room was mine. For some reason, I thought it important to keep the whole ten grand on me at all times. Five thousand in each pocket. There was a sense of power to it. A sense of freedom. A sense that quick choices could now be made. Plus, when I got in a jam of any sort, I flashed the money and it seemed to solve most problems. Presto! a room. This was new to me and counter to my former beliefs. I was conflicted. Maybe Bill was onto something. Money corrupts. A tiny capitalist inside of me squeezed my nuts.

With my temporary residence established, I soaked in the pleasantries of the ocean and called my wife a couple of times to check on the kids. The sizzle of surf – loquacious and meaningless – and the green waves slamming my body engendered an eloquent calm. On my second morning at the beach, I slipped on a rock as I waded out into the incoming waves. Down I went and there I stayed until I was washed to shore like a piece of drift wood or old rubber fishing glove. I was funded and had the right to bake in the sun and stoke my oceanic feelings into poems and images. No more soapsuds imagery or the squalor of uneaten meals as metaphors. New poems. And maybe a new job, like teaching poetry at some university to students who learned to write poems just like mine. It could happen I said to a gull staring at me with the intensity of an overweight child in the cookie section of a supermarket. It could happen. The gull was skeptical. It lifted into the air and dropped its payload into the shining sea.

My progress with my wife was of a different sort, as in no progress. Even with a continent between us, our grievances against each other continued to mount. Divorce was inevitable. So the hell with Bill and my wife, I recited during my vagabond strolls on the beach and on my way to a liquor store in the center of town. I was funded. I wrote poems about fat deposits on elegant China, sexy lip prints on wine goblets, insects in the drain, chapped hands, and owners who called me a knucklehead. You'd think someone would recognize a poet of haute cuisine with ten grand in his pants' pockets in this upper crust town. Not a chance. On my third day in paradise, I was holed up in my room and nursing a Canadian Club and soda when I started to scratch. When I lowered my boxers to observe the work of my fingers, I saw an army of red bumps marching across my lower abdomen with a party of scouts assessing my private parts in anticipation of a major attack. Allergy to sand? I thought. Mojo rising, I thought. It was time to head to LA.

**

I was scratching my groin pretty hard when Ray picked me up at the bus station.

"Bill thinks you're an asshole," he said, smiling and shaking my hand. "And Amanda thinks she might have the hots for you. The thing about having a degree in literature, scrubbing pots and pans for a living and writing poems turns her on. I think we should talk this over before going back to my place. And what gives with the scratching?"

"Nice to see you again, too, Ray," I said. "Would you like to hear how things are going at home?"

I gave my groin a hard and prolonged scratch and looked into his eyes. As always, they sparkled with mischief – whatever was in his head at the time.

"I could use a nice hot shower," I said.

"First things first," he said. "Oh, and congrats on your Foundation award. Dishwasher poems? What will those literary boards think of next? Then he laughed and slapped me on the back.

* * *

He took me to a joint called the Blue Flame buried in the warehouse section of downtown LA. A wave of nausea – spilled beer, piss, vomit and human desperation – found my nostrils the moment we entered. Though just around ten in the morning, the few patrons in the place had already passed out and were sleeping it off with their heads on their arms on top of the bar. The bartender on a stool behind the bar and absorbed in a morning tabloid, looked up and broke into a big grin seeing Ray.

"Honey," she said. It has been quite some time hasn't it? Daisy don't like that. Daisy get mad."

Daisy was truly a huge woman with an enormous double chin that shook when she took a few steps towards Ray and pressed her hand into his before launching it to her ample bosom. She attired her engaging bulk with an old and worn paisley smock that reached just below her bulbous knees. Her welcoming smile revealed a couple of missing teeth – one upper front and a lower incisor. After pinching Ray's cheek, she shot a glance in my direction.

"You like shots of mescal before noon, too?" she asked.

"Give us a couple of them, Daisy," Ray said. "You know I like to talk to my friends in a drunken state."

Because she let her eyes run down the length of my body, I discerned where her beauty resided. Her eyes were a lovely green – the color of the Carmel sea with their own brand of infinity – a singularity in waiting. When she turned to retrieve the mescal from the back bar, Ray and I climbed on barstools. The mirror behind and slightly above the bottles reflected the loss and hopelessness in the place. We were all wretches. Except for Ray. As usual he was a picture of success and taste: pressed white slacks, navy blue cashmere sweater, cordovan loafers with silly tassels.

When Daisy returned with the bottle, Ray made the necessary introductions.

"Daisy, this is another lost poet from the east driving to find salvation in the west," he said.

Daisy nodded and poured the shots. A bored look came over her when she poured out mine and took the money from Ray's hand. I inferred poetry wasn't her thing, and though I was tempted to recite *The Blasphemy of Pie Crusts*, the poem that led off my Foundation manuscript, I deferred. Instead, Ray and I performed the ritual of "bottoms up," winced at the strong mescal enflaming our throats and took a quick hit from the short beer chaser that came with the shot. Daisy leaned up against the bar as we performed the ritual. It brought a smile to her face and the energy necessary to return to her seat and pick up the tabloid. She left the bottle in front of Ray.

We got down to business. Ray's business.

"Look, Pete," he said. "This may sound weird and like I'm trying to spring something on you before you get your bearings in LA. But I've made a big decision. I'm tired of the crass and second rate writers I'm dealing with. There's no money in them, really. And I'm tired of all the literary politics to promote these knuckleheads. Tired of the scene. You know what I mean."

I nodded and scratched my groin while a man a couple of stools away broke into labored snoring. Daisy would have none of that. She left her stool, rushed to the offender and swatted him on the head with her tabloid like his head was a winter fly in a perilous existential condition.

"You can sleep it off, but no snoring, understand Harvey," she said. "No snoring in my place."

Ray poured another round and winked in Daisy's direction.

"Salute," he said as we clinked glasses before grabbing for the chasers.

The he continued:

"Look, Pete. I've already run what I'm about to propose to you past Bill. But he doesn't want any part of it."

"Part of what," I said.

"OK, Pete," he said. "Here's the deal. Amanda is one hot super number. She's not a one guy women and I doubt she will ever be. I do my best but I can't keep up with her. She's ten years younger and twenty years stronger. Maybe that's the difference. Maybe not. Who knows. It doesn't matter."

He paused, picked up the bottle, looked for the worm, poured another for himself and accepted my wave off. He picked up his shot.

"Cheers, buddy," he said this time before continuing.

"Besides, I need a break from love to start a novel that's brewing in me. That's right, Pete, a novel. You're not the only writer in here. Excuse me, poet."

I raised an eyebrow, nodded and scratched my nuts with passion.

"Go on, Ray, "I said. "Spit it out."

"My plan is to rent a flop down here for a few months," he said. "You know to test the waters of my creative soul. To see if I have anything that resembles art in me. I've talked to Amanda about it and I've built up you and Bill to her. And she's game."

"Game," I said. "Game for what?"

"Game to shack up with you or Bill or the both of you for the next three or four months," he said. "Of course, as I mentioned, Bill wants no part of it. So that leaves you. What do you say, Pete?"

I motioned for the bottle and poured myself a stiff one.

"Ray, are you nuts?" I asked. "I've even met Amanda. The reason for the trip here was to spend some time with you and to meet her."

I gave my groin a good rub and downed the shot.

"Well," he said. "You're spending time with me now and you'll meet her today. What do you say?"

I looked over at Daisy, settled into her tabloid. Three aliens on pogo sticks were raising hell in a suburban neighborhood. A cat revealed his mystical visions to its owner. The Governor of Utah kept a harem of plastic blowup dolls. Or something like that.

"I don't think so, Ray," I said. "I've got my own troubles with a woman."

"Hey, what has happened to the Pete I used to know!" he said. "Amanda is young. Sex is a form of exercise to her. That's it. Sure, we're friends. Maybe I even love her. Who knows? But right now, it's time for a change. Are you game?"

"Game for a shower and for getting out of here," I said.

"Ok, Pete," he said, "just wait until you met her. You'll love her."

* * *

Even on the threshold of divorce, my wife and I tinkered with our relationship in odd and unproductive ways. For instance, she had three fulltime platonic lovers. As she explained it to me, she needed more stimulation and adoration than I could muster. This was OK with me for I had been somewhat uncertain about sex and the appropriate amount of sexual activity since finding out the body was corrupt and unwieldy from a host of Catholic thinkers prior to and after the fall of the Roman Empire. The body is the temple of the Holy Spirit, not some funhouse of carnal pleasures. Or maybe it was after my psychedelic phase, man and woman in the "traditional" sense of marriage just didn't mean the same thing anymore.

The in-laws had their own views. Her father called his daughter promiscuous (not buying the platonic bullshit) and me a dope (not buying the platonic bullshit). My mom shook her head and blamed my predicament on the unsavory books I had read, including the poetry books.

I'll admit I didn't care for one of her platonic lovers –some old fuck, a professor of Romance languages at the State University College at Brockport, who often showed up at our house at dinner time. I caught his sexual interest in my wife from the start. He was old and ready for the grave, and she was a vivacious beauty. Who wouldn't blabber (which he did) about "eternal" ideas and the requirements of aesthetic beauty over a steaming bowl of Chef Boyardee Ravioli, if there was even a remote shot to find the sack with a young and supple "platonic" body.

It didn't take long for him and his incessant university-speak to gnaw my core and my fist to find his jaw one night after passing him a tuna casserole.

With the casserole puddle in his pants and the indignity of steaming noodles heating his private parts, I was called a barbarian by the two ethereal lovers and asked to get the "heck" out of their Republic.

Her other two man-children were OK with me. They just liked to help her with the laundry and stuff. One of them was pretty good at Ping-Pong, so there was some common interest between us. And the kids didn't seem to mind them.

I thought about these Greek goofballs on the drive over to Ray and Amanda's apartment after a parting shot of mescal. What the hell, I thought, maybe taking Ray up on his offer was something that would do me good, notwithstanding my sexual handicap?

***

Ray and Amanda lived on a palm-drenched side street off Santa Monica Boulevard not far from the ocean. When Ray and I entered the apartment, arm in arm, with the mescal in our bloodstream like a gorgeous senorita in a moonlit ballroom, Amanda was on her back on a weight bench and in the middle of a set of bench-pressing repetitions. Bill was her spotter. Spotting me, he said:

"Well, Mr. Moneybags finally makes it to LA."

"Come on, Bill," I said. "Let's kiss and make up."

He seemed stressed with his job as a spotter, grunted and took the weights from Amanda's hands, resting them on the bar above the bench.

"Ten sets of ten, Billy-boy at 250 pounds," she said, popping up from the bench and looking in Ray's and my direction.

Bill handed her a red towel and she took a quick swipe at her face before throwing it around her neck. With her eyes locked on me, she approached us.

"I'm Amanda," she said. "And I've heard all about you."

After blowing Ray a kiss, she stuck out her hand to me. She was stunning – long and sinewy with firm breasts pressed tight against her tank-top. She was in excellent condition. Her tanned and flat stomach rippled with the passage of invisible fish. I liked what I saw. I had never met an actual woman body-builder before and felt a tinge of excitement pass through me as I accepted her hand. She was all beautiful muscles and sweat. And though, I flashed on my own anemic attempt to lift weights in middle school, and the abused I had suffered at the YMCA for hoisting the bar sans weight over my scarecrow frame to the chuckles and derision of bodies oiled and bulging in a house of mirrors, stink and sweat, I gazed into her hazel eyes and understood lust at first sight.

As we shook hands she said:

"So, you're going to be the next famous poet from the next famous generation of famous poets."

She pressed my hand to the point of pain then planted a kiss on my cheek. Catching the surprise in my eyes, she pulled away and coiled into a boxing stance. She threw a few limp jabs in my direction.

"What can't you play," she said in a chiding voice. "I thought poets were spontaneous."

I gave my groin a good scratch, tucked into a crouch and came at her low and playfully swinging.

"Be careful," Ray said. "She's dangerous when playful."

When I turned to acknowledge his advice, she connected with a strong uppercut to my chin that sent me sprawling to the floor. Before I could get up, she was sitting on my chest and wedging her feet into the sides of my body. A drop of sweat from her pretty brow tumbled into my eye. I winced.

"Don't worry, honey," she said. "This is just a payback for poor, dear Bill. How come you stranded the poor boy with no dough when you have all that cash?"

"So that's why you nailed me," I said, "because of Bill?"

She laughed and for a brief moment lowered her entire body on top of mine. The sweet and sweated scent of Channel # 5 engulfed me. She whispered in my ear:

"More rough and tumble later, OK."

* * *

Later would have to wait. The itching around my lower abdomen and groin turned out to be scabies. Bill maintained that I had contracted them the night we bedded down near the rest rooms in a park south of San Francisco. It didn't matter. For the next ten days after Amanda's knockdown, I had to pour a bottle of Quell into the bathtub and sit in it. Amanda continued to court me, however. At night, she slipped out of her bedroom and watched over me as I slept or tried to sleep on the couch. Sometimes she kissed me softly on the lips and ran her fingers through my hair. Once when I opened an eye to her, she opened her white terry cloth robe and said:

"See what you're missing, sweetie."

With moonlight streaming through the window, I saw what she meant. My mouth watered. But there was nothing I could do but scratch and listen to Bill snore on the floor beside of me.

Bill grew more and more upset. The Quell baths, the late-night visits from Amanda and the daytime drinking of gin we got into with Ray were taking their toll on him. He wanted out of the trip or to continue our journey south, maybe even to Mexico.

"Christ," he said to me one morning as I prepared my Quell bath. "At least let's get to San Diego. You know this scene here can't work out on any level. Ray's full of shit if he wants to dish Amanda for a shot at words."

I knew Bill was right but Amanda had me hooked on what she called "charming possibilities." Now and then I checked in with Ray for continued approval of his plan and received his final encouragement the day he brought me back from the last trip to the local clinic. The bugs were dead. He knew about Amanda's nightly sojourn to the couch but thought it was time for me to sojourn into their room. He suggested a swap. After Amanda returned from the couch with me and slipped into bed with him, he would exit the bed for the couch, so I could slip into bed next to her.

"Look," he said, coming to a stop in front of his apartment. "I'll take the couch for the night and you take the bed. Then we'll find out for sure if it's a go with her."

* * *

Swaps are tough to pull off. That night when I slipped into bed with Amanda and put my arm around her waist, she recognized me from the start. Rolling over toward me,

she whispered:

"Not here. Let's do it in the shower."

That sounded more than fine with me, and my body responded by breaking out in a trembling sweat. After a couple of passionate kisses in front of the bedroom mirror, Amanda abandoned her nightie, tickled me with raw flesh and ducked behind the shower curtain. As she turned on the faucets and let them roar, I got tangled in my jeans while jumping out of them like a contestant stumbling face first into earth during a potato sack race. I hit my face pretty hard on the toilet seat and managed to open a good size gash below my lower lip. Amanda shrieked at the thump produced by skull on toilet bowl and turned off the water. Ray burst into the bathroom with Bill right behind him. To my surprise, Ray acted surprised and incensed.

"What the fuck is going on in here!" he shouted. "Behind my back in my own house, my woman and a friend!"

I was about to say something when Amanda cried out:

"Oh, shut-up Ray and hand me a towel before I come around the curtain and level you. Level you all."

With disdain and vowing to leave in the morning, Bill shuttled me to the emergency room, allowing Amanda and Ray to settle their differences. An emergency room doctor with not enough coffee in his bloodshot eyes managed to close my wound with 14 stitches. When he asked how this had happened to me, I told him I had missed making it with a beautiful woman by inches in the shower of her and her boyfriend's apartment.

"Too bad about that," he said, dabbing the stitches with a cotton ball drenched in a brown disinfectant.

* * *

Too bad about that was my father's favorite expression. Anything humiliating or odd that happened to me while growing up was framed by *too bad about that* by my dad. After I shit my pants in kindergarten, putting up three fingers instead of one finger or two fingers to inform Sister May Ruler of which way I needed to go, dad summarized the unfortunate event (without even asking what three fingers meant to me) *with too bad about that*. Or the time, I came down with a wicked bout of diarrhea after drinking too much spiked punch at my first Arthur Murray 6th Grade Dance, dad weighed in with *too bad about that*.

As for what happened to Bill, Ray and Amanda after I left the hospital, I can only offer *too bad about that* as a form of impertinent closure. I never saw them again once we parted ways. Bill left LA that night in full fatigues on a redeye to New York City. The following morning, Ray packed a few things and went in search of a flophouse to write his novel. Amanda accepted that I would bunk with her until the stitches came out of my forehead. But no sex was part of the accommodations.

"No offense, Pete," she said, the stitches are a big turnoff and I don't want to be responsible for any further injuries to your person."

Once I returned to Albany, I got divorced, ran out of cash, became a single father with two kids, supporting them on credit cards, until I get back into the soap and suds of a restaurant.

I owned the Foundation a letter on how their money further my career as a poet. I couldn't imagine what might happen to me if I failed to execute that part of the deal. So I wrote it.

September 15, 1982
Dear National Literary Foundation,

Thank you for the money and your respect for my poems about the life of a dishwasher. I squandered all of dough on excessive drinking, including picking up the bar bills for friends, bums and strangers. I also used some of the money for camping equipment and travel. I contracted scabies and had to fork over dough to kill the bugs. (*Too bad about that*)

Recently, I was turned down for a $3,000 loan by the Bank of Albany (**see poem**). The loan officer informed me that banks didn't lend prospective debtors money for food. They said furniture and/or a car loan was something to think about and if interested please return. There was a small commotion and security personnel ushered me to the street. (*Too bad about that*)

I have moved on from writing about clogged drains, pie crusts and oppressive restaurant owners. Below is the first poem in a new manuscript, tentatively entitled, *White Man Appears on Southern California Beach*. Yes, I did spend time on Venice Beach and took up weight-lifting. To say I'm buffed is a slight exaggeration but no one at the YMCA will ever pick on me again.

I think the money had the appropriate effect on my writing.

Sincerely,

Pete the Dishwasher

(see poem)

Seagulls & Fishing Boats

Serotonin angels in
Magnificent arrays
Of astonishment
     The IQ of clouds
& the body as a
Mechanism of stress
Response I love you
& have founded (established
I guess) a
Small but successful
Art Gallery on the outskirts
/scratch that
On the prairies of SoHo which
Could lead to a
Discussion on
Globalization
& the outright
Politics of Being   I'm here
After all on
A sugar high of lost tomorrows
Engaged in the engagement
Of a hesitant response
To pierce through "something"
(Perhaps fog or opaque
Conundrums)
Like a quiver of metaphors
Into the land of OK as in
I'm OK
& transcendent
Despite the past & break up
     Of cellular conversations
     At sea

(see poem)

Plug Nickel

If the radiance of a thousand suns
were to burst at once into the sky
that would be like the splendor of the mighty one
I am become death
the shatterer of worlds. (Bhagavad-Gita)

Citizens of the world
I have a proposal
For you.
A clock is required
To warm you
To my notion.
You may count
To 60 with the aid
Of Mark Twain's river.
Let's start with a minute
Of your time
On this planet
Of laundry
And invisible polygons.

TICK TOCK
TICK TOCK

Let this precious minute
Pass
Then say:
30 MILLION BUCKS FOR DEATH!
Very good.
Let another go by

TICK TOCK
TICK TOCK

Fly by
With golden wings
Repeat:
30 MILLION BUCKS FOR DEATH!

Isn't it stupid?
Consider the nature of the body:
The perfect capacity
It has
To croak at will.
Repeat:
30 MILLION BUCKS FOR DEATH!
The question of a dime
A plug nickel
To support objects
Whose SOUL-LESS purpose
(Despite the
PEACE THROUGH STRENGTH
PREEMPTIVE STRIKE FIRST
Slogans)
Is to advance
The cause of planetary croaking
On a massive scale
Repeat:
30 MILLION BUCKS FOR DEATH!

ONE MISSISSIPPI
TWO MISSISSIPPI

How come citizens
We ignore solace
In the fact
In a mere 15 billion years
The tank of Sun
Reaches E
And good old Earth
With sagging breasts

Broken teeth
Plenty wise
Goes poof
Disappears
Or floats (maybe)
Like a happy snowball
In the knowledge
Its former citizens
Were pledged to natural
Death?
Repeat:
30 MILLION BUCKS FOR DEATH?

Do you suppose, citizens,
It is time to replace
Nationalistic ego boundaries
With the notion
Of a blue sphere
In a black void?
Could we use a second
Or two
To leap from the ladder
Of reptiles,
Declare by the saints
And sinners of neocortex
An end to 30 MILLION BUCKS
FOR WEAPONS PER MINUTE!

TICK TOCK
ONE MISSISSIPPI

Change the beat, citizens,
The beat of destruction,
Then funnel our croak bucks
Into a fund to support
A world party,
So we can hit the streets

And meadows
Hang out by the great rivers
With a jug
A joint
A kiss
And begin to dance
The next 15 billion years
Into existence.

(see story)

LENNY AND SARAH AS SENTENCES

Lenny lobbed a chunk of medium-rare prime rib au jus over Sarah's head in the parking lot of the Ramada Inn.

Sarah claimed Lenny threw the piece of beef at her in the parking lot of the Ramada Inn and it nearly took her hat off, a blue felt hat with a tiny orange feather, as it cruised by her head.

Lenny says that he tossed the medium-rare prime rib au jus so it would clear her head by an adequate number of inches and establish the fact that he remained upset over the fact she had barely touched her food or talked to him during their entire dinner rendezvous at Spaghetti Freddy's.

Lenny says he knows the difference between lobbed-tossed and throw-to-hit-someone-namely-his-wife.

He's a former athlete and outstanding dart player though he understands darts and beef require different grips, and if he were into repeating and/or revising sentences, he might enter the word "softball" into the semantic equation to account for his ability to lob natural objects over the heads of people that bug him.

Sarah says that a meal at Spaghetti Freddy's ain't exactly a rendezvous.

She says for her a rendezvous hints at something romantic and secretive.

There's nothing romantic or secretive about Spaghetti Freddy's; it just happens to share the same parking-lot-suburban-sprawl-polis as the Ramada Inn.

Lenny and Sarah are staying at the Ramada Inn because there are very many roaches in their apartment.

They live on the third floor of what is called a Triple-Decker.

Someone on the first floor left a chicken in his/her/their oven for months and had the audacity to seal up the apartment during the summer months with shades closed/windows down.

Ralph, from RALPH, THE BUG MAN, told Lenny after running out of the first floor apartment that there were more roaches in that downstairs apartment than he has ever seen.

Cite a number Lenny told Ralph.

Ralph told Lenny in the neighborhood of two hundred thousand.

"No way!" Lenny said.

"No way!" Sarah said.

"Way!" said Ralph, from RALPH, THE BUG MAN.

Lenny and Sarah had to get out of there.

That's why they're staying at the Ramada Inn on the landlord until he fixes the problem.

"I can stand an occasional roach," Lenny told the landlord. "I know it's the city. But when they get to playing the piano and fuckin' with the snooze-alarm button on my clock, I draw the line."

There are other difficulties between Lenny and Sarah.

Difficulties between couples seem quite ordinary.

Say Lenny's having a mid-life crisis.

It takes a long time to grow up and have a mid-life crisis.

Say Sarah's been quiet lately during meals with Lenny in attendance.

And Lenny likes to talk, especially during meals.

He might say Arafat this or that while munching on a carrot or launch into a diatribe about recent interviews in obscure magazines on the construction of meaning and new ways of reading today's poets and writers before asking for additional whip cream for a strawberry shortcake.

For instance, Lenny knows that the title "Lenny and Sarah as Sentences" is a lame attempt at foreshadowing the actual words from which stories are made – this one in particular.

Sarah doesn't care about that, but she's generally a good listener though her mind will drift to a stack of laundry to be folded or a forsythia bush to be pruned or even to a flock of birds passing through her awareness, tempting her to sing.

She does get bored with food and tired of high-pressured clients worried about their stacks of money stashed inside electronic vaults.

"But that's your job," Lenny says.

Lenny could use some sensitivity training, don't you think?

"Talk to me," Lenny says. "Aren't you even going to talk to me?"

So Lenny starts to drift.

Should stories have problems and solutions (see poem) for characters to experience, he thinks, before asking for a doggie bag.

from *Altercations in the Quiet Car* (Lavender Ink/Fell Swoop, 2010)

(see poem)

FLUKE OF INSOLVENCY

this morning (meaning any random morning)
the world awoke without money.
during the night (meaning any random night)
the money disappeared from the face
of the earth.
though the face seemed more radiant
a world without money
was hard to swallow.
those who had gone to bed with their pockets full
of the stuff
found not a single coin
when they awoke. most panicked
when they discovered homes and cars
were devoid of the signs and symbols
that provided the feeling
objects were worth something
now they weren't sans explanation.
a few unlucky souls began to see
the trees, rocks, and minerals
their things were made of
and took sick; some died on the spot
when they caught a glimpse of something mysterious
and unattached to the concept
of value. it was a tough morning
for personal ownership. those who scurried
to banks to check on life savings
were dismayed to find fields of tall wild flowers
had replaced financial institutions.
in the fields were birds of every color and beak-shape
busy at breakfast. it was a horrible day
of the brightest light.
the people cried in the freshest breeze:
our stocks and bonds have become the clouds
above our heads. oh, it sickens

us to see how white
and innocent they appear. without a doubt
it was the greatest upheaval in a long time
with a few old minds
comparing it to the big bang
of Adam's rib.

from *Modulations* (Asylum Arts, 1998)

(see poem)

By Zero

I read somewhere
or did it drop
from someone's mouth
on a day when

the newspapers claimed
the gutters were filled
with blood
not rainwater
or spit from a collection
of new middle income

bums.

Something about writing
in the presence of death.
A suggestion

to fly
to abandon the speed of the typewriter.

If carp appear
if all you remember is the strawberry ass
of a deer strapped across the hood
of a car

consider these angels
or Boeings

that may know the way to heaven
though

the concern is not about salvation
it is about breath
the absence of fear

about the zebra that continues to visit
the dream
the one in which the Muse
rams her nakedness
into the neocortex

the one in which Lunacy and Balboa
gaze at the Pacific
like a couple of two-bit imbeciles

the one in which the lady loan officer
is eaten alive by the diamond
on her finger.

If you challenge time

swear on a stack
of Bibles
it moves by zero

death will reveal
a fly skipping
across the ceiling

is a small black stone.

from *White Man Appears on Southern California Beach*
(Bottom Fish Press, 1991)

(**see poem**)

Insight after Dinner at the Diner

I'm not into plot (**see poem**). I hate plot. Give me a sunset any day -
one with lemons, salmon, purple crayons and aquamarine
wading pools hidden behind one very long strip-mall.
Anything but plot. So here's what happened.

I was trapped in Sequence B. It was a small town full of
closed shoe and cigar factories. Each house composed of
feathers was blowing away. I yelled in to Heloise. "Hey,
Helly, the feather houses are blowing away." "So let them,"
she replied.

I heard the clink of dishes, glasses, and plastic silverware.
A dull clank reminding me of romantic macaroni. Hash in a can.
I picked up my cigar from the end table. Recited constellations.
Grew impatient. And recalled the last letter sent to me by
my father.

Dear Son,

I'm heading out to sea. It's infinite out there
you know.

Love,
Sailor Jack

"The pea pod," I said to myself. "The pea pod!" - once or twice more
in a manner imitating dawn.

from *Under the Sky of No Complaint* (Lavender Ink/Fell Swoop, 2013)

(**see poem**)

An Attempt at Couch

I've dismissed cell phone trees as underweight
Beyond the legal limit of height
This is a poem with a plot
The form of the plot is the line
The reader understands the setting is the imagination –
The branch of consciousness that creates the world

There are rocks and soil in the margins of thought –
The house of a celebrity after a mudslide
The intention of the writer is to take an afternoon nap
With the cat
Language is the main character
It precedes the starting gun of the spacetime continuum

Words ignite stars
Being is an ontological term not a fire extinguisher
Who we are is a question language must address
There are suppers and candlelight dinners for culture and exegesis
How quaint in an era of digital takeout and restrictions on caloric absorption
Still there are reasons to talk and rename the enterprise of being here

Words are not fools
They have the stomach to consider past present and future roles
Take the rich for example
They turn words into telecommunication companies for profit
Can you hear me now
Talking heads multiply like fish and report on the state of the world

The ability to record and watch 15 TV programs at once is an industry standard
I'm feeling sleepy in the chaos of choice and debilitating action
Denouement has me by the balls
So the plot not of the poem but of the plot is a cast of villains
Who controls whom for material advantage and gain
See it now on Xbox Live (**see Book 2: The Year I Wanted to Be on Television**)

from *Techniques in the Neighborhood of Sleep* (Spuyten Duyvil, 2016)

.

Reader's Notes and Artwork

GALLERY A

PAINTINGS
BY THOMAS HAINES

Arrows of Eros - Oil on MDO Board - 24"x 36" - 2005

Canoe - Acrylic on Masonite - 18"x 24" - 2003

Gill Williams' Dream - Acrylic on MDO Board - 48"x 48" - 2004

MOTHER NIGHT - House Paint on MDO Board - 96"x 48" - 2003

NIGHT FIELDS - Oil on Canvas - 36"x 48" - 1987

Night in Day - Oil on Canvas - 24"x 30" - 1986

Ocean Birds Abstract - Watercolor on Paper - 18"x 24" - 1998

Self Portrait in my Cold House - Oil on Canvas - 28"x 24" - 1986

BOOK 2

HETERONYM INTERRUPTUS

MEET DUCK MARTIAN

According to postmodern legend, Duck Martian was hatched on the grounds of Walden Pond after the end of WW2. Who really knows? Data on Martian hatchings is notoriously unreliable. For those of us who know him (or it), it's a bit of stretch to believe he (or it) was hatched by the pond made famous by Henry David Thoreau (**see story**). More than likely, his (or its) spacecraft crashed into the pond around the dates that he (or it) claims as his (or its) birthday in his (or its) present form. The Martian is a shapeshifter, and has enjoyed, via an illustrious career, the benefits of having assumed a myriad of shapes, including cactus, rock, soda bottle, beer can, congressman, congresswoman, woodpecker, etc. etc. It's safe to assume that he (or it or now she) squirmed into the form of a duck once climbing from (or his, its, her) craft on Walden Pond into a brace of mallard ducks.

There is nothing in the legend of the Martian that indicates he (or it or she) was especially adept at shapeshifting. He (or it or she) was (and is) an ugly duck (ling). Some contend that he (or it or she) doesn't look like a duck or even a Martian. They based their judgements on the following physical description provided by a painting by the renowned Martian artist, Atomic Tom Haines and subsequently reproduced as the front cover of the Martian's first book, *Napkin Apologies,* published by the renegade and highly sensitive literary magazine, *Fell Swoop: The All Bohemian Revue.* According to the penetrating vision and adroit brush strokes of Mr. Haines, the Martian's head resembles a push broom detached from its pole. His thin wooden head is beset by an incredibly long nose which curves like a ski jump after its perilous descent from the crossbow of his crossed eyes. A lower lip is quite fat as if someone struck the dear Martian in the face with a soda can. His black beady eyes seem somewhat radioactive and focused on the absurd realities and predicaments of daily life. His preferred style of clothing includes goggles, snorkel, short sleeve madras shirt, cutoff jeans and bright orange flippers.

There is no reliable, imaginary and/or legendary information on when Duck Martian started writing or why he chose to do so.

An Interview with Duck Martian

By Richard Martin

RM: Is it true that your favorite TV program, now syndicated and which aired from 1963-1966, is *My Favorite Martian*, starring Ray Walston as the Martian, along with Bill Bixby of Hulk fame, and Pamela Britton?

DM: Absolutely not. My favorite program is *Here Comes Honey Boo Boo.*

RM: Elizabeth Hurley and Daryl Hannah starred in the film version of the original TV show. The film was released in 1999 with a budget of 65 million. It grossed about 37 million at the box office. Do you think the bust at the box office was a referendum on the public's skepticism about Martians on earth? And, by the way, did you have the opportunity to woo and date either Ms. Hurley or Ms. Hannah?

DM: "Maybe: to the first question. What do you think to the second question?

RM: Who translates your poetry from Martian into English?

DM: S. Zivvit 57, author of *Angry Red Blues*, issue #7 of *Fell Swoop: The All Bohemian Revue.*

RM: Is S. Zivvit 57, a Martian?

DM: Why yes he (it) is.

RM: How come he (it) can translate Martian into English and you can't?

DM: I'll take the next question.

RM: Sorry, I have no further questions.

DM: But what about my oeuvre?

RM: Yes, what about it?

Selected Poems of Duck Martian

Duck's Manifesto

Part 1

I love poetry.

Part 2

I love my poetry.

Demographics

too many people period

The Absence of Data

Take your superhighway
of information
and shove it

window dressing

the avant-garde
sits
in my yard

(from *Napkin Apologies*, Fell Swoop #48)

MOLECULES

The elephant stomps in
demanding
my saxophone.

The house is brilliant
in the dream
and the white flakes
outside are bombs.

If my brain slips
I will fall through a sidewalk
of homemade chocolate.

Hello China!
Renounce the speed of light!

Zip up the zippers
and forge a silent e
on the backs of clouds.

Quick
look around
which objects smile
which objects frown?

Profit Sonnet

They're laughing it up in the Boardroom
They're laughing it up in the Bored Room
They're laughing it up in the Boardroom
They're laughing it up in the Bored Room
They're laughing it up in the Boardroom
They're laughing it up in the Bored Room
They're laughing it up in the Boardroom
They're laughing it up in the Bored Room
They're laughing it up in the Boardroom
They're laughing it up in the Bored Room
They're laughing it up in the Boardroom
They're laughing it up in the Bored Room
They're laughing it up in the Boardroom
They're laughing it up in the Bored Room

DOOMSDAY REPRIEVE

The world is still here
Get used to it

PASTRY

All the moments
of your life
pass into this moment

which passes, too
donut?

(from *Doomsday Reprieve*, Day 24 in boink!; Lavender Ink, New Orleans, 2005)

INSIDE THE HEADS OF MALFORMED LEADERS

The significance of waking up
then falling back to sleep
in a swirl of ancient feathers
trips digital alarms

Those bolted to bronze chairs
respond to an urge to drive pink sedans
through cities where shoppers shuffle
through bags filled with mysterious items

THE DIFFERENCE BETWEEN A BARD AND A DUCK

A bard sings
A duck quacks

On the Isle of Dead Hierarchies

600 miles up
the new space tool detects cow farts

Quick Cosmic Song

Does it work
or doesn't

A billion radio stations
tuned to an alien's voice

Silence
&
Rhythm

Volcanic microbes
& lots of time
equal me

Lover of flowers
& bird whistling
now
in budding tree

O O O O
OH OH OH OH

There is a violin
in each word
a tuba
or someone playing the saw
with delicate fingers

Quietly
in front of cameras
claim
earth
is an only child

waiting for siblings

(from *The Rise and Fall of the New Media*, Fell Swoop #91)

Souvenir Valium

Looks good between the bowling trophies and self-help books

Gross National Product

Reading poems on the job
Improves production
Increases the sale
Of small cars

Writing poems on the job
Creates the happiness
On a madman's face
When he taps
The moon
With a gentle hammer

Reciting poems on the job
Improves the air
Incites the necessary riot

CAUTIONARY TALE

Age is irrelevant
The wiles of gravity
And the speed of light
Are known

LOST

Sometimes I don't know where my mind is on a given day
That's the line
Those are its words
This is the form

(from *Souvenir Valium*, Fell Swoop #93)

HOMONYMS

My genius is full of holes
It's Tuesday
A wren's egg falls from the sky
Things break
I'm breaking
Into a rash of blue yolks
Call the doctor
Call the medicine man
Call the correct time
My genius is full of wholes

Breaking News

Splinters of media fester in my head

Oh, Boo Hoo

Issues
Bring
Tissues

(from *Synapse Picnic*, Fell Swoop #100)

Love Buns Revisited

A terminal dose of immaturity
Beefcake
A few missing teeth

Bake at 350
For a nanosecond
Of Wannabe

Oops!

Over we go in the vortex boat

Neural Directory

Get it over with
Put a chip in my head

Insurrection of Charming Behavior

Leap beginning
The chasm of new steps
Is starting over

The sun is up
The crazy youth inside of tired feet
Is you

Stampede
Into the moment of rebirth
As birth

There is a long list of things
To repeat
Begin with vigorous love

(from *Automation Holiday*, Fell Swoop #106)

E

Ebullient

Ezra

Elusive

ee

Efficacious

Eliot

Erotic

Ethos

Eminent

Egad

J

Jasper

Johns

Jungian

Jungle

James

Joyce

Jostle

Juggernauts

Jubilant

Jujube

L

Licentious

Likeability

Lovely

Love Handles

Lilliputian

Languor

Lugubrious

Loneliness

Left Bank

Linguist

Z

Zany

Zodiac

Zippy

Zygote

Zonked

Zephyr

Zealous

Zigzagger

Zap

Zilch

(from *ABC of Duck*, Fell Swoop #116)

ABSTRACT HYSTERIA

for Bill Lavender

1

It's time for some tainted exegesis
A hot dog eating tournament
The ladder of despair
Fantasy
& delicious anticipation

Internet fries
Ever hear of them
2

Me & the dog
You & the dog
The splash of color in your eyes
Daunts/haunts me
I'm a stump of redress
Not an abstract expressionist

3

History fabricates
& creates
My joints are
Dis
Jointed

Melody of appeal
Apply here

Spicer Update

I'm not writing for the morons of this generation
I'm writing for the morons of the next generation

Powder Keg of Baloney

Mortality
Causes
Conflict

Nothing
Roughs up
The eternal

(from *Abstract Hysteria*, Fell Swoop #126)

Literature for the Damaged and Young at Heart

Did you say vortex
Or Zarathustra

Slap thine distractions five
Thus spank Language

Umbrella

Imagine water molecules of the cosmic soul
As raindrops in the minds
Of Geo. Washington & Al Einstein

Pretty Flowers
Let's eat the pretty flowers
Like dinosaurs caught in yesterday's downpour

A Sampling of Duck Haiku

Ocean Daze

Beach littered with stones
Great Black-backed gulls mesmerized
Under a pink sky

Hail Spontaneity

The mind approaches death
With the mind that survives it
What I'm thinking now

Goosebumps of Antimatter

Mind prefers the void
The cataclysm of history
Dogwoods in blossom

Counting Asteroids

Do the math
The universe has enough rocks
To squelch us
In our tracks

Mother Earth Says

Patriarchy is an asshole

Epidemiological Reduction

According to an international panel of experts
Living is detrimental
To one's health

Slobber

Honk to disconnect
Prior to drooling

REM Couplets

I ate a cookie
I ate two cookies

It's happening in the digital mind
Consciousness missed or pissed

The handlebars of past mistakes
Wobbled fiercely

The eyebrows of a misdemeanor
Pressed for a holiday of love

Night stole my identity
You called the cops

Found Options

Laser Toenail Fungus Treatment
5 Ways To Have A Great Vacation All By Yourself
Activate Your Data Mask
10 Habits That Make You Fat
Style Struggles Men Will Never Understand
9 Gadgets That Will Make You Love To Cook
Remove Malicious Spyware
6 Common Foods You Can Actually OD On
Could You Be Doing More For Your Allergies
19 Secluded Beaches Worth The Trek

Maybe Today After Tomorrow

Why (k)not
s

(from *Maybe Today after Tomorrow, Fell Swoop # 143*)

DUCK PARAPHERNALIA

Duck Martian Discography

Napkin Apologies	Fell Swoop #48
Doomsday Reprieve	(See Day 24 in boink!; Lavender Ink (New Orleans, 2005)
The Rise and Fall of the New Media	Fell Swoop #91
Souvenir Valium	Fell Swoop #93
Synapse Picnic	Fell Swoop #100
Automation Holiday	Fell Swoop #106
ABC of Duck	Fell Swoop #116
Abstract Hysteria	Fell Swoop #126
Maybe Today After Tomorrow	Fell Swoop # 143
Quack	A One Act Play (Lot M 3 Press)

Blurbobilia

"...I forgot to Duck (Martian)...!

President Ronald Reagan (**see poem**)

"...meant to be read while smelling burnt toast..."

Joe Sprang
Paradise Louse

"...with planetary intelligence, Mr. Martian plays volleyball with the legendary Bomkauf. Damn shame we have to reach back into the Briar Patch for Brer Duck, but then who would ever have imagined this state of both human events and Poetry's dismal showing in healthying up the language. In a gloomy landscape, humor becomes fresh air to breathe."

Peter Kidd
Igneus Press

A Message from Rene Descartes

Like most philosophers (see poem) I distain poets. Why just the other day I said to my friend Plato: "I really hate the bastards, don't you?"

He just grinned at me and said: "Rene, you dumb fuck, who do you think started the campaign on the worthlessness of poets?"

"Oh yeah, you," I said politely - remembering that all philosophy after him was a mere footnote.

But let's get to the heart of my comments in regard to *Automaton Holiday* by Monsieur Duck Martian dear readers. Everyone with a half of a rational mind knows that it was I who first pondered whether or not the "herd" and "suffering humanity" passing beneath my 16th century study's window were automatons. I don't see any mention of that in either Monsieur Duck's acknowledgements or during the course of the volume. And why is that? Is it because Monsieur Martian is so frivolous, caddy and careless about sourcing the ideas for his poetic creations (ravings)? I think this is a real possibility and don't give me no "merde" or back talk that proper credit is not due to me even when it has become quite apparent to those of us beyond the grave that the whole freaking 21st century is basically run and controlled by automatons - what with their iPods and iPhones and obsession with meaningless communication (see poem)

OK, I'll give Monsieur Duck Martian a small credit for blowing the whistle and claiming in the title poem of the book that the - how did he say it - the gig is up. It damn well is. Still, I'm not a fan of poets - even Monsieur Duck - and would put a contract on the lot of them if that was in my power. Cogito Ergo Sum, baby!

Rene Descartes

OPEN LETTER TO UNIVERSITY PRESIDENTS
AND ENGLISH DEPARTMENT HEADS

Dear Sir Ladies:
Don't you think it's about time to replace your present university poet
with me or one of my friends?
Let me blunt.
My mother used to smack me in the head
anytime I failed to bring home fresh bread from the corner market.

Catch my drift.
Things are stale.
Poems are stale.

The time for imprinting behind the waddle of a master is over.
Let me blunt.
As a duck I understand the innate attraction in falling in line behind a recognized
waddle
but Holy Quack
this must be resisted when it comes to writing poems.

By hiring me
or one of my watery friends
I guarantee this will not happen
because I vow
to chase anyone looking for a way
or a handle
to write an acceptable poem
right down the halls of academia
and out into their own experience
of the world.

Some will say this is too harsh
or possibly
not the money maker for the university
that the present system is.

Let me be blunt.
THE DUCK IS A DOWNSIZER.

But here's the thing:
New Space and New Ways will be created.
At the very least
before the next overthrowing
there will be some fun and chaos
and unabashed partying
in faculty lounges and classrooms.

Think of it.
Fun-loving poets in your midst again.
What a concept.
And not a single one of them with anything to say about how to write a poem.

My Sincere Quacks,

DUCK MARTIAN

(first appeared in *boink!*, Lavender Ink, 2005)

(**see story**)

Dog Pills

OK, listen up you mutts. I've decided to start this piece (tirade) off in an obnoxious manner (tone) because that's how I often feel, obnoxious. I mean look at the state of the world (yeah, the one we inhabit & created, not the romantic versions roaming around in our freakin' collective brain like pie-eyed /tie-dyed gurus). NO! This world: the one that has clouds with smoker's cough & polar icecaps as soft as the spongy spot on a newborn's noggin, & yeah, the one with manic terrorists (both sides) & the mad scramble for oil & God's approval (rating?), & outright control over others under various bullshit banners of meaningless nonsense (as if we weren't all made from the nuts & bolts of stars, twinkle/twinkle).

It just never stops. Like just moments ago via *The Telepathic & Séance News Bulletin,* I read about how the ocean is sick (& tired), & now moments after, I can't even remember what is making it sick. Buried treasure? Lost hydrogen bombs? Or just the damn chemical changes, induced in the primordial mother by our inexorable being of being just us ("hey, let's take another spin to the mall in our SUV"), it's undergoing during its swan song of coral reefs & intelligent life.

& it makes me nervous.

& so I said to my friend Thoreau:

"You know it makes me nervous."

& Thoreau said:

"Try one of these."

& I said:

"What are those?"

& Thoreau said:

"World anxiety reduction pills."

"Huh," I said.

"Yeah," Thoreau said. "Everyone in your world takes them nowadays. They spike one's energy while at the same time helping a fella to feel pretty damn relaxed while waddling through all the garbage, mayhem & death like a goddamn non-imprinting (lonely boy) duck. Scout's honor."

Who the hell knew Henry David was a scout or pharmacist?

"Hey," Thoreau continued, "if these babies were available at the Ye Old Apothecary Shoppe back in my day, I'd have been downing a few with the roots and beans."

So, I POPPED one I DID, one of his stash of world anxiety reduction pills, & what do you suppose happened to me?

Come on, guess.

OK, so you don't want to guess (or be a guest on *The Moron Channel*)?

Well, I did start to feel better, but with one (you would have to say) major side-effect. I began acting like a dog. Bark, bark. bark. Scratching behind the ears. Tongue lolling out of the mouth. Wag, wag, wag of tail. The whole dog bit.

Thoreau loved it & decided it was an excellent time to visit (or revisit) his famous cabin now at the height of its tourist season. But I was (bark) hesitant and unsure that a happy dog of a human (bark), sniffing around his state-preserved (bark) cabin & state-preserved (bark) effects – what with the (bark bark) digital camera & (bark bark bark) throw-away camera geeks taking pictures of his woodsy pad was the best thing to do with a transcendentalist wraith.*

"I don't know, Thoreau," I said, woofing it up & chasing my tail for kicks.

"Oh, don't be a pooper-scooper," Thoreau responded, kicking me in my mangy side. "Give Dip and Blondie a call, I'm sure they'd be up for a ride."

The wraith was right. Dip & Blondie were into it, & before I could say civil disobedience (sorry, bark), we all piled into Dip's machine & tore off for Walden Pond. While Blondie, Dip, & Thoreau pontificated on why Emerson, Hawthorne & Alcott chose not to join us, I stuck my head out the window without a leash around my neck.

For the moment, the world (bark) was a redolent blur.

* The impish wraith (the whole, Thoreau-as-wraith-routine {readers' right to (bark) know}came into being because my friend Dip, & his girl Blondie, and I are into séances {even before I started subscribing to *The Telepathic & Séance Bulletin*), & because of our New England roots [Go Sox], we started conjuring up old New England transcendentalists &/or at least we tried to (bark). As it turned out, Thoreau was the only one willing to come out and play. I think it may have had something to do with Blondie & the sexy way she said *transcendentalist* (maybe it was her (BARK) halter top and cutoff jeans) like it was a word constructed of hot-air balloons and simply waiting for a famous wraith up for a romantic jaunt through the luminiferous aether with her. But what the bark do I bark know.

from *Altercations in the Quiet Car* (Lavender Ink/Fell Swoop, 2010)

(see poem)

The World Is A Slob

Ronald a cognitive psychologist wakes up
Each morning with enough anger
To fill a brand new sports arena.
"The entire process is a fluid pig," he mutters
At his face when it reaches the bathroom mirror.
The world doesn't pay much attention to Ron's designs.
While he slept it ate a dagwood sandwich
Then took a little night ride past the neat structures
Ron had in place by the time his head met his steel pillow.
Ron has a thing for steel pillows.
For fun the world entered Ron's dream of simple
Underlying principals and burped.
It decided to follow a woman in red net stockings
Down a long dark corridor.
This was enough to blow away the knowledge
Ron had assembled in the lab.
A knowledge of fragments glued in the shape of a possible map
Which helps Ron move among the objects
Requiring immediate attention.
Ron is unsure of things as he eats his cereal and sips juice.
The world is a slob.
Messy.
The milk from his Wheaties drips from his chin.
It takes on meaning
For Ron..

from *White Man Appears on Southern California Beach*
(Bottom Fish Press, 1991)

(see poem)

They

They have seen the famous through the eyes baked
in the hot wombs of lost mothers
They have used the latest telecommunication devices
to call premier X and actress WHY
to attend a major event
in honor of an idea
that would persuade rational animals
to embrace irrational impulses
when the sky appears to a woman with tangerine breasts
to be something more than a blue vegetable
in a pot half filled with liquid philosophers

They have nothing better to do

They have tired of pushing metal carts
filled with root beer cans and discarded feather pillows
down main streets
under the watchful gaze of affluent bodies
pumping gas into sad cars
with nowhere to go

They have memorized the sidewalk rhetoric
repeat without hesitation
the exact syllable the moon whispers
to shapes that linger
by rivers flowing
through silk towns

They are here with us
whether we like it or not
They record what we think
when we think
the world is a porcelain gift
left on our doorstep
without consequences

from *White Man Appears on Southern California Beach*
(Bottom Fish Press, 1991, Binghamton, NY)

PAGE THIRTEEN

MEET ANT MCGOOGLE (see story)

Ant McGoogle runs the popular *postyourtreatise.com* website and is the publisher of *deadCpress*. A student of the mind, Mr. McGoogle studied Philosophy at the University of California at Berkeley in the sixties and retired from his profitable Stamp and Coin Boutique many years ago. His first book, *Headlines* (Fell Swoop #95) has been translated into a dozen languages and is required reading for those who prefer not to read. His second book, *The Ghost of Richard Brautigan* (Fell Swoop #124), has become a prized and rare collector's item (**see preface**). Some question the actual existence of Ant McGoogle, stumped by the fact that his existence may have been occasioned by his appearance in a story few have read. The only extant MRI (**see story**) of McGoogle's brain was sold on eBay three years ago for a hefty sum and subsequently has disappeared along with the buyer. However, there have been sightings. Recently, the online community, *Do You or Who Exists*, has partially verified through hacked satellite photos that Mr. McGoogle lives outside the outside with his wife, children and highly motivated abandoned cats in a RV on the outskirts of a town they have chosen not to identify.

An Interview with Ant McGoogle

By S. Zivvit 57 (see poems)

57:     Ant, your incarnation into spacetime takes place on page 140 in the story, *Dumbass,* in the short fiction collection, *Altercations in the Quiet Car*, by Richard Martin. I gleaned from that page you were a philosophy student at Berkeley at one point and had the foresight to post Martin's *My Milieu or Yours/Who Gives a Damn: Why I'm a Dumbass* on your website postyourtreatise.com. Assuming that Martin's stories are mostly autobiographical, do you consider Richard Martin a dumbass?

AM: Well, I can tell you this, 57, most, if not all, folks (**see story**) associated with the literary community think that he is. In fact, XJ Dailey, Editor-in-Strife of *Fell Swoop: The All Bohemian Revue,* many years ago upgraded Martin into a complete asshole, as well as considering him to be a dumbass from the moment they met.

57:     You've published two chaps with *Fell Swoop* – *Headlines* and *The Ghost of Richard Brautigan*. First, let's talk about *Headlines*, a poetic work on the musings and dilemmas known as the brain. Do you think the poems in this work of yours would help the current crop of Republican candidates vying to become President in 2016 contextualize and understand the crap pouring from their mouths due to their limited understanding of the workings of their own noodles?

AM: Look, 57, I don't mess with politics. It is a rigged game played by asshole billionaires. I will say that I'm good looking, smart, went to an outstanding university, own my own hair and have made a ton of money with my press, deadCpress (**see submission guidelines**), which is pretty incredible for someone who came into being on page 140 in a book written by a dumbass.

57:     Got it. What about your second work, *The Ghost of Richard Brautigan*? Were you really in touch with RB and did he give you a set of poems to publish that came from the other side?

AM: Brautigan doesn't get the respect he deserves by the smartasses in the poetry world of today. He was around during the San

Francisco Renaissance, and had a fairly good relationship with Jack Spicer (**see poem**), but went his own way. I love the hope, the sex, the fun and the cosmos in his poems. I'm not surprised that he is still writing and found a way to communicate with a being created on page 140 in a dumbass book. I'll just say, the earth is dizzy with Brautigan.

57: Last question, Ant. You mentioned your press, deadCpress, a moment ago. I know you publishedWilliam Kemmett's *Black Oil* in 2010 to wide acclaim. Do you have any other manuscripts you're considering?

AM: I have just begun conversations with poet Peter Kidd about publishing his manuscript, an incredible work chronicling his time hanging out with Bob Kaufman in San Francisco.

57: Sweet.

AM: You bet your ass, dumbass.

*Interviewer's note: Since my interview, Fell Swoop: The All Bohemian Revue has published Mr. McGoogle's latest chapbook, **New Digs**, as issue 146. A phenomenal work of Zeitgeist, panache, and utopian semiotics, it is offered to the intrepid reader in its entirety in **Appendix F.***

An Interview with Ant McGoogle
(in Martian)
By S. Zivvit 57

57:     Ant, your incarnation into spacetime takes place on page 140 in the story, *Dumbass,* in the short fiction collection, *Altercations in the Quiet Car*, by Richard Martin. I gleaned from that page you were a philosophy student at Berkeley at one point and had the foresight to post *My Milieu or Yours/Who Gives a Damn: Why I'm a Dumbass* on your website postyourtreatise.com. Assuming that Martin's stories are mostly autobiographical, do you consider Richard Martin a dumbass?

AM: Well, I can tell you this 57, most, if not all, folks (**see story**) associated with the literary community think that he is. In fact, XJ Dailey, Editor-in-Strife of *Fell Swoop: The All Bohemian Revue,* many years ago upgraded Martin into a complete asshole, as well as always considering him to be a dumbass.

57:     You've published two chaps with *Fell Swoop – Headlines* and *The Ghost of Richard Brautigan*. First, let's talk about *Headlines*, a poetic work on the musings and dilemmas known as the brain. Do you think the poems in this work of yours would help the current crop of Republican candidates vying to become President in 2016 contextualize and understand the crap pouring from their mouths due to their limited understanding of the workings of their own noodles?

AM: Look, 57, I don't mess with politics. It is a rigged game played by asshole billionaires. I will say that I'm good looking, smart, went to an outstanding university, own my own hair and have made a ton of money with my press, deadCpress (**see submission guidelines**), which is pretty incredible for someone who came into being on page 140 in a book written by a dumbass.

57:     Got it. What about your second work, *The Ghost of Richard Brautigan?* Were you really in touch with RB and did he give you a set of poems to publish that came from the other side?

AM: Brautigan doesn't get the respect he deserves by the smartasses in the poetry world of today. He was around during the San Francisco

Renaissance, and had a fairly good relationship with Jack Spicer (**see poem**), but went his own way. I love the hope, the sex, the fun and the cosmos in his poems. I'm not surprised that he is still writing and found a way to communicate with a being created on page 140 in a dumbass book. I'll just say, the earth is dizzy with Brautigan.

57:     Last question, Ant. You mentioned your press, deadCpress, a moment ago. I know you published William Kemmett's *Black Oil* in 2010 to wide acclaim. Do you have any other manuscripts you're considering?

AM: I have just begun conversations with poet Peter Kidd about publishing his manuscript, an incredible work chronicling his time hanging out with Bob Kaufman in San Francisco.

57:     Sweet.

AM: You bet your ass, dumbass.

*Interviewer's note: Since my interview, Fell Swoop: The All Bohemian Revue has published Mr. McGoogle's latest chapbook, **New Digs**, as issue 146. A phenomenal work of Zeitgeist, panache, and utopian semiotics, it is offered to the intrepid reader in its entirety in **Appendix F**.*

PEAPOD

The brain is now his theme
His dog
More or less
  That he walks
Each day
  With religious
Diligence
In a forest of
      Invisible trees
Their conversation is sometimes
Intense
Sometimes
Barely audible
Like flowers during
A phenomenological
Séance
It's OK with them
That the One
Became Two
     That history
Flows
Into a media black hole
The sky remains
  Steady
In constant transformation
It offers windows –
Plenty of them

Archetype of Silence

If he could see
Through his brain
The material aspect
Of it
To the space
(Possibly eternal space)
On the other side
Of it
    Or within
It
Like a veiled seed
     Material too
     But vacant
        OK with a few quantum
Jitters (no froth, please)
Then perhaps a conditional
Exploration is not
Purely imaginative
Like he's
       At some resort
Spa
       And presently
Engaged in a deep
Tissue message
       By a woman
With olive fingertips
And a voice soothed
Into cooing
The principle of not charging
Him or others for that matter
Who experience
A moment of stillness
       Rich with return

CAPTURED REVELATION

Ponder this
His brain says
On a night
  Of fireflies
  And antiques
The boutique of stars
You love
  The china cabinet
Of galaxies
In the mind's eye
  Your own existence
And
That of your favorite
  Chair
Are the result
Of an explosive twitch
In a tiny lump
Of space
During the era
Of primordial
  Chaos
Says who
He says
Opening the lid
  Of a fine
And elegant jar

No Signal

He lies down
On the couch
Of his brain
To confront
Problems
There is nothing
To confess in the act
Of composition
His brain whispers
As he wrestles weeks
    Weeds
  Sunshine
     A day of sterile
Raindrops
And silent thunder
In no particular
Order
He understands the
Waves passing
Through him
        Crest and trough
He has been to
The Mountain of Valleys
Without the compulsion
For souvenirs
        Though he prefers
Not to restart his computer
To enter thoughts
In a ledger of light
He's unsure
Of his options
When an hourglass
      Glowers

DESIRE

It's time
To consider
The nature
  Of thought
 The brain
   Demands
One night
Before sleep strikes
A pose
  Of a long-glided
Staircase
To climb
He's not up
To the
Task
But the brain
Persists
Think of the charm
Of invisible ink
It says
Looping ever so
Gracefully – swan's
Neck to fountain –
  From nothing
Or firing
Through you
Like pellets of ice
Bullets
Homeless neutrinos
Craving
Nothing but visibility –
Airwaves
Of talk
And blank page

Hollywood

He never thought
Of his brain
As a character
In his life
Until now
For years he used
Words like
  Occipital
    Temporal
      Hypothalamus
    Dendrites
     Synapse
To speak
Of his brain…view it
As lobes and regions –
Fields of vision
Ponds of hearing
Castles of smell and taste
The moors of feeling
And touch
But now his brain
Requires more –
Wants a bigger
More personal role
Spit-shined shoes
Dapper ties
More lines
And definitely more
Women
His brain cajoles him
On nights
He retires to his room
Alone

COFFERS

On rainy days
He lets his brain
Watch the tube
While he eats
Chips
  And sips
    Red wine
Until his brain
Feels woozy
  And addicted
    To talk
And news programs
There is trouble
Outside his brain
Men with guns
And high-powered
Weapons
Shoot at each other
    For God
  And Country
For wealth
And power
There are all
Kinds
Of reasons
  Explanations
 Rationalizations
And strategies
In the end
Everyone wants
Peace
  Tranquility
  And a good time
I'm a political machine
His brain slurs
Before nodding
Off

WISE GUY

He wants to say
Something
About the economy
Of his brain
And the people
In charge
Of its operation
There is a slew
  Of doctors
  And mystics
Invested (infested)
In his brain
That took a bath
  And lost
Their proverbial
Shirts
His brain is a small time
Operator   not
Exactly on the
Shady side
But in and out
Of shadows
Nevertheless
There is a lot
Of talk in the streets
About this bubble
          Bursting
Then that bubble
          Bursting
The whole space
Time thing
His brain complained
To him one night
Is about rapid inflation

So whaddaya
Expect from terra
  Firma
Some kind of
Guaranteed return

Therapy

He has to move away
From the bruised
Language of his brain
He thinks
   As a thought   in the
  Midst of thought
His eyes not exactly
   Bursting
   Awake
In the darkness
The sun delayed
For the moment
 Like someone
He doesn't know (who?)
Dashing in and out
Of a locked door
  Still he expects
That he is more
Than his brain
  Or a mystery
(He wants to say)
Unfolding
Like birds to song
Snow to fall   the speeding
  Cars of here to there

Headlines

I'm the infrastructure
Of thought
His brain proclaims
During a rain shower
 Of roses
 And peacocks
In a dream
Devoid of
 Magnificent umbrellas
I bet you know
Squat
His brain chides
During a jump
Cut
To apple skies
 And velvet
Wind (in the nectar
Of a kiss) about
Neurotransmitters
 And synaptic
Terminals –
How the self
Is nothing more
Than genetic juice
Without the Cartesian
 Certainty
Of a rational intellect
In the swirl
Of electromagnetic
 Sensations
All thought
Fires from Point
Alpha
To Point Omega

On predetermined
  Random circuits
(Got Whitman)
His brain
Assures him
As the radio alarm
  Pesters him
With morning
News

(see story)

Dumbass

Dumbass felt responsible for everything and he had felt that way for quite awhile. Most of those who knew Dumbass, and considered him to be a dumb ass, generally agreed that Dumbass himself thought that the responsibility jag started within a nanosecond of his appearance in the world. However, Dumbass is not talking to the media anymore (like a pampered celebrity) so verification of the trajectory of Dumbass' responsibility odyssey (via direct interview) is tentative at best.

Still there are shreds of evidence (including an out-of-print, not on eBay, difficult to find book) and plenty of hearsay, which is pretty much all the evidence you're going to get these days, plus a recently surfaced treatise on the internet attributed to Dumbass. Let me start with a shred of evidence. Take the following entry from his mother's diary for example:

I blame Dumbass for the mess my life became

Mom-blame and its link to responsibility is always productive, and in the above fragment from Dumbass' mom's diary, his mom is undoubtedly referring to the lack of opportunities thrust upon her due to the daily and monumental care involved in raising Dumbass as a child. He wasn't exactly easy to raise, what with his penchant for self-inflicted bruises and wounds – nasty boo-boos, really, that came from bouncing off chairs and walls like a rogue electron in full spasmodic motion when trapped inside an imaginary box (hearsay).

"Why the number of times I had to take Dumbass to the emergency room," his mom told me, before lapsing into tears, "pretty much ended my chance of making much of myself. And when Harry left…he just couldn't stomach Dumbass, you know, especially after his gravity (grave?) experiments took hold of his attention around the time he turned seven or eight…the ones, yes, that he describes in his book *I Didn't Mean to Hurt Myself or You for Christsakes*…the ones in which he repeatedly jumps out of our second storey apartment window, at times with a feather in his hand or a lead ball or some object he let go of at the moment of his descent, only to discover, again and again, that feathers and lead balls whether or not they rush to earth at the same speed, don't break or sprain ankles. This type of craziness was a little over the top for my neurasthenic husband. So the bastard, how do you say, skedaddled."

After some more tears, a quick check on my ID (was I or wasn't I employed by Fox News), an awkward moment when I asked: "Who the hell did he think he was, Galileo," she continued:

"It got tough on me after that and I still regret, and you may write, UNTIL THIS DAY, drugging him with my tranquillizers and leaving him outside the main tent of the Big Apple Circus – one night in the pouring rain like an overgrown baby Moses – during one of its vagabond stints in our fine city."

Dumbass took to abandonment like a tanker spill to a pristine coastline. Even after metaphors and similes for waterfowl and pure flight were rinsed free of slime, he knew that the weight of the world fell on his shoulders like plummeting twin concrete elephants dropped from a phantasmagorical sky crane because of his odd behavior in familial and social situations (he didn't exactly warm up to the circus crowd) or milieus as he referred to them in his treatise *My Milieu or Yours/ Who Gives a Damn*, with the accessible subtitle: *Why I'm a Dumbass – a treatise* that received little attention until an enterprising philosophy student from Berkeley, Ant McGoogle, established *postyourtreatise.com* as a viable sight on the Net for your quotidian treatise lover. A bit of a visionary and smart editor, McGoogle replaced the title of Dumbass' treatise with the subtitle.

It goes without saying when treatise lovers found the site and the list of options etc. (Aristotle, Martin Luther, John Locke and a pantheon of ETCS. ETCS. to chose from) they couldn't resist clicking on *Why I'm a Dumbass* by Dumbass. According to Ant McGoogle, Dumbass' treatise garnered a lively number of hits right from the start, in the neighborhood of 200 to 300 per day.

"It's almost like there's a Dumbass craze going on out there among treatise freaks," he told me over the phone recently.

"Really," I said, "a Dumbass crazy, huh?"

"Sure enough," McGoogle said. "And I think it has to do with the simple eloquence of Dumbass' treatise. What I mean is that Dumbass lays out the facts of why he is a dumb ass in a methodical and persuasive manner, the hallmarks of any decent treatise, before concluding that in fact he is a dumb ass. And of course embedded within this appraisal is his heavy sense of being responsible for being such a dumb ass. Here, go to the site and see what I mean."

After a minute (filled by Ant whistling *The Weight* by The Band), I brought it up on my laptop, clicked on *Why I'm a Dumbass* by Dumbass, and read the following:

I'm a dumb ass. Why is this so?
Let me explain.

"See what I'm talking about," McGoogle chortled over the phone. "Isn't that simply beautiful or beautifully simple?"

"In a way, I guess," I countered.

"Oh, come on," Ant McGoogle admonished. "Dumbass proceeds from those simple opening lines and presents the hard core facts:

- The burden he placed on his mom and dad by jumping out of windows
- The burden he placed on friends by jumping out of windows
- The wives he lost via his swan dives from various heights during mundane arguments
- His life-long struggle with defying gravity and/or searching for magical portals in solid objects, door jams, walls etc., with his head (screaming head, some might say) accelerated at full speed when things weren't going his way
- His remorse."

"Yeah, sure," I said, letting McGoogle rave on:

"It's a gorgeous argument that he presents for his condition or maybe the condition of *dumbassness*, which he nails at the conclusion by subtly returning to the opening line of his treatise, and with the slightest, legerdemain-like tweaking, transmogrifies it into the final line of pure awakening: "Yes, folks, I'm a dumb ass."

"It'd be an honor to meet him," I said, before euphemistically hanging up the phone.

from *Altercations in the Quiet Car* (Lavender Ink/Fell Swoop, 2010)

(see preface)

The Ghost of Richard Brautigan
Preface

The Ghost of Richard Brautigan offers ten new and previously unpublished poems by the late Mr. Richard Brautigan to interested readers and passionate devotees of the deceased writer. Scant attention is paid to Brautigan's work today, and it is my hope that these new poems will spark a renewed interest and appreciation for Mr. Brautigan's oeuvre.

To my chagrin, I didn't come in contact with Brautigan's work until the obscure (reclusive) poet, short story writer and antimemoirist, Richard Martin, sent me a copy of his highly unacclaimed antimemoir, **boink**!. The reclusive Martin (some say he spends his days in an undisclosed turret writing nasty notes to critics (**see story and poem**) and small press publishers) sent me his antimemoir after reading my highly acclaimed first volume of poems, *Headlines* (*Fell Swoop*, Issue 95). For those unfamiliar with *Headlines*, I run the popular website *postyourtreatise.com*, and I'm also the publisher of deadCpress. How I missed reading Brautigan is a testament to my shoddy education and/or devotion to musty texts while studying for my Philosophy degree at Berkeley in the sixties. With Descartes, Kant, Hume occupying my attention, I didn't tune into poetry and the well-known writers in that genre during the late sixties and early seventies. Regrettably, I was a late baby bloomer.

In "Day Four" **of** *boink!* Martin credits Brautigan as the writer most influential in the creation of his non-seminal work. In a nearly incomprehensible letter to me, he claimed that he happened to be reading Brautigan's *Trout Fishing in America* on the day a nasty nor'easter slamming the coastline of New England, specifically Boston, prevented him from going to work (yeah, right). In fact, "Day Four" of *boink!* starts with a poem Martin dedicated to Brautigan.

More Love

for Richard Brautigan

This morning I put my love poems
into the little stack of loneliness
        they made and read them

like a lover with feverish eyes
Pale, purple hosta flowers in my garden
cooled my vision

Because there was a gentle breeze
in the backyard
Because there were birds, squirrels,
airplanes, cars
and men working with hammers
and saws on old houses

The pale, purple flowers
of the hosta
became women in sexy bonnets
(ones I'll never meet)
swaying down streets
during annual parades

Martin is correct in his eventual assessment (I threatened him with bodily harm) that *More Love* is a lousy, throw-away poem. However, it did pique my interest in Brautigan, and I quickly devoured *The Pill Versus The Springhill Mine Disaster*, *Trout Fishing in America*, *In Watermelon Sugar*, and *Rommel Drives On Deep Into Egypt*. Like Martin, I enjoyed the whimsical joy, sadness and satire pervading Brautigan's work, and while working on a set of "homage" poems in this present volume (imitation born from respect) – and besides how could I ever follow up or match the success and praise *Headlines* had garnered (some critics even suggested that I set "brain" research back at least ten years) – a most unusual thing happened to me.

I wish I could claim or blame a nasty addiction to séances and/or the sport of entertaining spirits of the dead, for what I'm about to disclose, but séances or soirees with the dead never thoroughly captured my imagination and/or interest. To the point then, while at work on the "homage" poems (imitation born of respect), I did have an unsettling dream that the ghost of Richard Brautigan had partied in my head one night while I slept, and during the course of the party had pulled me aside for a private conversation.

"Ant," Richard said. "I want you do something for me."

"Yes, Richard," I said, "What is it?"

"Ant, I want you to stop by the Post Office later today and buy me a package of postcards and steal one of its pens. I feel like writing again and when I'm done you can have the postcards and do whatever you want with them."

"Come on, Richard," I said. "I don't mind you choosing my head to party in while I'm asleep. But after that it seems a little crazy that a ghost inside my head during a dream could be you, and particularly a "you" who wants to write again."

"What's not crazy, Ant?" he said, "Just do as I say. Buy the postcards –leave them on a table or counter in the lobby – and when I'm done, I'll slip them into your postal box."

"You have a postal box, don't you, Ant," Richard asked.

I just gazed at him in astonishment.

"Sure," I said

"Here, take a snort of this," he said, passing me a flask, before continuing:

"Ant, find a place for them in your new book. *The Ghost of Richard Brautigan* might be a cool title for it."

I took a hit from the flask and fell back into the coma of sleep. With some reluctance, when I got up the next morning, I did as the ghost requested. When the 10 postcards appeared in my postal box sometime later, I suffered a minor nervous breakdown, and, eventually under some intense therapy, came to accept that I had written the newly discovered Brautigan poems myself during a hallucinogenic hiatus in my normal routine as a retired entrepreneur.

The ghost of Richard Brautigan thinks otherwise.

(see story)

Fat Asses Working the Desk

Carla's ass took up three good-size desk chairs, and she didn't like people either. It wasn't always like that. There was a time when her ass just spread across two good-size desk chairs, and she sort of felt skeptical about people. No one can remember, not even her mama or an omniscient author like myself, when her ass could occupy a single, good-size desk chair, but if it ever had, it's a shoo-in neighborhood assumption that people to her, during her period of a normal size ass, were just people, and maybe she even liked a few of them or deigned to consider their feeble requests for help and service. But who cares, for this isn't about an especially happy individual or a category type of an individual or one (real or just category) that really tried to be less than outright hostile to those seeking sundry services for sundry needs.

No! This is a person (or category of people) that you and I are dealing with right now in a variety of essential and/or common places. Let's say a dental office or a large urban medical center to give a setting and place from which Carla can operate from with her repertoire of blank stares and snickers. Maybe, she's installed with all the grandeur of a disposed queen (or evil step-mother) at the customer service desk at Sears or Tweeters or the new IPOD Emporium and Donut Shoppe in your strip-mauled consciousness – yes ubiquitously there, as a visible, luminescent being in the Heideggerian sense of Madam DaSein, in other words (full light bulb strength and everything), a being-in-the-world (fully hyphenated) with a bad-ass grin and inherited gene pool that undoubtedly mutated (way back when) under the stress of living and consigned by fate to grow and multiply in the service sector like freaky toadstools on damp, lightless lawns. The kind of "shroom" you've met (not taken) before with *sneakered* toe, knocking the head off into kingdom come, only to find more of them on your lawn next year just like (and I'm begging this analogy to hold up, hold water, stay strong, and weather the onslaught of this rush of words) fat asses working at desks somewhere and ready and bonded to cause you (yeah, or me) discomfort for asking the simplest of questions, as in, like mine (man) to Carla during a recent visit to a large urban medical center:

"Excuse me, Madam. Can you tell me what floor the MRI unit is on?"

"Maybe."

"You see I need a MRI for my head."

"What, did you fall on that big old thing or something?"

"Not exactly, Madam. A house alarm went off in my ear."

"Now how did a house alarm go off in one of those big floppy ears? Did you forget the code or something?"

"Really, Madam, I don't think that is any of your business."

"But you think it is my business to tell you the floor where you can get your big old head magnetized?"

"Well, that's your job, isn't?"

"Who the hell gave you the right to say what my job is or isn't, big-headed, floppy-eared boy?"

"Well, there's no reason to be hostile?"

"Oh, yes there is!"

"And why is that?"

"Because you and your big old damaged head are standing in front of me asking a bunch of dumbass questions when the sign just above my head tells you where to go and how to get there."

Now obviously there is something fake or phony about the above conversation. Not the part about my home alarm going off in my ear and turning the sound chamber into a post Stones (early) concert buzz that failed to dissipate after a few days. But generally, the overall exchange between fat ass and me seems to stretch the parameters of what dialogue under these circumstances would entail into the realm of exaggerated play that could backfire on me (as the writer) and sweep the reader(s) into a sudden and destabilizing moment of insight or conviction that namely the writer (me again) may be nothing other than a fat ass working at his desk. (God forbid).

Let's get out of this jam (OK?) by considering one of your encounters with some fat ass working the desk– one that's dawning on you now and appears at first blush to be almost totally different in verbal quality than the deconstructed (not even a chance) bit of tomfoolery from above, in that this fat ass (as in some fat asses) may not even talk, or even refuse to talk, at least for those first few uncomfortable moments you're (yeah, you) standing in front of them. Yep, there you are (blushed-arrived) shifting from foot to foot, clearing your throat, and suddenly thinking you've got to pee, and what an unfortunate time for that, which would undoubtedly mean losing your place in the *Waiting to Talk to A Fat Ass* line and imbibing the concomitant remorse that comes from not taking your dose of *Flomax* (picture a herd of old men on Mountain bikes in the Rockies sucking down spring water from plastic jugs) or any such drug that allows you to function in the public eye (sore) without drawing unnecessary attention to yourself.

So, Judy (her name this time around) is wrapped up and absorbed in a bag of chips (got *Doritos*) while watching her accomplice (multi-tasking, Carla that is) do her nails like both of them were on holiday at a city beach or something before Judy finally speaks, but not to you or at you, but to her wind-blown accomplice, in a fairly affectionate manner as documented by Mr. Omniscient (as requested by you) in the following manner:

"Well, Judy, honey, what are you planning for the weekend?"

"Not much, Carla (complete naming coincidence). Maybe, grill some kielbasa on the hibachi and chase Randy around the apartment with a dust broom."

"You're a stitch, you know that, Judy. Chasing Randy around with a dust broom! I like your style, girl. Maybe, I'll switch from target practice on my significant other with my trusty BB gun this weekend and lock and load with some dusty feathers for him in honor of you."

And you don't even have a buzz in your ear (or a hope in your head) Nope! You're just standing there at the return desk at Sears with a worthless appliance a vile relative gave you. And the talk goes on and you've got all the time in the world, so you lean a little closer to it and detect the delectable sweets of fetid breath in the whirr of chip-chomping teeth.

I'm wrong again (outstanding). That's not your fat ass working the desk, but another version of mine (you say), like I have some uncontrollable need to control the multiple examples of fat asses working their desks. Which begins to make this a bit tedious, and even if I did sneak in another fat ass and call her yours, I never intended to catalog fat asses… or even imply (which I have) that fat asses necessarily are women. I know what side of the political correctness tracks to live on. So please just drop the *a* from Carla and *y* from Judy before adding an *e*, which I did (no shaking of *thee* head), before settling into the junkyard, jackhammer, surround sound melodies of magnets (**MRI – Fifth Floor**, turn right from elevator, walk in under **HAZARDOUS MAGNETS IN USE** sign to receptionist desk) pinpointing fine grain, and not so fine grin, chunks of metal accidentally lodged in my head for some unknown reason.

from *Altercations in the Quiet Car* (Lavender Ink/Fell Swoop, 2010)

(see poems)

MEDLEY

An old woman
Tightens the squirrels
she finds
in her fists

MARTIAN WINTER

Man beats woman
Woman beats child
Child beats dog
Dog beats off

REASONS

Instead of deodorant
he uses hamsters,
one under each arm.

This makes the hamsters
very happy as they
feel useful rather

than just pets. "Yay!"
is how they feel
about underarms &

Martians.

BEERHEADS FROM OUTER SPACE

for JVS Miller

The nights are blemishes
here where our retros
kiss Mars, but the night we

heard about the Beerheads landing near
The Belmar Bar & Grill & taking
applications for space

employment with light years
of benefits & Milky Way rays of hope,
my only hope was that we

were somehow eligible.

From ANGRY RED BLUES (*Fell Swoop* #7) by S Zivvit 57

(Translated from the Martian and into English by Joel Dailey)

(see story)

Folk

Menfolk hitched up hisfolk pants a nanosecond before womenfolk hitched up herfolks. Menfolk didn't know what a freakin' nanosecond was and didn't much care, though womenfolk had a nice ass and looked better in hitched up pants than menfolk looked in hisfolk pants any day.

Menfolk said to womenfolk: "Youfolk look mighty fine in them hitched up pants. Ifolk know wefolk just goin' out to rake leaves and all, but still womenfolk, youfolk look hot."

Womenfolk said to menfolk: "Raking leaves is not about myfolk fine body displaying itself through myfolk hitched up pants. Besides, myfolk pants have to be hitched up, not in deference to myfolk fine ass, but because I'mfolk surely the menfolk in this sorry ass family."

Babyfolk giggled at that. Babyfolk knew what a nanosecond was (kind of like Platofolk in Menofolk knew whofolk hefolk was), and though babyfolk knew, babyfolk couldn't explain it too well (even to layfolk) and opted instead to ignore specialized details about piddling time, and drew, in a black and white spiral notebook, a picture of the sun wearing red shades and smoking dizzy clouds through a blue pipe. The sun also donned a single orange tooth (crooked as the ruts of wisdom), and on a closer inspection of the drawing, onefolk could see that babyfolk had drawn tiny insectfolk crawling up droopy sunrays like storm-weary spouts.

Babyfolk also wrote a fistful of words on this drawing of light, sprinkling them like literary raindrops – hyperbolic ones (the size of mutated Smith Brothers' cough drops) that signifier and signified the following: STOP GO TRAFFIC LOVE MOMMYFOLK DADDYFOLK.

When menfolk and womenfolk viewed babyfolk's drawing, theyfolk felt immense pride. Neither menfolk nor womenfolk could draw much. Menfolk could draw a large foot, that's about it. Womenfolk was into abstract cherries and liked the word *jubilee*, when associated with misshapen berries, a tad more than shefolk liked menfolk.

Youfolk see readerfolk, menfolk was a big pain in the ass. When it came to hitching up pants and working around the house, everything was such a big deal. Raking leaves, fixing steps, building a new porch, patching the driveway were all somehow connected to traumatic experiences with home repairs menfolk had experienced as childfolk while working with hisfolk dadfolk many years ago. Dadfolk was a perfectionist when it came to home repairs and improvements, but hefolk just lacked the patience to teach menfolk (as childfolk) how to do anything without yelling and screaming like some bansheefolk at menfolk (as childfolk). Menfolk (as childfolk) had dreams of dadfolk hitching up hisfolk pants before commencing to do the necessary dadfolk (as menfolk) jobs around the house. Menfolk's momfolk didn't participate in home repairs and by the luck of the draw on love, menfolk had fallen (like lead leaves) head-over-heels in love with womenfolk before realizing that womenfolk knew tons of stuff about home repairs, and when womenfolk hitched up herfolk pants, shefolk meant to accomplish and complete some task without fooling around and/or complaining.

It's not that womenfolk minded fooling around (and not even getting to the repair jobs) because fooling around with menfolk was damn good fun and had produced babyfolk whomfolk womenfolk loved immensely. But since the arrival of babyfolk, menfolk couldn't hold up hisfolk end of the bargain in the *Fooling-Around-Department*, and womenfolk had little tolerance for menfolk's traumatic stories about sawhorses and ballpeen hammers. And let mefolk be honest here, readerfolk, womenfolk hated the pants hitching up contests menfolk perpetrated on herfolk before even hauling garbage and trash to the curbside. Womenfolk knew menfolk questioned hisfolk manhood and was threatened by the manhood womenfolk possessed in greater abundance than hefolk possessed.

How else could womenfolk understand menfolk's constant refrain:

"Womenfolk," menfolk said. "Are youfolk aiming to hitch up yourfolk pants again in front of neighborfolk?"

"Youfolk know I'm not menfolk," womenfolk said. "Pants hitching up is all in yourfolk mind."

"Bullshit," menfolk said. "Ifolk can hitch up my pants faster than womenfolk."

"Please, menfolk," womenfolk said. "Enough is enough."

"No it ain't," menfolk said. "Come on, let's see whofolk is faster."

from *Altercations in the Quiet Car* (Lavender Ink/Fell Swoop 2010)

(see submission guidelines)

CALL FOR SUBMISSIONS

deadCpress
2532 Pirate Cove Road
Suite 400
Ocean City, Florida 34982

Publisher: Ant McGoogle
Editor: Randy "Bud" Playfield (**see story**)

Submission Guidelines: There are no guidelines. Ant will contact you; you are not to contact Ant. Ant gets very upset when he receives an unsolicited manuscript (and he's not that fond of solicited manuscripts either). Randy "Bud" will search you down and put the beat down on you if you send Ant anything.

However, please donate to the press in donations of at least $1000. If you send less than that, Randy "Bud" will search you down and put the beat down on you.

Those we do publish are sworn to secrecy. When they rat us out by sharing their work with others, Randy "Bud" searches them down and puts the beat down on them.

If you've ever attended a writing workshop or have gone to a special place in the world – often an exotic place – to learn to write a poem, Randy "Bud" will search you down and put the beat down on you.

Mission Statement of deadCpress: Ant and Randy are the best poets; you're not.

To date deadCpress has published one volume: Black Oil, by the legendary poet William Kemmett. Mr. Kemmett searched out Ant and Randy and put the beat down on them.

(**see poem**)

POST COMPUTER FAD

for Jack Spicer

There are no metaphors for dread.
You can't use rats
or the fact government agents play
with the drinking water.
Buying a sack of lemons at the grocery
thinking the moon is a heavy word
won't help.
Freedom piles up.
Don't confuse it with snow or garbage
and there no ground wires.
Pointing to the gravity in feet
means nothing.

Each must decide the fate of radios
When to consult ghosts
how to server the Martians.
It is real.
Words are knives
wrapping things is
pointless.

from *White Man Appears on Southern California Beach* (Bottom Fish Press, 1991)

(see story and poem)

CHASING INTELLECTUALS

The critic didn't like me, well, maybe not me, but my work, well, maybe not my work, but my stories, well, maybe not my stories, but my characters, well, maybe not my characters, but my settings, well, maybe not my settings, but my style, well, maybe not my style, but my sentences, well, maybe not my sentences, but my words, well, maybe not my words, but my thoughts, well, maybe not my thoughts, but my consciousness, well, maybe not my consciousness, but my unconsciousness, well, maybe not my unconsciousness, but my collective unconsciousness, well, maybe not my collective unconsciousness, but my role or place in the collective unconsciousness…nevertheless, the critic didn't like me.

I saw the critic at Starbucks on the corner of X and Y. I observed the critic through a window made of transparent maps and adventures. He was dressed for summer in a white and blue pinstripe suit. He had a straw hat on, one with a black ribbon circling its crown, and he wore white bucks with red soles and heels. There was a crowd around him – admirers, each with a coffee, unique and different to suit their taste buds. I was good at coffee identification. I spied the following brews through the window, my head pressed against a transparent map of Greenland: pumpkin spice latte, mango spice latte, kiwi spice latte, plantain spice latte, very-berry spice latte, guava spice latte, papaya spice latte and stinky fruit spice latte.

Without a doubt the critic had astute and discriminating coffee drinking friends and listeners. The critic was listened to – he had an audience. His literary ideas, penchants and proclivities were important – the culture – the literary culture –was under siege by audacious, tasteless and meaningless plots, or no plots at all – just detours and deconstructions, word play, inside puns and jokes and a myriad of allusions.

I entered the coffee shop to hear directly what the critic had to say or reiterate, and to not just think about what I had read (with my head pressed against a transparent map of Greenland) – what the critic had said about me, how I was a misfit, a hopeless nihilist without a cause, that my adjectives smelled bad, that I had no sense of direction, did not appreciate the plights – the daily existence – of the little man and little woman, that my exploits on the page to set the narrative on fire were jejune and regrettably exhibitionist, which, unfortunately, caused a flamboyant disorientation in the reader's sensibility, causing some readers to commit low-level crimes, turn to drugs or commit to love-making in the town square. But there was more, much more. According to the critic, a reader reading my "stuff" (just once) could return the reader to TV, video games, fighter pilot lessons or a blind trek deep into the Himalayan mountains to secure a rare audience with a hermit – a prescient Tibetan monk who knew like the void in his mind that I was a fool who dabbled in the absence of story and meaning.

After ordering a double espresso, I took a seat close to the critic and his crowd of admirers and perked my ears like a dog in a silent alarm factory. The critic was at it. The critic was talkative.

"You see," the critic said, "I don't like the Big Guys – LMNOP – or the little guys – abcde – that like to write like or imitate the Big Guys – LMNOP."

"You must understand," the critic went on, "the *text* is an exercise in meaning and purpose. It's a workout in style and insights that allows the reader to evaluate and re-evaluate the world. I'm talking here, of course, of the real world – the one which we all inhabit – not some imaginary one, some half-cocked or partially rendered one – but the real one, with all its inanities, stupidities and tragedies, so often presented to us – rightly or wrongly – through the filter and manipulations of Big Media – the one in which we maintain our existential and quotidian lives."

"Now dear friends," the critic continued, "say X marks the Spot for the Spot is the quotidian and from the quotidian (Jack and Jill went up the hill – didn't they, don't we all) come the stories of serious interest to me – stories that under the white-lightning strokes of the master craftsmen reveal secret doors, passages and wormholes into the everyday forgetfulness of our lives – stories which lead (they can; they must) to a deeper and better world, a world with options never before realized."

The critic took a sip of his pumpkin spice latte and adjusted his straw hat so it sat square on his large and glowing head. He looked at his audience and the rapt attention in their eyes and on their faces. They were jack-o-lanterns parked on the steps of each and every one of his words.

"Finally, let me frame it in this way," he said. "We – you, the reader, and I – are engulfed, ensconced, submerged and entombed in the crushing and irresolvable problems generated by a species (us) that left the Great Pond eons ago and are presently lost in a directionless, unmapped polis of confusion, ambiguity, violence and despair, and all the noise that goes with it. We all know the score (what do you think headlines are for) and any writer worth his or her salt must leap into that vat of noise, confront it, mine and excavate meaning and set down with a sparkling pen a message that thrills the eyes and ears and inspires hope. And it is my job to squeeze "texts" in this light, to press down on them like an almighty rock, interrogate them and judge them to be worthy or not."

I had heard enough, quickly swallowed my double espresso and went outside. It remained a pleasant day of stick characters and pastel faces. Everyone on the street was completely plugged into their favorite telecommunication device of choice. The trees hummed and unattached modules of abstraction moved up and down the street like an invisible convoy of small trucks. I waved to them, but they ignored me. I took my place behind a street bench and thought about what the critic had said. Maybe he was right. Maybe I should view my last book – *Where Is It Going?* – in the light of his interests and concerns. I wasn't sure, so I waited.

When the critic emerged from Starbucks, I stood up.

"Hey, you," I shouted, and chased him down the street.

Excerpt from Where Is It Going?

For some years now, I have written two to three page novels (not short-shorts) which pummel meaning, ridicule personal relationships and demonstrate the devastating effects of climate change on specific regions of earth. Although I have not been able to give up my day job, as the saying goes, based on the royalties from these novels, I have derived immense pleasure (yes, consider me Joyce Carol Oates in miniature) from the number of novels produced within any given month.* Besides, I don't mind being a page at the Albatross Public Library (APL). It doesn't kill me or anything, putting books back in their proper places in the stacks. In fact, I enjoy and have mastered at least one of a page's favorite hobbies – getting lost in the stacks for hours. I know how to kill the clock thumbing through oversized art volumes of Rembrandt, Van Gogh, Picasso, Magritte, Michelangelo and other great talents, while totally ignoring the staccato tremors of the page bell at the front desk, which attempt to muster my attention for some mundane task (*Get thee to a nunnery* [Hamlet, 3.1]-{read: Post Office}, *page boy!*) exploding in the head of Ms. Smith, the Head Librarian.

from *Buffoons in the Gene Pool* (Lavender Ink/Fell Swoop, 2016)

(**see poem**)

BAND-AID FOR MY BOO-BOO

I can't help what they like or don't like
I said to the critic in me – the one with a stuffy nose
ashplant & electronic cigarette   Liar
someone yelled from the cheap seats
window open for an April breeze
blood moon obscured by clouds – clouds of snow
another said   What's that she called from across the street
Make it personal   Make it real   Make it new
It seemed like the right time for the wind
to roar through hemlocks   (out back)
A gang of garbage can lids harassed
the slick street   Engines succumbed   subsided
We hid inside until morning – cosmic wise
mostly different

from *Techniques in the Neighborhood of Sleep* (Spuyten Duyvil, 2016)

(see story)

Whoopee Cushion Meltdown

According to *The Divorce Manual* (TDM) by Randy "Bud" Playfield, Albert should have been divorced by now, but he wasn't. What a shame, most of his divorced buddies momentarily thought when momentary thoughts surfaced in their individual or collective consciousness. Albert was a good guy. How come he couldn't be divorced like them, living the easy (as in hassle-free) life, as they poked into the ashes of night, searching for new love? What was Albert's wife about any way? Was she some kind of masochist or something?

The Divorce Manual or the TDM, as they called it, mapped the way for any man to land on his ass outside his home or castle. "Bud" really understood what got to women – what they absolutely refused to accept in a long-term, interminable relationship. All any guy had to do was to follow, consistently now, the guidelines set forth by "Bud" Playfield. Guidelines, such as (Chapter One, "Grave Intestinal Disorders," page one, bullet 15): *One must burp vociferously after every meal, even breakfast, even after a continental breakfast, even after a continental breakfast at a swank hotel during a romantic get away weekend.* What was so hard about that, his alimony-swaggering buddies wondered as tiny, nearly invisible phoenixes formed and took flight from the ashes of their hopeless longing? And come on, some of the other bullets, from at least the upper GI portion of the bullets (and no, *we*, as in the royal *we* of omniscience, will not pursue the Lower GI portion of "Bud's" bullet-crazed Chapter 1 for the simple sake of propriety and taste), seemed easy enough to accomplish with at least some practice and/or diligent attention. Give a scan:

> • *One must form burps into simple words and/or commands, such as, Yes, dear; No, dear; Bring me the paper; Fetch food* (Bullet 16)
> • *One must make sudden and frequent stops at convenience stores and pharmacies for Tums, Rolaids, Maalox and new brands of antacids* (Bullet 10)
> • *One must run from said convenience stores and pharmacies, brandishing a jug of Maalox, and with great glee unscrew the cap while saying: "It's time for a slug on the jug."* (Bullet 11)

Yes, it took some practice, some will, some fortitude, some screw fortunately dislodged from the assembly of the mind to approach the mastery level, that level that instigates, better yet, baits a woman (and let's say a damn good woman) to narrow her eyes, cringe and dial her lawyer up on the cell. Playfield didn't pull any punches; he warned the faint of heart straightforwardly in his introductory remarks:

Yo, dunderheads, as in be forewarned lamebrains, the techniques offered to you in my manual are not for every Bozo Tom, Bozo Dick, or Bozo Harry. A guy can get hurt applying these techniques (think back to your youngster days when you used to make fart noises by flapping your arms [you ambidextrous sons-of-bitches] and know this; them days are gone in terms of " isn't that cute" etc…as in Mommy dearest, perhaps claiming: "Look at my little dear making fart sounds. I wonder who taught him that," as she rang the bell of her old man with a flour-peppered rolling pin) especially in the age of Whoopee Cushion Meltdown and polite speech.

So what gives with Albert and his wife, Lindsey is a fair enough question to pursue and thank god Albert was up for that task via dialogue and a few beers with his friend, Ding Dong at Mike's Bar & Grill, a favorite haunt for those recently released from the bonds of matrimony and alive to the flight of imaginary, reconstructed birds of fiery hope. Ding Dong (aka, Walter D. Slipknot, attorney at law, whom by the way was christened Ding Dong by the throng of unattached patrons at Mike's after admitting to a ringing in his head, not from any rolling pin, but from an unopened bottle of Dom Perignon applied to his noodle after working his way through Chapter 2 of the TDM – "24/7 Insults" (especially bullets 10 – 15 on subtle but noticeable weight gain) by his wife, Minty, a hell of a woman, who loved the bubbly but who had finally come to the end of her love affair with Walter D.).

Albert was first in with the words:

"Look, Ding Dong," he said, "Lindsey simply absorbs my burp speak or at times just grabs the gaseous verbiage and twists it into invisible balloon-like animals, some of them ferocious enough to chase me up and down the stairs and throughout the house."

Ding Dong looked into the flat halo of his Bud-light draft as if it had oracular potential, lifted his head slightly from it, side-glanced his friend with palomino eyes and scanned the environs of Mike's. Sure enough (death/taxes), Mike was slumped on the back bar with his hand still clutching his whiskey glass, and the dark interior of the joint remained a sojourn into the dark, despite the faint and erratic holiday lights draped like beauty pageant banners across the tattered posters (framed/unframed) of once gorgeous "beer babes" now flickering into the oblivion of neglect.

"You're bullshitting me," Ding Dong finally said. "Burp speak drives them all nuts!"

"I'm not kidding, not Lindsey, she seems to thrive on it," Albert said. "If fact, she belched *dipshit* at me just the other night after downing a six-pack of Miller-Lite ponies while painting the kitchen."

"That's pretty advanced," Ding Dong said. "I'd be pretty frightened, if I were you."

"Tell me about it," Albert said, chugging his Genny draft. "As for Chapter 2 in TMD, I've had limited success at best from that. In fact, the infamous bullets on "poundage" nearly killed me."

"How so?" Ding Dong inquired, while following the flight of a confused, hummingbird-size phoenix into the spent neon lights of MIKE'S GRILL on the front inside window.

"Well," Albert said, "I had barely dipped into the advice from Chapter 2 – you know the opening bullet on insults connected to inevitable and inexorable weight gain: *One must start out slowly when addressing weight gain by asking in a matter of fact way, for example: What happened to our scale dear* (bullet one) – when Lindsey engaged me with a full and aggressive response."

"What did she do," Ding Dong asked, pounding his left ear with a half-made fist and ordering another round.

"She tied an anvil around my ankles while I was sleep, and when I crashed to the floor in the morning, I had the good fortune to read: *Here's a present of weight for you, Buster.*"

"Yeah, it sounds like you're up against a real marriage pro," Ding Dong said.

"Tell me about it," Albert said, throwing his beer glass at Mike to startle him into serving his thirsty patrons.

from *Altercations in the Quiet Car* (Lavender Ink/Fell Swoop, 2010)

PAGE FOURTEEN

MEET AL PANTS

Al Pants is a used car salesman (**see poem**). His dad was a used car salesman. Like his dad, Al prefers shined cordovan wingtips, grey suit, pink dress shirt and indigo tie. He keeps his black hair combed straight back from the forehead and in place with an abundance of mousse. He often chews on a swizzle stick in deference to giving up cigarettes. He claims he was born in 1961 in Lyle, New York, an upstate town famous for its residents' addiction to staring at dirt. To this day, Al loves to stare at dirt. Besides racquetball and arranging flowers he's allergic to, he enjoys writing the occasional sonnet. He's unfamiliar with the term "metamodernism," but when he coughs or sneezes loudly in a public place, his face hints at a slight resemblance to Mr. Ed. Al has been married and divorced at least three times to women with advanced degrees in Physics, Astrology and Analytic Psychology who all tired quickly with his mundane performance in the sack (**see story**).

During a 2012 trip to the great city of New Orleans for the annual National Used Car Convention and Lemon Festival, he accidently bumped into X.J. Dailey, Editor-for-Life of *Fell Swoop: The All Bohemian Revue*. As fate would dictate, Mr. Dailey enjoyed the advantage of owning numerous vintage used cars over the years. This common love of secondhand vehicles induced Mr. Dailey to buy a Pimms cup for Mr. Pants and vice versa. Well, one round led to the next and before long XJ and Al were swapping stories about used cars and those they knew who benefited from driving one. And thanks to the glorious impropriety of secretly recording another's conversation in bars, restaurants, church socials, track meets (you get the idea), a segment of a recording (I assume from Al Pant's phone) has come to light and is now in my possession.

Start Recording:

XJ: No shit, you know that loser, Richard Martin.
Al: Yeah, I sold the weiner a real lemon.
XJ: You say you write an occasional sonnet?
Al: Yessiree, my lady.
XJ: Call me a lady again and I'll order you another Pimm's cup.

Al: Did you say pimp's cup?

XJ: Call me a pimp again, and I'll bust you in the chops.

Al: Did you say your favorite food is pork chops?

XJ: Listen, you dumb bastard, send me a manuscript of your sonnets and I'll take a look at them.

End Recording.

That is the extent of the transmission. However, it appears this accidental encounter at the Napoleon House led the esteemed (steamed) editor of Fell Swoop to publish a collection of Al Pants' sonnets, entitled, *The Year I Wanted to Be on Television*.

An Interview with Al Pants

By Claudia May Nostril (**see poem**)

CMN: Al, may I call you, Mr. Pants?

AP: Sure, why not?

CMN: Well then, Mr. Pants, I've read your sonnets and found them to be ludicrous, mundane and somewhat sexually arousing.

AP: I'm not sure about the sexual arousal bit you peeled off them. I gave up on sex years ago (**see poem**) and have been living as a celibate for years. And I don't buy into that sublimation bullshit (**see poems**) i.e. that my libido (**see story**) is packed inside my verse and consequently I'm satisfied. I ain't satisfied.

CMN: Your response to my question is unsettling to me. I feel flush in the cheeks.

AP: Yes, I can see that, but could we get back to my work, the clock is ticking (**see poem**).

CMN: Yes, you're quite right. Name three sonneteers you admire and who have also influenced your work.

AP: Shakespeare, Berryman and Berrigan.

CMN: Have you met any of these gentleman in your travels or on a used car lot?

AP: Yeah, I hung with Shakespeare once in an alley with his pointed shoes and his pen.

CMN: How did that encounter (**see poem**) go?

AP: The great bard nailed me just below the shin with one of those pointed shoes and told me to get the fuck out of his alley.

CMN: And that inspired you?

AP: More or less, yes. At the very least, it goaded me to write the sonnet, "Medical Codes."

CMN: Well, Mr. Pants, may I call you, Al?

AP: Sure, why not?

CMN: Well then, Al, in keeping with the mandate of less interview time with a Heteronym the better, I would like to thank you for your time and less than honest answers.

AP: Claudia, honey, I'm a used car salesman for chrissakes.

The Year I Wanted to Be on Television

by Al Pants

A Selection

Medical Codes

After the selfie with a forsythia shrub
I jumped up and down on a pile of leaves unfortunately
in a moving vehicle with a sign that read: Moe's Tree Service
At the hospital the doctor thumbed through 68,000 ICD 10
medical codes to describe my injuries how they occurred
and what I may have said in the ambulance
on the way to the hospital
Code W 61.01XA: bitten by a parrot, initial encounter
Code V 95.43: spacecraft collision, injuring occupant
Code V 97. 33XD: sucked into a jet engine, subsequent encounter
Nope   Nope   Nope
"I can't find a code to describe you and your injuries," the doctor said.
"Maybe when the wind dies down," I said.
"Huh?" the doctor said.

Recently Used Vagaries

The end of my rope is a personal favorite
Sun through a peephole of understanding   understands
We could look up the unknown words in our minds
write them down in alphabetical order
use them to our advantage when strangers
knock on the door
It has been getting better since I changed
my name to   Al Pants
Grey in color was my only horse
Now what about the prodigy on the corner
who hocks images for a buck   I wrote this sonnet
while playing the Bach-minuet in G major on the piano
Breakfast is always at half-past 5 in the morning
The poetic whistle in your mouth is mine

White Sandwich! White Sandwich!

You're not the first totally dedicated and complete sexual being
I ever knew so little about   The dream
a younger man mocks me   He knows
what you like   The list is long
and we'll all need passports
I've never been to the Caribbean   or points humid
In the movie if this is one
I'll play Narcissus and live with Cleopatra on Galapagos Pond
Minus the sea-doos the water is gentle mirror-like
I've never been to Greece either
The owner of the Greek Diner in town calls
a fried-egg-ham-no-cheese-no-butter-on-white-toast
a White Sandwich   and screams White Sandwich!
White Sandwich! whenever I order one

Just a Few of Them

AA-12 (US-Automatic Shotgun-12Gauge AK-47 (USSR-Assault Rifle -7.62x39mm)
American Arms PK 22 (US-Semi-Automatic Pistol .22LR)
American-180 (US-Submachine Gun – 22LR, .22 Short Magnum)
Apache Revolver (France – Multi-Purpose Pinfire Revolver – 7mm.27)
Berretta 8000 Mini Cougar (Italy-Subcompact Semi-Automatic Pistol – 9x19mm Parabellum)
Blazer R8 (Germany-Straight-Pull Bolt-Action Hunting Rifle-7.62x51mm NATO)
Blunderbuss Blunderbuss Blunderbuss Blunderbuss Blunderbuss Blunderbuss
Browning R75 (US-Light Machine Gun – .03'06)
Colt Mustang Pocketlite (US-Subcompact-Semi-Automatic Pistol – .380 ACP)
Glock 17, 17L, 18, 19, 20, 21, 22, 23, 24, 25, 26, 27, 28, 29, 30, 31, 32, 33, 34, 35…
Gyrojet series: assault rifle, carbine, derringer, rifle, lancejet, light machine gun
Hua Qing Minigun (Peoples Republic of China – 7.62x54mmR)
Luger (Pistole Parabellum)   Luger Carbine 7.65mm   Luger GL 1907
Milkor Stopper (South Africa – Single-shot Grenade Launcher)

DISTRIBUTION OF THE GREAT AMERICAN POEM
for XJ Dailey

I've been growing stacks of unread poems
next to the Chia plants and *Bird Songs Bible* in my room
They mostly require solitude minimal soil an occasional
raindrop of nightfall Sometimes they talk lodge complaints
cramped with moon lost lovers those times in Paris
and Amsterdam penniless without smokes the habit
of metaphor in unrequited bones or mouth off
Spare us that poets as legislators of the world bullshit
I can't say I blame them the seed packet warns
that many will not flower or avoid becoming hostile
even if an audience for them materialized in the post-
apocalyptic milieu of OMG and LOL
Language will always be in love with language
I tell them Live for that

(The) de/DUM 5

14 lines can be broken into four sections 3 quatrains and a couplet
Rhyme scheme: AB/AB CD/CD EF/EF/ GG or ABAB CC
10 beats per line alternating unstressed and stressed syllables
Three quatrains contain four lines the couplet just two lines both rhyme
First quatrain establishes theme/idea (my lover is a knock-out
and doth torture me) 4 lines AB/AB
Second quatrain develops theme/idea (my lover thy wickedness
is hot because….) 4 lines CD/CD or AB/AB
Third quatrain rounds off theme/idea, i.e. possible consequences (my lover
doth see me in a new light and requires certain behaviors methinks
I'm unfamiliar with) 4 lines EF/EF or AB/AB
Couplet summarizes theme/idea or introduces a fresh look at the theme/idea (my lover
thou hast changed thine locks on doors and no longer respond to entreaties
via text messages) 2 lines GG or CC

(see poem)

THE DIFFERENCE BETWEEN
USED CARS AND LANGUAGE

Seaweed

and

the new graffiti of waves

splash over my feet

Downtown

the young maestro strums a yellow guitar

and dreams of the V-8 engine (**see poem**)

The country moves like a hurricane into itself

Cans of laughter

and

reels of mistakes later

the history teacher takes of his shoes

The rest is tv

The way it talks about itself

what it's up to during this period of gimmicks

and power

On an ice floe my favorite etymologist straps three words

a red scarf

and

a Band-Aid

The content miser shaves in a froth of form

Hallelujah

Vowels in the waiting room of the lung hospital

appear ready to escape

histrionics

There's sunlight on my dancing hand

Hallucinate

Deep in the alley poets decide on pick-up-sticks

or

the I Ching

Give a listen to the bells and tolling clouds

"Come on down and drive this baby,

if you don't believe the flashing odometer!"

In a series of blue don't cross out blue
As far as new worlds…
Close your eyes
and
count to ten
Capture the flag
Jump from roof to roof (**see poem**) in your neighborhood
Applaud the sounds spinning around dissolved objects
Kiss the tree anyway

from *Modulations* (Asylum Arts, 1998)

(**see story**)

WHO THE HELL HASN'T?

The day Jack's wife, Esmeralda, walked out the door, she left his ears ringing with a parting shot: "I never had an orgasm with you."

"Ouch," Jack said later that night, looking in the bathroom mirror at himself. "Women really know how to hurt a guy."

He ran a comb through his thinning brown hair and checked the bumps on his lower inner lip with his tongue. He looked deeply into his eyes. *We're tired*, they said. *She won't be back.*

Jack and Esmeralda had fought for years about food, politics, the weather, God, education, art, medicine and children. In fact, Jack told his friend, Leroy, that it seemed like he had been fighting with Esmeralda since the moment after their first kiss of deep attraction.

"Go figure, Leroy," Jack said. "It seems like that's all I've ever done – fight with the wife."

"Who the hell hasn't?" Leroy said.

Jack and Leroy worked together at the Mundane Manufacturing Company (Plastics Division) which manufactured stuff for the populace. What kind of stuff? All kinds of stuff! Stuff you see in *Wal-Mart*, *Home Depot*, *Kitchen Inc.*, *Electronics Today*, *Total Auto* and *You've Got To Have Medical Supplies*. Stuff the populace needs to patch the holes in their lives, houses, teeth and selves. Jack and Leroy made the stuff that required plastic – or at least some of it.

Does it matter?

Did it matter to them? No.

Leroy's wife had left Leroy months earlier after posting her 95 Theses on the door of his monk room. Leroy reduced the parchment and kept a copy of it in his wallet. Sometimes he took it out of his pocket at break time and read some of the theses to Jack while they powered down packages of mini-doughnuts with machine coffee. Henrietta's statements weren't exactly David Letterman like, but the first few went:

1. You're not a real man.
2. You're not a real man.
3. Etc.

Theses 50-84 documented a host of poor Leroy qualities:

50. You're not much of a plumber.

51. You're self-involved.
52. You're kind of stupid.
53. You're bald.

"Look, Jack," Leroy said, wiping white sugar powder and crumbs from his mouth. "My woman was just too smart for me. She confused and overwhelmed me with her theses, and I didn't have the slightest chance to improve."

Jack took a slug of motor oil and threw a pensive rod. *Women are smarter than men*, he thought.

Leroy broke into a sheepish grin before reading Theses 85 – 95.

"Go," Jack said. "I can take them."

"Here…here…goes," Leroy said, his voice unsteady with alarm.

Clutching the folded document, he read:

85. Never had an orgasm.
86. Never had an orgasm.
87. Etc.

"I know your pain, bro," Jack said.

Jack felt empty and isolated. The house wasn't the same without Esmeralda. He especially missed their fights about weather. Esmeralda loved hurricanes more than tornadoes. He was fond of tornados. Esmeralda enjoyed large hailstones. He preferred small ones. Small for Jack meant ice cube size – something you gather from the yard and driveway, put in a whiskey glass, and pour Jameson's over. Large for Esmeralda meant asteroid-like or at least big enough to replicate *Disney on Ice*. She loved figure skating, even when the skaters were dressed like Goofy and Minnie and the grand old Mouse himself.

Jack was a Democrat.

Esmeralda was a Republican.

Esmeralda believed in God.

Jack didn't.

Jack had liver problems.

Esmeralda drank herbal tea.

Esmeralda wanted kids.

Jack wasn't sure.

Esmeralda championed Hopper.

Jack dug Pollack.

Esmeralda went to college.

Jack finished high school.

"O the fights we used to have," Jack intoned to an empty house.

Outside the window, a full moon on a balloon string floated higher into the night sky. Esmeralda saw that moon, too, and wondered why.

Jack fell asleep.

Esmeralda didn't.

from *Buffoons in the Gene Pool* (Lavender Ink/Fell Swoop, 2016)

(**see poem**)

HAMPTON INN THOUGHT PAD

> for Thelma Ritter

A classic resource of backyard entertainment

An underhand stroke

So many carbs, so little time

The dominant poetic voice of the last six seconds sends one

> final text,

"TV's a smart way to control ants…"

The clown wig's a flagrant self criticism

Boyhood of furies & flurries

Clouds in projectile vomiting puppy dog shapes

"They come to visit not to stay/Return our bottles every

> Day"

The Opaque redensify Omaha

Where & when the Point of Accuracy trumps the Point of No

> Return

Claudia May Nostril (*Fell Swoop* #136/137)
Claudia May Nostril is the best-selling author of *Me and My Thoughts*.
 (**see poem**)

IMPORTANT BUSINESS

1

Yesterday, during my walk
Around the block,
The inevitable headline
Appeared in my head:
Sex Is Over

Spring was out in the neighborhood
As I tried to name the flowers
I knew by name
A dog, both large and small
And black and white,
Galloped past me
With a rabbit
In its mouth

Could this be
My autobiography
If I were a registered voter

2

The subjunctive case always
Paints a smile on my face
I never did think highly
Of grammar

I'm not sure why
I was born a Catholic in a prayer book of rules –
Lived as a monk
In a variety of sentence
Exercises
Said my prayers
And took on the fears
Granted to me

3

Cicero felt relieved
When sex pulled up lame
In his life
He was not a horse
But sixty-years old at the time –
Viagra unavailable in Roman
Drugstores

The science
Or thought
Of prolonging
Sex
Indefinitely
Was not
An option
Or desire
For him

4

Desire tricked Buddha
Into Enlightenment
I've read of his palaces
And sun-sprayed chariot –
The lack of youth he feared
Before retiring from
The world

The grandeur of emptiness exists
Just as form extends content
Beyond itself
Is a rule for audacious
Syllables
Uneven as I go
Is for the captain in me

5

My wife's name is Peaches
Actually, it is Alice
So I call her Peaches

Once I returned from my walk
I shared the headline
In my head with her
She smiled and said:
"How many years ago was that?"
She knows how to downsize
The news

6

I'm not sure if Cicero
Had a wife or not
And if he did
How she responded when he exclaimed:
"Look, darling, now I can get down
To some important business
And concentrate for once,
Goddamn it!"

(see poems)

SHELL GAME WITH STAMP

Right up through my toes
the brain runs its scams
Which day of the week is it
Pass the TV toilet paper   will ya
OK the odyssey of 13.7 billion years
wears thin on the nerves
But I wasn't born yesterday
or the day before yesterday
in yesterday's toupee
I'm a red-blooded American
with belt-loosened trousers
on a paid holiday
traveling toward what I'm saying
in a stolen limousine
Make sure you mention that
to the congregation of rats
ratting me out
I'm under indictment am I not
for issuing the following statement
The pansies of literature make whoopee
in the outhouse of retroactive fantasies
In the current environment
who could manage more Freud than that
Text me the preferred escape route
from myself
My pet peeves are in the mail

from *Techniques in the Neighborhood of Sleep* (Spuyten Duyvil, 2016)

SUBLIMATION MATINEE

I'm lost in the imagery of love
Years have bent time into silence –
The way drunks negotiate sidewalks
In the shadow of being here
I'm a pagan of space

Let's recall passionate nights
The youth of bodies drenched in sweat
The all night fuck
Things like that
Under the umbrella of Venus

We met on a superhighway of chance
In a season of indolent weather
Flowers framed our antics
Birds flew fast into naked mirrors
I grew into your reflection

Used words to touch breasts
Dropped to my knees in a hail of kisses
It's so easy to be lonely
Drift into the parade of animals
Counseling the mind

Look the world is a battlefield of false gods
One side shines a gold Mercedes
The other dusts a desert of death
Stars litter intelligence
Remake dreams into dreams

Of something else
The indigo blouse you favored
After naming your cat Twilight
The way you said: *Address Eros*
And nothing more

(see story)

Model T Junk

Melvin was a horse of a semi-tolerant man (true grits) with a slight limp, wry smile and a sarcastic bank account. Let's start with the limp – focus our gaze on his *Gunsmoke* gait. No, he was never shot but did enjoy *Gunsmoke* (Chester Goode never shot himself in the foot on the show), both the original episodes and reruns, and did model his limp after Chester's. In fact, Melvin was somewhat of a fledging aficionado of the show and knew the following pertinent facts thanks to *GunsmokeNet.com*:

- Chester Goode was played by Dennis Weaver from 1955-1964
- Chester was not Marshal Dillon's deputy
- Chester slept on a cot in the Marshal's office
- Chester once said to Doc: "What's the matter? Somebody pull you through a knothole."
- Chester could sing and favored the song* at the end of this story

Melvin also knew that Chester's stiff right leg (the same as his) was never explained but the reason for his limp was fairly well known to those who knew or associated with him (a number considerably less than the total number of *Gunsmoke* TV episodes). His limp came about through the antics of being an impulsive, daredevil teenager. OK, he fell through a skylight of a brand new middle school built across from his boyhood home after scampering to the roof and pounding his chest like King Kong, an annoying habit that he kept up through high school until he flunked out of East Jesus Tech in his sophomore year in college. It was while he was at this illustrious two-year institution located somewhere in the panhandle of Texas (during beer bashes and hazing rituals, and yes, pounding his chest etc.) that he developed his view that Time (father, mother and the whole kit and caboodle of possible offspring and relatives) was a highly compact and extraordinarily dense single moment (which we'll {referring now to the fragmented self receiving a small stipend to record this tale} get to or not). Undoubtedly, Melvin's plummet down three whistling floors (landing in front of the sign: **All Visitors Must Report to the Main Office**) could have killed him. But it didn't, though he could never shake the feeling that his right leg had turned into bone dust.

It took some time for a wry smile to take control of Melvin's face (after all, research has identified over 50 smile types, the most shocking being the most common, the sincere smile, commonly known as the "Duchenne." As bizarre as it sounds, a French scientist by the name of Guilliame Duchenne {my jaw is already feeling weird} unlocked the mystery of the sincere smile by experimenting with the heads of individuals who met their death at the guillotine. Using electro-simulation, he discovered that the zygomatic major muscles actually run down the face to connect with the corners of the mouth. These muscles pull back the mouth to expose the teeth; they also enlarge or expand the cheeks. Meanwhile, the orbicularis oculi muscles narrow the eyes and cause wrinkles to form in the corners of them. When the muscles work in unison, presto! a genuine sincere smile appears on the face of an individual with a head still attached to the his/her body. Interestingly enough, we can control the zygomatic muscles, but not the orbicularis oculi, which is why saying CHEESE always leads to a fake smile because nothing happens to the "eye" muscles when saying CHEESE), edging out a host of competing smiles, such as the heartfelt smile, tightlipped smile, smirk {though close to wry} and the counterfeit smile.

The "wry" smile with its bent up or twisted shape suited Melvin, and did convey a sense of predictable irony and/or something grisly humorous in his brain, provoking his facial muscles into this all but standard smile on his face. Frankly, the smile revealed a scrap of interior monologue lodged in his brain like a broken record:

I'm no genius, but at least I know that most people are insufferable idiots. Trapped idiots in a host of idiotic dilemmas…dilemmas bridled with idiotic headings or captions – *The Universe Is Nothing at All* (deliberate author intrusion into Melvin's interior monologue: please see addendum at end of story concerning this heading or caption);** *What is the Purpose of Life; Should I Become a Raging Capitalist or Not*.

And when the metaphorical needle jumped its groove, Melvin thought of the intense travails of buying groceries on a regular basis, making periodic visits to hardware stores, raising children and trying with a modicum of success to sustain a romantic life or as the masses (Melvin preferred "herd" over "masses") would say – getting laid on a regular basis.

Melvin disdained all of the above and so copped to a wry smile – a smile that he seemed to enjoy displaying to all in his environs like an intricate tattoo (describe one of your own) or a scouting badge (Bear Igloo) stitched to a sleeve of battle fatigues.

As for the sarcastic bank account, well, it mostly registered a balance of zero or default below zero (and let's be honest and stultifying current here: No one will ever raise Melvin's Debt Ceiling), which could partly be attributed to his numerous marriages (anything after one is many) and his prodigious ability to create offspring on the dole.

Melvin explained his sarcastic bank account to his wife (#4), Gigi, by stating the obvious (at least to him):

"Gigi," he said, "the bitches before you took me for everything. To say nothing of my offspring."

"Please," Gigi counseled. "Don't call you former wives bitches. It makes me feel uncomfortable. It's just sadly wrong."

"OK, honey-child," Melvin retorted (snorted). "But that's exactly what they were."

"Can we move on to another topic?" Gigi countered. "You know talk about something else."

Being an excellent topic-shifter (rather than shapeshifter) that was just the opening Melvin needed. With a loving and hungry gaze in his eyes (toned down wry smile) – Gigi was quite a looker sporting a snug t-shirt (inscribed: Ain't No Housewife {front} But Have An Un-medicated Craving for Old Men {back}) and an imitation leather mini, which she wore as sort of a uniform while lounging around the house or out on the town – Melvin moved into a familiar tirade mode. Tirade mode meant three things:

A. A discourse on the imprisoned male libido. While at East Jesus Tech, Melvin took a course in Developmental Psychology and had the opportunity to read dangerously little about the concept of the libido in the works of Freud and Jung. As he confided to Gigi during a previous tirade, "I remember sucking on a peppermint stick, darling, with some other classmates doing the same, just to piss off the professor, but I'm still not sure if he was talking about the oral or the phallic stage at that time." Nevertheless, Freud edged out Jung in Melvin's mind, for in the end, he considered the libido a primary instinct or energy force lodged in his id, rather than a form of psychic energy created via duality and manifested in the life process as striving and desire. And Melvin saw his own libido from a bird's eye view. From lofty heights, it was surrounded by an extremely high fence, an electric fence with barbed wire lacing the top in a bird nest design. He could see the libido just pulsating and gyrating without the ability to escape. Of course, Gigi helped him to interpret this aerial view: "The electrified fence represents your ego defenses, silly. The fence, honey, zaps (represses) your sexual/psychic energy, thus imprisoning your libido." Melvin hated to blame his so called "ego defenses" on the toxic effects civilization (read: parochial school education) had on his magnificent brain, but what other choice did he have?

B. A discourse on his theory that Time was simply one big moment and on days when his libido broke out of prison (which did happen, especially during Leap Years), that the big moment Time was no more or less one big sexual moment and that the one big sexual moment contained all the various planes and periods any loving relationship moved through during its cruise through the one big sexual moment of Time. He would often move into this discourse by simply stating: "Doll-face, don't you remember how we moved through our classical period (Greek and Roman) of lust and love – our love fest orgies etc. on the grounds of the Acropolis and Parthenon – before entering the Dark Ages of our love. O, honey, how terribly alone we became in our unenlightened period as lovers. You in a separate tower, me in a separate tower, with nothing more than the light from the illuminated manuscripts we created to keep ourselves busy in the penetrating darkness." Usually, Gigi got up and left the room sometime during the reiteration of option B, choosing bed after spewing disparaging appellations at Melvin (Bozo...Loser – due to the humiliating fact that Melvin conflated his past loves and marriages into his present marriage to her. Glimpse Gigi's interior monologue: *I'm still in the pro-orgy stage with you, you dumb shithead*). But if she stayed for the duration of the tirade, she listened as he described the Sexual Renaissance of love and how that (like a well-greased tectonic plate) slid right into the Romantic Period of a relationship. As the moment demanded (the big sexual moment of Time), things got out of whack again during their Modernist Period (fragmented, individualistic and crazy) before joining the ranks of quirky and kinky love during its Postmodern phase.

C. And Melvin just literally came up with C (creative bastard) – a few minutes ago at a new pub in town while downing an IPA Harpoon with Gigi – and decided to go with (test) this new tirade, without so much as offering Gigi a choice of Tirade A or Tirade B – a standard practice before the spontaneous creation of Tirade C.

"Yep," he said. "There's a lot of males – athletes and congressmen – sexting-texting their 'junk' to a lot of unsuspecting women out there in cyberspace. What do you think of that development, honey sweet pants?" he said.

But before Gigi could control her rolling eyes and had the chance to respond, he continued:

"Why it's the damn devolution of civilization, that's what it is. Cell phones and shit are bad enough – bad enough to launch us back into the House of Trilobite, honey sister. But sending one's 'junk'…?"

Then Melvin paused, taking a furtive look at his own "junk," providing the opportunity for Gigi to say:

"'Junk' sending, dear, is just another manifestation of the male libido trying to escape its imprisonment (astute reference to Tirade A)."

Melvin scratched his bald pate over that.

"You think so, honey delicious?" he said. "And the women, you girls, what's your stance on receiving 'junk' via cyber delivery?"

"'Junk' mail?" Gigi cackled. "Well, I wouldn't say it would be our first choice in potential photos for meeting a perspective mate or arranging a date."

"Damn, honey fantastic," Melvin said. "So you wouldn't mind all that much?"

"Probably not," Gigi said. "After all, a woman's libido is not in jail and we're less attached to 'junk' than you might imagine."

Melvin scratched his bald pate again, took a long hit on his beer, before setting it down on the bar and fixing his eyes on his beer swilling wife.

"Trouble is, honey buns," he said, "I'd be a bit afraid to sex-text my 'junk.'"

"Why?" Gigi said, with a twinkle in her eyes.

"Because," Melvin said, "I fear that my 'junk' is little more than Model T 'junk.'"

"Well, it sure the hell is," Gigi said, patting (actually tempting) Melvin's thigh with lascivious fingers. "Why for all the excessive cranking I have to do to raise a lousy spark in you, I consider that a damn understatement."

"Oh, honey love," Melvin said. "It ain't that much of a strain on you; is it?"

"Putt, putt, putt," Gigi said, relaxing her upgraded sexy grip on his thigh, before ordering another round of beers.

* Chester's Song

> Run rabbit the dog's gonna get you
> You gotta get away
> Run rabbit run the dog's gonna get you
> Run run you gotta get away
> The rabbit ran
> The rabbit flew
> The rabbit tore its tail in two

(from *GunsmokeNet.com*)

**Addendum

According to a recent book, *On Being*, by Peter Atkins, a British science writer, the something that we assume to be (and the Libido is certainly something) may be nothing at all. This has to do with the original chargelessness (spell check options: changelessness, carelessness, changelessness') of nothingness, and how for some unknown reason, this chargelessness was dispersed into positive and negative charges during the Big Bang, which in the end, however, sums to zero or chargelessness' nothingness (**see poem**). The same sort of thing plays out with matter and energy and dark matter and dark energy. Again, things end in zero. Zero harbors nothing, and something (snacks, dog food, Melvin's stages of a relationship) is simply the appearance of something and really nothing at all.

from *Buffoons in the Gene Pool* (Lavender Ink/Fell Swoop, 2016)

(**see poem**)

QUANDARIES

Someone's eating my shirt
and stuffing my socks

with garbage.
Clocks tick

and those at the office
discuss the size of the claws

on tv.
Coyote is stupid and drops

the idea of death
in the drinking water.

Coyote is bright and steals
the mouth of the president.

Meanwhile the red apple
rolls into a sonic dream.

The cosmos is chaos and the winos rejoice.
I would like to scream

with a chorus of bafflers
the brain's wiring won't support

a trombone of wintry birds.
The men in the yard

swear by long shovels
they're digging for words.

Because I was handled like meat
grilled onto ceilings

and fried off floors
I have things on my mind

like lost notebooks
when I piss on my leg.

from *Modulations* (Asylum Arts, 1998)

(**see poem**)

ENCOUNTER

Each morning we discuss my age and IQ
I'm older now and my brilliance
(Once the fodder of talk show hosts)
Lives as a trophy on the mantel
With your dog show awards

I could spell almost anything
Words like *metonymy* and *eurhythmy*
Were my specialty from birth
They just entered my mind like important ideas
When Mom powdered her face

Or vacuumed rugs
Ideas we like to consider
During remarkable celestial events –
Strange tempting lights in the sky
Remember those we saw

That night in the desert
During our annual campaign for greater
Nudity in dry climates
Key ideas like *transcendence* and *immanence*
The history of our involvement

As green plants or underwater specimens
Your belief in the transmigration of whales
My own commitment to comedy and the afterlife
Conversation defines us
Sometimes when the word "random"

Pops from our mouths simultaneously
We stop to fill notebooks with
Serendipitous words: *cerulean crepuscular*
Because we met while walking
Blue-eyed dogs at twilight

(see poem)

Fast Cars

in his brain
grease gods from Detroit
dig holes
and plant trees
with vinyl roots

tenacious
the roots suck
dreams into leaves
shaped like billboards

as advertisements
they display
violent products
to those
driving by
in fast cars

from *Modulations* (Asylum Arts, 1998)

(**see poem**)

ROOF AND SKY

1

Bird wings & banana trees
In the courtyard of green umbrellas
Word impressions
Throw a dollar bill into the cigar humidor
I'm a fragment
You're a big sack of something:
Wheat flour   pasta   hurricane
The mind balms its injuries
Sunshine hat – you fool

2

Take that the fountain sings through frog-mouth
Cracked slate   &
The haircut cost 18 bucks
Further not farther into the dilemmas of TV
Information fat cats take holiday on sunken boat
On the weathervane of charm –
A nickel's worth of attention
Kiss me with your *shoo* hand
Music we like

3

In the alphabet corner of common sense
Leroy plays his trombone
Agent X arrives from Honolulu
Metallic planes shiver in the metal rain
Again another report of IQ plumbers in the paper
Out of tissues
Lost keys
Rhythm of disjunction flows through feathered brain
Wait time back in ten minutes

4

Imitation harmony distorts the vowel concert
We talked in a complicated way about complex things
Freedom turned into Proposition Secret
Count the votes *damn it* formed government
Exhaust pipes in every pot
Chicken hysteria in the streets
Barkers for sex   Dream
Animal sound asleep
In this way I caught your eye

5

Por Favor
On a rooftop of turistas in the sun
Chewing gum
The shadow of my head on a white page
Blue thunder memory lines somehow
The world in a block highway of words
Cranes build other skies
& the piano player ain't my dad
Honky-tonk stride fingers of pure spirit

6

Contagious text in the heat of false argument
Then a collection of gray buildings for sale
Cars inside radio curlers crawl the streets
Much happiness
& hot sauce to boot on variegated oysters
In time with the tempo
A hat full of Z   Stopwatch
Perceptions near the finish line
So grows the melon of awareness: Iron lace

7

The mystery of each syllable explodes praise
Austrian crystals on a brass string
A shack for consciousness & complaint
Just the other night at the Carousel Bar
We all got dizzy
We must sing
Interstellar message declares the answer
Is a question
Wind across rooftop – gusting beautiful forms

from *Under the Sky of No Complaint* (Lavender Ink/Fell Swoop, 2013)

(see poem)

POETRY OF THE MASSLESS

1

I have nothingness
And an antiquated To Do List
In a hip pocket
Yesterday I was a factoid

2

Forgot I was in the mountains
On top of one
Conversation intense
Until mid-afternoon

3

It had to do with neurons
In the brain
Their own peculiar star date
Odyssey into existence

4

What a trip
A wave of majestic adjectives
How to modify "positron"
The menu of snow at the garden door

5

Mountains project enlightenment
Not the tainted kind
Samsara of you and me
Slush in the streets

6

It's a matter of degree
Depends on the temperature of coffee
The improvisations of painted lips
Language and its desires

7

We live in territorial chains and beliefs
Have plans to remake coherence
Into something tangible
Creator inside of us without an agenda

8

I could say I'm on a slope
Dodging the rocks and fantasies
Of memory
With a modicum of self-control

9

I could say I'm a fan
A devotee of the arrow of time
Have (at times) calculated
The tattoo of minutes on the soul

10

There are plenty of things to ponder
When it comes to ideas about things
I used to be a hunter
In a forest of soundless wings

11

Get it
Here or there
Visible to invisible
My place or yours

12

The mind tracks the universe
To see where it's headed
The universe muddies the mind
Are we there yet

from *Techniques in the Neighborhood of Sleep*
(Spuyten Duyvil, 2016)

ABOUT DIK TATER

The only known photograph of Dik Tater is actually a drawing of him by the world class artist, Tom Haines, on the back cover of *Against News*, Fell Swoop #83, the Dik Tater's only known work. Mr. Haines is the proprietor of Atomic Tom's Studio and Cigar Museum in downtown Binghamton, New York.

Mr. Haines reveals the facial characteristics (also neck and a hint of shoulders) of the Dik Tater as if he were caught in a violent windstorm or a recent hurricane that destroyed a sad city. Dik Tater's head floats above the city like the Snoopy Met-Life dirigible. In a simple swipe of his pen or pencil, Mr. Haines reveals Dik Tater's huge Alpine forehead – a forehead that provokes the sensation of an albino-like boulder set in place above Dik Tater's scratchy eyebrows by a heavy crane. His eyes are piercing clear and transparent, suggesting the ability to see through masks and other paraphernalia of the unknown. They indicate the glasses resting on the bridge of his nose are a sham and/or a style statement. Within the lenses, however, a series of fish, footprints, and golf tees form a reflected parade beneath the Dik-Tater's eyes. His hair shares the motif of pick up sticks after a fistfight or stubborn linguine surfaced above a pot of boiling water. Stubble covers cheeks and neck. His lips mime the candy lips available on Halloween. Though the drawing is impressive, there is one disturbing highlight. In the center of the Dik Tater's forehead, there is a clean, neat and round bullet hole, suggesting that the Dik Tater is a member of the undead. The hole is open to interpretation. Perhaps it is a portal, a portal of insight, into the Dik Tater's only known publication, the aforementioned, *Against News.*

An Interview with Dik Tater

By Ghost of Richard Brautigan (see poems)

GRB: Mr. Tater, are you a dick? (**see story**)

DT: I'm not sure I understand the question. But for the record, I spell "dick" "dik."

GRB: Oh, come on, Tater, everyone knows you were called the Ring Leader of Bad Behavior during the glorious years of *The Big Horror Reading Series*** in Binghamton, New York. One patron of the series went so far as to claim that you openly encouraged the audience to commit random acts of poetry in the streets of the beleaguered town.

DT: If memory serves me the correct cliché, I did coordinate and host a number of the readings during the Big Horror series. I did tell a few rowdy souls to sit down and shut up, but that's about it.

GRB: Methinks you're full of shit, Mr. Potato Head. There is ample evidence – video clips – of you controlling Big Horror meetings and loud-mouthing your way about whom you wanted to appear at the series. In one telling video moment, a member of the Horror clan, late for the meeting, runs into the backroom of Swat Sullivan's, where the meetings and readings took place, dives headlong onto the floor and after rolling across the floor and coming to a stop, poses this question to you: "Who made you George Washington?"

DT: Lighten up GRB, you're getting your ghostly form bent out of shape.

GRB: There are also reports that an AKA of yours is "Dancing Head." As the Dancing Head, you ripped off your shirts at some readings and worked yourself into such a frenzy that you often lapsed into a tachycardia and had to be escorted into an ambulance after someone called 911.

DT: OK, I'll admit the muse and music of poetry on occasion possessed my bones.

GRB: That's more like it. OK, before I ask you about *Against News*, I would like to know if that is a bullet hole in your head, and if so, are you a member of the Walking Dead of Poetry? Or, if it is not a bullet hole, is it by chance a portal, and you are a pioneer time traveler?

DT: Let's just say I travel the time realms when it is to my advantage.

GRB: It must be obvious by now, Tater Tot, that I'm not the one interviewing you due to the fact that I'm not here. But besides that, please clue me in about *Against News.*

DT: As the title suggests, I'm against the news. The news has slid away from verifiable facts into sleazy opinions. It is a construction of Media Empires and serves the sole purpose of keeping the populace misinformed, afraid and bummed out. It is often accompanied by Big Pharm commercials hawking drugs with suicidal effects and other alarming side effects (**see poem**) in the human body. If people desire that, I offer a simpler form via my poems. I hope that everyone enjoys them.

GRB: You're quite the SOB.

DT: Right on, GRB.

AGAINST NEWS

BY DIK TATER

A SELECTION

CHEESZ WHIZ SPECTACLES

the criticism monkey slips the last judgment
into onion dip and proceeds
to the park to play three men
in a pink Cadillac
i refer to my own poems on desolate landscapes
and gratuitous crackers to revive misty sails
movement's arrow
the time the woman with
a new watch kissed the forehead of ivory
REM or the antiquated levers in skinnerian
laboratories to convince the art patron
not to invest in pharmaceuticals
player piano scrolls
blue frisbee of dawn floating in my hand
prose chickens
the hope in the next book read
presence and what we have to say about it
scholars of ice proceed in an orderly fashion
through the car wash the possibility
of a sitcom of verbs franco-
phile
beauty the body wears each day into the blast of sunrays
the effect of bulldozers on a young child's mind
phenomenological reduction in or out
the brick factory quiet in the
harbor of despair vortex
vortices the plumber arrives
with the kitchen sink self-referential

ovulating mirrors for the heretic of dreams
trip alarms and the american flag stuck in a snow bank
OPUS OPUS HOPELESS
the fool of scratch off tickets home at last

PRODUCT NAME

i'm a screen and no one alarms me
the majesty of planets disarms literary analysis
why not squirrels romp in the hemlocks and
the invasion of meaningless death stumps capitalists
you could fall asleep applauding the installation
of tvs on jet airliners – sitcoms through the clouds
loss of cabin pressure during flawed laugh tracks

welcome to a stunning consciousness and lack of focus
don't be bitter an egg every day is good for you
foster a relationship with ancestors
the sky did turn black/could turn black
the asteroid necklace of being-in-itself is a dead give away
if you like really long sentences raise your hand
tipsy is not the answer to the problem of time

don't complicate voice by reciting mysteries like eons
engage the aether cynics and magicians of light
you're not a professor yet so wait
radio frequencies with your initials impose fines
on personality whiz on by
become the gorge you long for
kiss the women laughing at you

there's a convention in town and you're not invited
hang in there despite the denouement of political capital
in the white noise of it all find friends
absurd absolves absurd
spice variety
accept the fact they've named a drug after you
concentrate on writing false prescriptions

55

word species into rambling here
the theory of could arrived in his morning brain
sudden white flowers in her neighborhood
time for coffee
or they could make love in digital sunshine

vines of affirmation grew the wild procession
of obscured trees
throw open the window and make the first mistake
'tis the season of chin music
we want the fast embrace of beautiful hands

mist the trance of transparency with enigmatic smile
walk the plank romantic
into the unknown region just created
o wispy planets tattooed on canvas walls
the speed limit used to be 55

the mind snapshots data stream into want
and hurricane
we need to drink drinks with red umbrellas
inside the bell jar the message glowed
like fireflies into metaphor deciphered

welcome to the self-referential palace
fine the atmosphere claims to tonic spirit
we are not more than here
in this location of thanked sky
revel in the rain slate fragments

POWER FAILURE

1

new poems explained on television
      no intuition
in the way the dishwasher clanks off
ripe political flavor
      of the month
a series of statements latched to
the kingdom of keys
          finding out
space encapsulates the desire
to rewrite the monologue all this
and more
      when mother regains
  control of her vehicle

2

crossing the bridge merry
friends
rehearse
their debt to spontaneous
songs
lingering
in the flower bed of yesterday's
kind discourse
on the art
of elaborate motives bang
the lights go out and city
trucks revive
a version of literary history
written by a hostile gang
of academic comedians

3

sizzling
on a page
of charcoal periods
a pond of white trees
evades the pretense
of continuity

HILARITY OF DISTRIBUTION

all pronouns feign excuses to witness
(   ) absence in (   ) piece carlos
understands once a pine was all
aglow but the story ended enter
the cathedral of maidens
on the buoyant charms of the rich
after a trinity of relationships
and brilliant critical exegesis
(i.e., the folklore of language is cunning and sparse)
confusion reigned and a lone horseman
raced into the next town
without (   ) mailbox of clowns

say exhilaration and night weave
a dream through rosemary's head
rules are rules
the refrigerator hums and a mouse
whips past the man with a bundle
of correspondence in (   ) arms
letter A claims to understand more
about mayan excavations than the next guy
letter B contains a sonnet if written
by a twelve year old boy rosemary
will shift in (   ) sleep as (   ) book tour
begins in the heart of the sun

margins appear to challenge
the couple responsible
for the catalogue of summer dresses
soft breezes attend the sullen model
walking down the pearl runway without shoes
without a calendar or a fixed star
to guide the magnificent hi-jinx of sailors
(   ) grimaces

thinking of the price of admission
to watch (   ) traipse down a loading dock
where back orders of stylish shoes
ponder (   ) final dilemma

DIGITS

1

memory eats smoke for dinner
time in a short glass of whiskey
cash on the jukebox
the world not hurricane of nonchalance
magnolia is a word
2

building blocks for love in our hands
stark slate graves in spring rain
noble horse chestnut tree in blossom
the mind leaps
pen aches

3

dreams invented automatic writing
then the war of commercials began
i bought a ford
you hopped a hayride to mars
love fogs the windows of life

4

yesterday demands the perfect dilemma
on a sliding scale of make-believe
enter the purple dawn
in the warp and woof of words
bird it up

5

closure is not a sequence of numbers
or parlor of feathers

4x4

blue monkeys trouble aesthetics
i'm alone
others storm heaven flashing union cards
tit-for-tat mom always said
when a tour bus detours into the past
passengers respectfully turn off cell phones
o hopeless sea (   ) save me
like wind talking to windows

we reach the summit of our collapse
and begin to feel better   thank god
night startles us into thinking we're here
we should behave

it's easy to claim women wink at you
with boulevards of sun in the pockets
it is a bright and gorgeous day
now for some exercise

GAUCHE PICKPOCKETS

like a bucket of fresh
milk

waterfall gadzooks
check the auto-spell

awake to what's happening
the media of inattention

while

technological advances reissued
in time for the spring parade
you know what i mean
you've see it before

stood in line
waited
even paid for it
light

as synthetic androgynous
actor/actress playing

flicker-flack
remembers the lack

(see poems)

#1

Dear Marcia,

When I was thirsty
I licked water droplets
off your breasts
after we swam
in the naked lake
of dreams.

Me and your gumball breasts
I used to say
like a sexy grammarian
blowing bubbles of syntax
into the cosmic air.

You were beautiful in
and out
of the water.

So was I.

Your lover boy,
GRB

#2

Dear Rimbaud,

I'm doing fine as a ghost.
How about you?
Just the other day I reread
Une Saison en Enfer
Great as always, bro.,
especially, *Delires II:*

Alchimie du verbe.

Let me know
when you're on Facebook,
so we can post
hopes and broken dreams
once again.

I remain a big fan.

Au revoir,
GRB

#3

Dear USA Government,

Since when did all Democrats
and Republicans in Congress
need to be
complete assholes
in the hip pockets
of special interest groups
and lobbyists?

Remember we are the people
and we're pissed off.

Even us ghosts.

Power to the people,
GRB

#4

Dear City Workers and Psychotherapists,

Like everyone else
in Ghost-land before me
I had some big potholes
in my being
that needed filling
with the steamy macadam
of love.

Don't get me wrong.
There were plenty of days
on the road less traveled
that were smooth
and lush with lips
and kisses.

I'm just saying…

Turn on the juice,
GRB

#5

Dear Death,

My mind moved so fast at times
(like a light bulb of Einstein
like a stray thought
in a wolf pack
of Jack London)
I thought you'd never catch me.

But you did
didn't you,
you persistent bastard?

Regrettably yours,
GRB

#6

Dear Universe,

I've heard the story
about how you broke down
and cried
when you were just
a kid universe
after your tricycle of stars
was stolen by another
kid universe –
a parallel one, someone said
with similar stars
and happy meals
for citizens.

I've cried too
like a star
whimpering fried
and oozy light
even when I was
a big kid.

Beam me up Scotty,
GRB

#7

Dear Telecommunications Industry,

Call me a reactionary
but you should have
called it quits
after the Princess phone.

I for one
(out of the millions and millions for one)
savored glints of sunlight
in the eyes of beautiful women
on their way to work
down high-heel streets

before their eyes succumbed
to bitter iPhones.

Busy signal,
GRB

#8

Dear Populace-at-Large,

I understand you're pissed.
But did you know
poems travel through the mind
at the speed of light
and you have to be pretty quick
to nab one?

Even I,
a ghost with a fully activated
twilight of consciousness,
stand on invisible toes
to catch one
and write it down.

Poems even zip
through heads
like juiced molecules
on a date of
magnificent collisions
during sleep.

Yes, ghosts sleep.

Relatively speaking,
GRB

#9

Dear To Whom It May Concern,

I can't remember
what I intended to say.
Perhaps,
I bequeath all that
I was
and left behind
to each and everyone one
of you.

Or maybe,
The orange sun
would enjoy a lollipop lick
by a very cold tongue.

You decide.
Gifts are gifts.

Your friend,
GRB

#10

Dear San Francisco Poetry Renaissance,

It's time for another one.
What do you say?
I'll get Rexroth on the phone
and ask him
to assemble the old gang.

Until then
I'll be fishing
with Spicer.

Thanks for the memories,
GRB

(Transcribed from postcards by Ant McGoogle)

(**see story**)

DICK

Dick was tired of being a subject, not of a sentence, but of vast experiments that had turned him into a certified – as opposed to uncertified, unofficial, fake, faux, inauthentic, sham, scam – blithering idiot.

The first experiment involved getting Dick some parents and having them raise him. The experimenters (so called scientists) behind this experiment interviewed various individuals caught raging in convenience stores or neighborhood bars and/or praying vociferously in churches still requiring hats, dollies, napkins, or some form of paper product on the heads of women. Thelma of Doileyville and Al of *I'll kick your teeth in* after three shots of bar whiskey with chasers – who reigned supreme on the end barstool in *Jack's Pub & Arcade* – were chosen after taking a set of strenuous personality tests while earning a small fee – green stamps and coupons for free oil changes and front and rear alignments for their participation.

The tests revealed that Thelma and Al could get along up to five years before inevitable marital disintegration. Thelma and Al were told by the experimenters (so called scientists) that they were an ideal couple and obviously ready to marry and raise a child. This seemed fine with them, and when handed a baby by the experimenters (so called scientists), they expressed more joy than surprise and graciously accepted a ten thousand dollar check as start-up funds to get married and raise the infant. "There's only one condition to all of this," the experimenters (so called scientists) said. "You have to name the baby, Dick."

"Fine by me," Al said.

"All right," Thelma said.

And together they gazed at the infant and said:

"Hi, Dick."

(Now just suppose Dick's fate was simply to be the subject of a sentence rather than an actual subject to be experimented on by experimenters (so called scientists). Then Dick's fate or tale could be reduced to a line like this: *For many years, Dick didn't know that his name was slang for the male sexual organ.*)

Thelma and Al lasted four.5 years together before they thought it best to return Dick to the experimenters (so called scientists). They did have some problems finding the harmony point between hard praying and hard drinking, but they didn't get along too bad. It was mostly, Dick. You might say Dick was a dick. At least that's what Thelma said when returning Dick to them (so called scientists):

"He's just an impossible little kid who does endlessly strange things."

Al piped in: "Well, for example, the little dick thought he was a bull for a couple of months."

After some knowing nods by the experimenters (so called scientists), Al continued:

"Yeah, a raging bull, and so like he runs into walls and crap, knocking stuff over, you know lights and knickknacks onto the floor before pretty much knocking himself out."

"Ok, then," the experimenters (so called scientists) said, taking Dick back.

After some intense debate about his choice of animal and their choice of a name, the experimenters (so called scientists) agreed that he was still a bit too young to consciously understand the implications of his name. The fact that he could be a dick had more to do with the gene pool acting out than anything else in their opinion.

For the next few storybook years, the experimenters (so called scientists) raised Dick themselves, feeding him human growth hormones with burgers and fries. Dick got huge (no lie), and by the time of his high school years, the experimenters (so called scientists) had set up their next experiment, naming the study: *How Would Dick Fair in a Catholic High School*?

After finding a couple (via ads in *Psychology Today* and the Love Advertisements in various tabloids) who had always wanted a child, but couldn't, and installing Dick with them, they hypothesized that Dick would have a good time but probably be expelled by the end of his sophomore year.

As experimenters (so called scientists) go, they were pretty smart and on the money.

Dick got his ass kicked out of the Catholic school (St. Mike's of Scranton) at the beginning of his junior year for not containing his mirth, glee, guffaws and belly-gut laughter when it was his turn to read in "round robin" fashion from a text called *Why Wait Until Marriage?*

When Sister Mary Hickory asked Dick to explain his inappropriate laughter and behavior, Dick said:

"Me and most of the girls in the class has already done the dirty deed."

Later, in the principal's office, while completing the expulsion paperwork, Sister Marie Hickory informed Principal Xavier the Meek that she was almost as shocked by Dick's atrocious grammar as by his lascivious antics with the female enrollment.

Over the years, the experimenters (so called scientists) ran plenty of other experiments and tests on poor Dick. There was one in which his own son, after jumping off the school bus and surrounded by his kindergarten classmates, asked Dick the following question:

"Daddy do you know your name means penis?"

Tough experiments that took their toll on Dick.

from *Buffoons in the Gene Pool* (Lavender Ink/Fell Swoop, 2016)

> **Binghamton University Libraries – Connect-Discover-Create – enter Big Horror Poetry Series into Search Box to locate the Big Horror Poetry Series DVD archive.

(see poem)

Side Effects

1

All
medications cause
depression I may
be in a bar
talking with a stranger It
has been a week of intellectuals
in plastic bags and the karma of
retribution The movie deal is off the table
The summit of the powerful canceled due to the
weather It snows on Jupiter if you believe in lies
There are various things in my wallet I can track my
packages by telepathic numbers open up a small restaurant with parking receipts
There was the day you mistook my mind for a carnival I spoke
in small boats and rabid colors Lights flickered I gave up on Thomas Edison
before you Candy apples and Ferris wheels without a predicate There is an abandoned mining
town in my sentence structure In the grass a supple flag monitors the action We knew
each other through the love beads stolen by the aristocrat I arrived at the watering hole with
a gold tooth and hall pass Reality stalks perception By the time I got through high school the
author was dead Victims of the ego clashed with victims of the ego Night pranced across the
     field of

2

sleep

GALLERY B

PAINTINGS
BY JAMES DE CRESCENTIS

Shadow Fire, acrylic, ink & gesso on paper, 30"x22"—1991.

Falling Through The Net With Waves, acrylic & ink on paper, 41"x26"—1991.

Tricks On A Blue Face, acrylic on paper, 30"x22"—1991. (in private collection)

Rainforest, acrylic on paper, 30"x22"—1992. (in private collection)

Passage, acrylic on canvas, 30"x30"—1992. (in private collection)

Under The Ocean Floor, acrylic on masonite panel, 48"z48"—1992.

Wally's Café, ink & sand on canvas, 18"x14"—1994. (in private collection)

Walking Backwards, acrylic on paper, 30"x22"—1995.

Reader's Notes and Artwork

Book 3:

Pipeline Interviews

Interview with Joel (XJ) Dailey
Editor-for-Life of Fell Swoop: The All Bohemian Revue
November, 2014

Martin: I'm here in New Orleans with XJ Dailey, unrivaled poet and renowned editor of *Fell Swoop: The All Bohemian Review*. OK. XJ, is 2014 the 30th anniversary of *Fell Swoop*?

Dailey: Well, I don't remember too much about it to tell you the truth. I think it was 1983 when the magazine began. That would make 31 years of continual publishing. The first issue came out in the summer of 1983.

Artifact Insertion: Title Page of One FELL SWOOP

ONE FELL SWOOP

Joel Dailey
1601 Burdette St. #4
New Orleans
LA   70118

We welcome correspondence……………………..

This issue is dedicated to the pure spirit
of Ted Berrigan, 1934-1983

One Fell Swoop: The Word From

Louisiana
Ohio
New York
Oregon

Japan
Massachusetts
Texas

This magazine has been
Acre Press (ed)

Dailey: The second issue came out in Amherst, MA. in early 1984.

Martin: Fell Swoop 2?

Dailey: Yeah.

Martin: Is the magazine still published under Acre Press?

Dailey: Sort of…but I don't put that on the magazine anymore. We
                also published a chapbook through Acre Press.

Martin: Yeah. In fact, I think I know whose chapbook that was.

Dailey: It was your chapbook.

Martin: Yes, *Between The Eyes.*

Artifact Insertion   **A Remark About Toilets**

His remark about toilets
was taken seriously.
The police removed women from the streets,
and pretty soon men were required
to carry red umbrellas.
He stared at clouds
wishing the reporter
had asked the pigeons in the park,
about the world,
the present danger,
the policy of chaining convicts

to the personal computers
in homes,
where love was reduced
to a pet dog
staring at ripe bananas
on top of the refrigerator.

Richard Martin
from *Between the Eyes* (Acre Press, 1984)

Martin: OK…back to the summer of '83. What was the reason for
             starting Fell Swoop? What was going on in your head at the
             time?

Dailey: Well, Ted Berrigan died in the summer of '83. I remember
             thinking I should do a magazine. And I did. Most magazines
             don't last very long but this one has. Although, I wanted to
             quit many times. I quit smoking instead.

Martin: Berrigan. Was he a big influence on you?

Dailey: Yeah, he was and still is…not only as a publisher, but his
             writing.

Martin: Berrigan founded and published the magazine, *C* … a
             mimeograph operation.

Dailey: At the time, I didn't know anything about his magazine.

Martin: When you started Fell Swoop?

Dailey: I didn't know anything about *C*, really.

Martin: But I think there is a connection between *C* and *Fell Swoop*.
             Do you see the connection today?

Dailey: Ah…we go in for the retro-look…which means we have lousy

production values and Berrigan's were pretty down to earth…
though 8 ½ by 14 mimeo.

Artifact Insertion: Some "C" Notes   May 1964   X

"It's 6:15 a. m. May 22, 1964, just about a year since "C" magazine first
appeared, and just as that I was scrounging around for money to buy stencils,
stamps, paper, etc. (not to mention pay the rent buy food pepsis etc), so today
I'm rushing up to finish this so I can scrounge up some money to buy the
paper for the issue (number 8) that Lorenz and I are going to pick up thirty
dollars-worth of paper today."
(Ted Berrigan Papers, Syracuse University)

Dailey: Now with all the e-magazines…you can't even hold in
        your hands … ah, *Fell Swoop* now looks like a lost cause …
        a throwback. Writing is online for the young people
        today. Swoop would never go online. We don't even accept
        online submissions. Our submissions are mailed to a PO Box.
        There aren't many magazines left that take submissions by
        mail. You have to submit through an online engine.

Martin: How do you feel about that?

Dailey: I don't like it. But I'm old. A dinosaur. There are a lot of
        things I don't like about the world.

Martin: I refer readers to your poetry for an exhaustive list of what
        bugs you. For now, where does the magazine's name come
        from?

Dailey: Well, it comes from *Macbeth*, a Shakespearian reference. In
        the play, MacDuff's children are murdered and when he
        returns to find this out he says:

        "—All my pretty ones?
        Did you say all?—O hell-kite!—All?
        What, all my pretty chickens, and their dam,

At one fell swoop?"

I should put that quote in the next issue.

Martin: Definitely. Let's talk about XJ the editor. Speak about your editorial life. What are you looking for when you put the magazine together?

Dailey: I look for poems that are creative, amusing, innovative or experimental. I used to get a lot of crap in the mail. Lots of junk. People hadn't seen the magazine, obviously. Now I don't get so much because everyone is submitting online or to other places. I have my regulars and once in a while a new person shows up over the transom. I like stuff that is satirical in nature. It's amazing how many writers don't have an understanding of satire or as a dimension of it in their work. They just don't understand it. They just want to be famous, I guess. They're like gunfighters. They want another notch on their gun…another publication. We rip up and throw away a lot of stuff that comes in the mail. I use the editorial pen. I'm the editorial board. I'm the publisher. Much much better that way.

Martin: Yeah, you have told control.

Dailey: I can tell when I open the envelope if I'm interested or not.

Martin: That fast?

Dailey: Yeah.

Martin: A couple of lines?

Dailey: Just by looking at it. It doesn't matter at all about the name on it.

Martin: Who are some of the regular contributors that have appeared over the years in the "Swoop."

Dailey: Some of them have died.

Martin: Who are they?

Dailey: Oh, Anselm Hollo died. Andrei Codrescu died or is he still alive?

Martin: Andrei is still alive.

Dailey: Oh, right. He moved to Arkansas. He is as good as dead up there.

Martin: Clark Coolidge?

Dailey: Clark Coolidge is alive at the moment as far as I know…out in California.

Martin: Fielding Dawson. Ed Dorn.

Dailey: Dorn died of pancreatic cancer. We should have done a Dorn issue. At the time he was in the magazine, we weren't doing single author issues yet. We should have done a Berrigan issue…too late on that one. We did a Berrigan memorial issue (#84) We did an Anselm Hollo issue (MINIGOLF # 17) and also Clark Coolidge (*Hoppy Poems* # 60; *The Human Bond* # 115). We did a lot of Richard Martin issues and various and sundry individual author issues: *Scooch* by John Miller (#62); *Cauliflower or Bust* by Tom Weigel (# 75), to name a few.

Artifact Insertion: from the "linoleum tattoos"   Edward Dorn
                                                                       ABORRENCES
                                                                       15 Jan. 1985

                                                 <u>He spits, therefore he is spittle</u>

                                                 Of course, all futures are loaded.
                                                 The Eighties will be seen
                                                 as the last bit of paradise
                                                 hoving out of view:

the opportunities for truly im-
mense fraud, the widespread
cupidity in the appreciation
of contrasts – "Have, Havenot."
These will seem The last of the dream,
a beacon of magnitude
in the acres of time.

from 6 *Fell(ed) Swoop(ing) – the 'wrong planet' issue!*

Dailey: I solicit for the individual author issues.

Martin: Well, including the individual author issues," Swoop" is up to
                134. 7* in terms of issues.

Dailey: 134.7 on your FM dial with no end in sight.

Martin: That's a relief to your readers. Let's talk about your
                introductory remarks to Swoop issues. You started piping
                off in them about what to expect in an issue in *Fell Swoop*
                # 5 (*Five Swell Foop*) while also laying on them other things
                crossing your troubled mind. Right?

Dailey: From the Editorial Dusk.

Martin: That's right. I found some of your poetic/world beliefs in your
                introductory remarks by reading "Swoop" over the years.

Dailey: I don't know. I never read them.

Martin: May I treat you as a hostile witness? I don't know. I remember
                reading a statement to the effect that Swoop went after
                poems on the razor's edge – one side greatness; the other size
                garbage. Poems could swing either way.

Dailey: What issue was that? Isn't that a short story by Somerset
                Maugham, "The Razor's Edge?"

Martin: I guess I'm referring back to poems that enter the trash bucket
                – the ones on the wrong side of edge.

Dailey: You mean yours?

Artifact Insertion: *NINE FELL SWOOP*
                        The Post Mardi Gras/Pre Nuclear Blast Issue

YET ANOTHER EDITORIAL PEP…

O yeah, time for another editorial two-step right across the velvet (velveeta?)
ballroom of yr. consciousness…Here's the Swoop's latest burnt offering:
gusting opinions, doom-saying fantasies, attitudes & altitudes concerning The
End Of It All…Welcome to the Post Mardi Gras/Pre-Nuclear Blast Issue!

As one R.S. Posey scribbles from California, "I have seen the fault line &
it's not a pretty sight." O well, Earthlings our #9 chews on the Apocalypse,
personal, impersonal, generic, regular, irregular, unleaded…

Don your purple crash helmets, Ladies & Gents, & prepare for Impact
with the Future. I gotta run – THEY are trying to get in at the back door—
aardvarks 4 rent, X.J. Dailey

Martin: Ok, now that we've cleared that up. Do you send notes or
                rejection slips back to those who send you poems?

Dailey: Sometimes. I had this one guy who kept sending me a packet
                of poems every week and they weren't very good or right for
                the magazine. The cynical, satirical, and sarcastic nature of
                the magazine wasn't right for his work…it was like he was
                unaware of what appeared in *Fell Swoop*. But he kept sending
                me a packet a week, thinking he would wear me down…like
                a used car salesman. Eventually, I wrote him and said: "Look,
                keeping writing and send back to me in a year. His poems just
                weren't right for "Swoop". Maybe they belonged in the New
                Yorker.

Martin: Have you ever been published in the New Yorker?

Dailey: No, I never sent to *The New Yorker*.

Martin: Why not freak the Poetry Editor out and send him (?) some of your work?

Dailey: Ashbery sometimes appears in *The New Yorker*.

Artifact Insertion: "NO" FOR AN ANSWER

At the height (6 even) of my powers I dive
    flippers aside
Bullseye tonight's meatloaf with speargun
Avoiding future disappointment & regret
You bet yer rusted out tailpipe
    or Parkyerkarkus

The Present is monogrammable & its summary
    finding Bursitis
                du Jour
Me personal
Initially
It's for you

If John Ashbery's writing is the consequence
    of an on/off
            faucet
I'm a moist unstable storm cell raining fire
    on your lawyer's
            codpiece
I'm "Talk to a Human"
A disobedient mole on Chubby Checker's pecker

Joel Dailey
from *Industrial Loop* (Lavender Ink/Fell Swoop, 2013)

Martin: Let's twist again…What about the satire from the poets in Fell Swoop? What are they criticizing?

Dailey: Well, they aren't all mocking things out. Some are just writing poems with interesting lines…poems that are unpredictable…surprising. You know Bill Berkson has a poem in the most recent issue. We did a single issue…a ways back in time of his. Unpredictability. Do something different with the genre. Not the same old crap you see coming out from the writing programs. We're interested in poems that attack the narrative poem rather than a poem about the time your brother almost drowned and you saved his ass. You know there's a Yale Younger Poet that used to work down here and he went out and got an academic job. He got all these accolades from the Academy of American Armchairs. Probably got a membership card…knows the secret handshake and has six or seven books out. But his work to me is not that interesting, although it is rewarded by the Poetry Establishment. I think really the "Swoop" started at a time…in the Seventies, when I started by own work, there were a lot of so called underground magazines…small press magazines. You know Walt Whitman never received any awards for his writing… not that I'm comparing myself to Walt Whitman. HE HAD A BEARD AND I DON'T. I HAVE THE FACE OF IMMORTALITY. HE HAD THE FACE OF DEATH. The small press movement back then allowed writers going in different directions than the careerist poet places for their writing. All kinds of writing. Now a lot of that has gone online. My feeling is that nobody reads the online stuff. I sure don't. But again, I like to hold a book or magazine in my hands. But the internet offers cheap, endless, economical publishing of unnumbered pages.

Martin: And there are just so many online journals out there now.

Dailey: They proliferate.

Martin: They multiply.

Dailey: Like rabbits – fucking rabbits.

Artifact Insertion: SON OF FLARF

for Marge Perloff

My goal   fondle the Fruit Loops,
   escaping detection
For instance, hypervigilance unfettered
To confine the goalie, my goal is
As in, floating drywall

My ghoul is to exceed all expectorations
Picking up where the Jesus left off
Point is, don't be that carrot
Hot in the argyles   I flog the
   Inflatables

Joel Dailey

from *Industrial Loop* (Lavender Ink/Fell Swoop, 2013) (**see Appendix E**)

Martin: Holding the magazine or book is still an important
                   dinosaurian skill. Another great T-Rex activity is going to the
                   PO to mail out your poems. Kurt Vonnegut wrote that
                   he loved putting a story into an envelope, putting a stamp on
                   it, and going to the PO. He loved standing in line, talking to
                   his neighbors etc. during the wait. And the super young are
                   now prowling the music stores that are left in the world for
                   vinyl albums…finding out the sound quality is better than
                   digital. There's a little retro thing going on. It's hard to enjoy
                   the "palpable" online.

Dailey: For you and me.

Martin: OK…it's time for my afternoon medication. Now there is more to the "Swoop" than just the poems. Talk about its construction. You rarely see a poem sitting on the page without cutouts all around it. At times, it seems that the cutouts comment on the poem or enter into a conversation with it.

Dailey: Well, I cut out a lot of little headlines…strange pieces of language from the newspaper and tape them around the poem…sometimes with pictures – beautiful women, political leaders, old men, athletes, movie stars etc. They often have nothing to do with the poem, ostensibly. Sometimes they do. But generally, I'm not cognizant of that or working intentionally to pull it off. It's accidental. Some people think it distracts the reader. A page in "Swoop" is like a collage…a mild collage. But I don't really get that much feedback on it.

Martin: How long does it take to put an issue together, start to finish?

Dailey: Not long once I start rolling, though I don't always do it in one shot. I always have stuff coming in. I kind of have a deadline in mind when it's going to be done. Sometimes during the construction of an issue I'll write someone or send an email requesting work. There's a guy up in Canada, Stuart Ross. He's a Canadian and he likes the magazine a lot. So, I'll send him an email and say: "Look, Stuart, stand me some stuff." Despite the fact that he is Canadian…a good, clean Canadian and quite a force in Canadian literature. Most Americans are amazed to find out that there is a Canadian Literature. It's up north… across the border. You need a passport to get there. There was a time when you didn't need a passport. But with all the poetry terrorists around you're forced to have a passport, even for our neighboring countries: Canada, Mexico and Wyoming. You need a passport to get into Wyoming. I read that online.

Martin: Pretty soon you'll need one to enter any state in the Union.

Dailey: There might be even a little toll.

Artifact Insertion: **4 TINY POEMS I WROTE ON MARCH 15, 2014**
by Stuart Ross

On the edge
of the highway:
a giant eraser.

*

Where did it go?
What?
The piebald
dog who
invented
the stapler.

*

The air came in
the window. I
breathed it
carefully.

*

Later on,
A helicopter
collapsed
on the dance floor.

From *FELL SWOOP the 131.6*
aka the ritchie martin review

Martin: Let's talk about your writing for a little bit.

Dailey: CHEESE!

Martin: One of the things I've noticed is…

Dailey: CHEESE!

Martin: Yes, your poems are cheesy. But before we consider that, I've also noticed you don't publish many of your poems in *Fell Swoop*. You have a couple of single author issues, but not many single poems in the issues. Why?

Dailey: I publish some individual poems in "Swoop" under fake names. But still not often.

Martin: I recognize a couple of the fake names: Joe Cabeza, Claudia Nostril. But not too many by Joel or XJ over 134. 7 issues. And you are the "boss" when it comes to satire and pushing the envelope of language and poetic form.

Dailey: Well, I just came out with the single author issue, *Touch Typing in 10 Lessons*. And a few years ago, I published through Swoop, *Forty-Five Minutes to Air*. But mostly, I try to publish my work elsewhere.

Martin: That's right, the artist Chu Mee did the cover for *Touch Typing in 10 Lessons*. And of course, you've been widely published in magazines and now have at least 22 books for readers to enjoy. And your style has certainly changed but humor and satire are consistent elements across your oeuvre.

Dailey: Oh yeah.

Martin: I mean the poems in *Mars 1953* are pretty funny.

Dailey: Those are prose poems.

Martin: Am I on the right track here? Were humor and satire part of your work there from the start?

Dailey: Well, in the beginning I wrote deep image poems for a while. Poems first published in my book, *Exploring Another Leg*, which Pentagram Press published in 1975.

Martin: *Exploring Another Leg* was prior to *Mars 1953*?

Dailey: Yeah. *Mars 1953* was my fourth book. At the time of "Exploring" I was under the tutelage of David Kelly, famed and longtime poet-in-residence at SUC at Geneseo.

Martin: So you explored deep image with him?

Dailey: Well, you know, he didn't make us write deep image poetry. I just happened to be an undergraduate at the time and he was my poetry teacher. His work an interests were influential because that's what I was looking at and studying at the time. Since then, I've advanced, developed into complete incoherency – my response to the contemporary world. I would say my work is an incoherent reflection of the contemporary world.

Martin: Your poetry fragments and shatters what we think of as the contemporary world?

Dailey: Yeah, Olson's idea of experience being fragmented by the contemporary world. I agree with him.

Martin: In his introduction to his translation of selected poems by Pierre Reverdy, Kenneth Rexroth poses the following question: What is Cubism in poetry? He goes on to answer it, stating: "It is the conscious, deliberate dissociation and recombination of elements into a new artistic entity made self-sufficient by its rigorous architecture." Does this statement reflect in any way the manner in which you construct and write poems? If so, please explain how it does and/or what precisely are the techniques employed by you to create your work, and most recently, your outstanding 52-line poem, "Aberrant Follicle"?

Dailey: First of all, early this morning my dog, Earl, nearly vomited into Hillary Clinton's mouth and coincidently, Ice Cube is my favorite actress……In other words, part of Rexroth's definition of Cubism fits the glove for my "technique," but the artist who really parallels my method of composition (sounds pompous, huh?) is Joseph Cornell with his mysterious, unpredictable boxes. The field of a Cornell box unites objects which are dissimilar, stray, seemingly unrelated. The thing is, these items in the box ARE unrelated, but the viewer attempts to conjure up meaning, to create an acceptable narrative – not that different from how we interpret experience. We want experience to make sense – even though it often does not. One of my favorite/most hated common place sayings is "Everything happens for a reason." No, it doesn't.

Martin: So, with Cornell, Olson and a tad of Cubism in mind you construct your poems via language that challenges the reader to conjure meaning from stray and seemingly unrelated images, associations, phrases, concepts, and ideas?

Dailey: Yes, and I wear a hard hat when I'm working.

Martin: I have seen a photograph of you in a hard hat, and quite frankly, you'd be the "ringer" on almost any construction site. But let's stick with the creation of meaning and/or challenge to the conventional notion of meaning (what makes sense etc.) via your poetry. What do you expect from a reader of your work, and what does your poetry offer the reader in return?

Dailey: As a teacher I often preach that all literature ought to do two things: entertain and instruct……My hope is that these works I create entertain through humor, at least initially, and that they also point out empty facets of our 'culture,' some   of which I wholeheartedly embrace and value. Sharp and not so sharp satire can certainly be critical at the same time as it's humorous.

Collisions of words, phrases and ideas can create spontaneity on the page and in the air. I always want to make the poem itself an experience – instead of writing a poem about an experience I once had. In my view, poetry needs to move beyond re-telling a narrative – put it in prose if it's a story…..I expect a reader to be first entertained and then curious about taking a second look at the work in question….

Martin: How does your poetry differ overall from the "language" poets writing today?

Dailey: Anselm Hollo once said to me something along these lines – if language poets lack a sense of humor in their work, the work is cold and not very interesting…..I agree with that. Maybe some of the Lang Poets were too much theory, overweening theory, will you stop with the theory?

Martin: Forget theory, reading a Dailey poem is similar to gazing into a shattered funhouse mirror…a shattered mirror of culture and experience.

Dailey: And it's bad luck for anyone reading my poetry.

Martin: Bad luck? I don't think so. Victim of a good laugh is more likely.

Artifact Insertion:

ABERRANT FOLLICLE

My issue-oriented campaign

Thumb on the scale

Each moment unprecedented   yet soon dented

Courting relevancy

Action rising

Alarum within, carrots without

Bring to a furious boil

Figurative Fog replaces Literal Fog

Fog Lobby launches protests

Dramatic emphasis

"Put Your Head on My Shoulder" before ISIS lops it off

The occupants steep in Routine

A backlash of belief

As in, resilient gum Arabic

Non-affiliated

Serious disarray compounded by olive loaf

'off duty'

Gone porky swattin'

Dramatic New Footage replacing Dramatic Old Footage

Play less more often

To so digress

It's Shakespearean, possibly Orwellian

Intertextuality – cheese it!

The equipage, cursory   nearly bucolic, pastoral

In vacant lot or in pensive mode

Traumatic centipede

Nature's way

Falling down the stairwell nonstop notion

Propelled by adversity

Now re-thinking Nuevo Laredo

Tighten it up

Re-thinking egomania

Driving the financial markets to outer Fresno

More than an evocative nudge

Fantods several

The violent yoking together of heterogeneous objects

'top priority'

The population snack ready, trigger happy

Latent prints discernible on the butterless toast

Ornate burpage

Unlikely combinations yield feeding frenzy

A second apparatus

The turf   planet Earth

A dim bulb

Strewn leaflets attesting to the facts

Overhead luggage may have shifted during the flight

Lines shift overnight

Tension released

In the name of National Security

'glue gun'

Veins varicose point toward the Future

Joel Dailey

Dailey: Right. Readers do find my work humorous. It reflects many
                things…the media…the way people relate or don't know how
                to relate. But really, it's an incoherent fragmented world that
                we inhabit. And it's no surprise to me that people frequently
                go insane and go back to where they got fired and shoot
                everybody. Because the world doesn't make any sense to them.
                Their experience doesn't have any roots…any root system…
                this happens…this happens… then BOOM. I think we can
                look forward to more of that in our society, unfortunately.

Martin: Yeah.

Dailey: Look, we live in a society that teaches violent resolution to problems. When there's a school shooting, everyone is whoa… whoa…why did that happen? Our children are raised… taught to resolve their problems by violence. They play violent video games by the time they are able to walk. What's the big surprise? We've brought them up to be that way. That's not satire. That's what is really happening. That's the kind of world we've created and it's messed up. Everyone is enraged every time a school shooting happens. I think we can look forward to more of them in the future. That's a grim prediction but I don't see why we should think it should stop. As a matter of fact, some of these "shooters" that go into schools have seen what previous "shooters" have done and think it's kind of cool. That's part of the motivation…to get on the news and in this fragmented, crazy world become the top story.

Martin: We're certainly drenched in horrible information from all angles of the media. Shootings, terrorism, bad weather, global warming, the economy…the daily diet. You have no idea what's going to happen when you step out of your house each morning.

Dailey: Well, at least you know there will be trash collection.

Martin: OK, it's all fucked up and fragmented and you go out swimming into it as a poet…always with pen or pencil and a small notebook or a folded piece of paper and harvest the language fragments in the environment…phrases uttered at the supermarket, on the streets, in private and public conversations, colloquialisms…dialect…internet and newspapers. And you create…and for me, a poem of yours is almost like a life raft. I'm fortunate to get many of your poems in the mail prior to publication. And the art of your work astounds me…how the various "fragments" the "leaps" the "humor" the "satire" come together as a whole…not in a sense of closure…but in the sense of a map to understand and read the human condition and new frontiers of language. I often think XJ is the guy who knows how to take the elements of what is fucked up…gone awry and put it together in such a way that a chuckle, a smile, a belly-gut laugh are possible… some hope even…considering laugher inspires hope. OK… enough of how great you are…(I usually reserve that kind of praise for myself). Is there any connection of how you see yourself as a poet and how you see yourself as an editor?

Dailey: Well, I don't really publish too many poems that are like mine. I guess there aren't too many poems that are like mine. I have said in another interview that happens to be online that the Fell Swoop mission is to destroy American poetry. Although, we do publish fiction…short fiction…for the most part rather conservative in nature. Destroyer of American Poetry is what it says online. Camille Martin did that interview with me. It probably needs to be destroyed.

Martin: Well, it's destroying itself, isn't it?

Dailey: Oh, yeah, it's caving in on itself. I believe that is true. The American Academy of Armchairs would not believe this to be true. They have a rather conservative view of what a poem is. I think those kinds of poems have been written over and over and over again. I'm not really interested in someone's narrative angst about the human condition and what the "I" in the poem is saying or doing. I like to think that I've moved beyond the "narrative ego." I look for work from people who have also moved beyond it or are attacking it in some manner.

Martin: Rimbaud said the I is other.

Dailey: He said a lot of shit and became a gunrunner.

Martin: The I is other.

Dailey: Rimbaud gave up writing, became a gunrunner, got TB, and cashed in his chips. Think of Samuel Beckett's work. He won the Nobel Prize in Literature. I became aware of his work in high school through an English teacher. He didn't teach Beckett to the class but saw that I was fucked up enough maybe to appreciate Beckett's work. And you know the basic message of his works…is the human condition is born in suffering and it's not a good condition to be in and life is absurd and meaningless. And yet, the guy went right on writing plays, poems, and novels. He kept on writing about the same thing over and over. If he really believed in what he wrote maybe he would have just blown out his brains. So, there was something that kept him going…kept the fires burning inside of him. And the kind of stuff he was writing about would never be accepted. He forced his way into the establishment of what was accepted in literature. He forced his way in…he kicked open the door. I think he was quite surprised that he was successful. According to a biography I read, he was afraid publishers would lose a lot of money on his books. Of course the reverse was true. Although, it was true for his first few books. They lost a lot of money.

Martin: He was Joyce's amanuensis?

Dailey: Right, right.

Martin: Where do we go after *Finnegan's Wake?*

Dailey: Go blind! Unreadable!

Martin: OK, that's 30 minutes. Call it a wrap. It's time for the Quarter, a cigar, and Pimm's cup.

Dailey: Part 1 only.

Artifact Insertion   *My Psychic Dogs   My Life*

A little about myself
Remove shrinkwrap
I suffer from dumbass narrative cling
Fell down
Correct nervous stance
Attendees were petrified with tongue depressor
citywide
Indent willya
Ahead of our fucken right selfs
The garage tilts epidermis pull ninny
I just knew it
Such that you dast not dog bounce
Enhance & Flatter   eat cheap   leave
skidmarks
Had feeling
I know God called me to plunging neckline
Wait'll took sick
Whosoever you may Person B
ing fastly
Index trajectory half incline to agree

Joel Dailey

from *My Psychic Dogs   My Life* (Lavender Ink, 2008)

Fell Swoop: The All Bohemian Revue ended its magnificent 34-year run in May,
2017, with double issue #154-155, *THE POCKET RHYMING DICTIONARY*,
edited with unmitigated joy by Joel Dailey & Clara Mae Nostril.

By way of introduction to the double issue, Mr. Dailey writes:

"On behalf of this enormous poetic project, I would
like to thank and acknowledge my co-editor, Dr.
Clara Mae Nostril, PhD, MA, MFA, DA, MBA, for both
her invaluable input and her legendary output; she
is also well known for her shotput athleticism!
Compiling this POCKET RHYMING DICTIONARY has been
an especially challenging endeavor, for a) it simply
will not fit into the average consumer's pocket, and
2) nary a rhyme will be discovered herein. Proceed
with caution, dear word pioneers!"

WE WON'T GET SWOOPED AGAIN!

INTERVIEW WITH PETER KIDD
PUBLISHER OF IGNEUS PRESS
NOVEMBER, 2014

Martin: I'm here in my home in Boston with Peter Kidd – poet, landscape artist, novelist, and publisher of Igneus Press. It's a day before Thanksgiving and raining. Welcome, Peter.

Kidd: Thank you, it's nice to be here as always.

Martin: It's great to have you back in Boston for a few days. I'm still trying to get into my head that you live in Texas now but things change. We could talk about the many things you have accomplished as a life-long New Hampshire resident and in Boston during over 60 years of living in the area before your move to Texas. But let's start with Igneus Press. This is a signature and ongoing accomplishment of yours, a press that arose out of your work as poet and a keen mind for a new direction. Talk about Igneus. When did the press come on the scene?

Kidd: Well, it got started in Cambridge in 1989-90 when we were all meeting at the Stone Soup Poetry Series at Charlie's Tap on Green Street. And I looked around and I seemed to have a core group of friends (poets) – friends I had been involved with for many years, some with a book or chapbook out during the eighties, but now we were a little bit older – 15 years or so older than the young writers at Charlie's Tap, and we were stumped at where to go with our new work. I ran a small business, a landscape design/build business and had small business skills so I leapt forward and said let's do it ourselves – a press that is – rather than like an Old Yankee with hat in hand begging at the bank. So the idea and direction were born and Igneus came into being with a book by Wally Butts – W.E.

Butts, our dear friend.

Martin: And that was in 1990?

Kidd: That's the year it came out. So '89 was probably the year we
               started conspiring and I remember Bill Kemmett was in the
               back of my car after a reading at Charlie's when I started to
               go over the idea with Wally and he said: "No, this will never
               work."

Martin: Yeah, I sort of remember you saying at one point that Bill was
               opposed to the idea.

Kidd: He was a skeptic. He said it couldn't be done.

Martin: And why did he think that?

Kidd: Well, first of all he is the Prince of Sigh.

Martin: Right, the Prince of Sigh.

Kidd: In other words, how do you move the rock up from the bottom
               of a mountain to the top of a mountain?

Martin: Yeah, the "Myth of Sisyphus."

Kidd: Yeah, yeah, the "Myth of Sisyphus." But Wally had a wonderful
               manuscript, and to my mind, it remains the best book he ever
               did.

Martin: What was the manuscript titled?

Kidd: *The Required Dance,* and so we started in. Wally would come
               out every weekend to my home in Bedford, NH, and we worked
               on it. We sifted through the poems and decided on a few
               tenets that made sense. We wanted to be diverse and tuned
               to our concern for the human condition. We wanted to be a

cooperative press and draw in a group of close friends who had had access to one another for 30 to 40 years. So that was the spirit Igneus grew out of, and out of that spirit it was launched with the publication of *The Required Dance* in 1990.

Artifact Insertion:

Why *The Required Dance* now…because this is its time and to wait any longer and it would be stillborn. Why W.E. Butts…because he's like the first bite into an October apple. These poems are offered up in that mystical musical cadence of the neighborhood of the soul. They are warm, concrete, and incandescent. Whether they take place at a nursing home, at a church with his daughter, alongside a creek, or a corner store in Boston, they are always compassionate and incarnate two qualities difficult to come by in any age. To Butts, the world and its events are surreal enough and his poems are a wonderful sifting out of meaning. Butts has worked long and hard for such a complete book, and in turn, voice. *The Required Dance* is exciting for the world of poetry and the world at large because it represents a right direction for poetry, a poetry that is trustworthy and seeks to share its universe with the reader-listener.

Peter Kidd, Publisher, Igneus Press

The Balance

For James de Crescentis

I am visiting someone in an apartment,
located around the corner
from a long row of broken-down tenements.
At either end of that block
is a liquor store. We have little money
but, in celebration of my return
from New York City to Boston
we roll two dollars worth of pennies,

and go to one of the liquor stores to buy beer.
The gaunt, black cashier taps his jeweled,
long-nailed fingers on the counter suspiciously,
picks up a roll, balances it
in his slender palm and says,
"Man, there ain't no fifty cent in here."
He opens the roll, counts the pennies
and he's right—forty-eight.
I envy this ability to know
the full measure of a thing by its weight,
no more—no less.
Between us, we have two pennies.
On the way back, I notice
a disheveled figure sprawled across the steps
of a boarded-up brick building.
I'm told he lives there, has for years.
He's luckier than most.
People give him things, take care of him.
Later, we drink beer and talk
About women we thought loved us once.
I want to say something is terrible and wrong,
that there's more to this evening
than our carefully measured desperation,
then realize, I am at peace
in a friend's home.

W.E. Butts
from *The Required Dance* (Igneus Press, 1990)

Martin: What came next after Wally's Book?

Kidd: Well, it wasn't long after that I published Peter Laska. P.J. Laska is
             an excellent West Virginia poet whom I had known for a while. We
             entered into a project and then, all of a sudden, the Prince of Sigh
             wasn't sighing anymore and wanted to do a book, too.

Martin: And what was Kemmett's first book titled?

Kidd: *Flesh of a New Moon* is (was) an excellent book. So I took
              Kemmett's manuscript and sent it to Laska, and Peter took the
              two books to Kinko's and paid to have them typeset, and then
              sent me the hard copies, and I paid to print them. Then we
              started to get around with the books. Wally's broke through
              right away in Boston. Sixty people came to the launch of it and
              I walked away with $400 in book sales.

Martin: So Igneus started, more or less, in a bar in Cambridge via
              conversation among friends who were poets? And it took off
              from there.

Kidd: And with me saying: No whining! No whining! in poetry.

Martin: Right. No Whining! Create your own thing…your own
              scene. And then three books came out from Butts, Laska, and
              Kemmett. I'm curious about the name, Igneus. How did you
              come up with that name?

Kidd: Well, I first thought of Black Bear Press and searched out
              other presses and found some similar imprints, and so I went
              to the Bedford library and pulled out a Latin Dictionary. I
              started going through it and came to "igneus" which was
              spelled i-g-n-e-us; that which comes from fire. And I said:
              "oo!" that's great and underneath igneus was "igniculata"
              or sparks and I thought if I ever wanted to do a magazine or
              broadside I could use that term. Well, I loved the word and
              idea…you know passing through the initiation of fire and
              seeing what is carbonaceous…what is left after you go through
              that purification of fire…so that was the philosophical push…
              the metaphysical push….whatever.

Artifact Insertion

Peter Laska is an intensely sensitive man with a heart wider
than the Interstate. His intelligence is a stringed instrument

that cannot be outsmarted or ignored. And while West Virginia plays a major role in his works, it is by no means the alpha of his resources nor the omega of his vision. Through a combination of submission and compassion for the human condition, he offers us hope for a dignity and decency in this life, to me the major job requirement of a contemporary poet of stature.

Peter Kidd, Publisher Igneus Press

The Secular Humanist Phones Home

Warm tangos of sunlight
interrupt the telephone
on the mattress

the room smells of coffee
and cigarettes
before breakfast

I'm here on the Sabbath
looking at the text
of my worse regrets
both a father and a son
but not The Father
and The Son

past forty
I retain a belief in knowledge
as my true belief

I hear the pendulum
swinging
in the vestibule

I restate my position –
religion for the dead

socialism for the working class

this doesn't mean
the alcoholic priest
is not a friend

Hello!

Give me an outside line, please
maybe this time
I'll be understood

P.J. Laska
from *The Day The Eighties Began* (Igneus Press, 1991)

"Bill Kemmett's *Flesh of a New Moon* echoes voices of
nature, be it mineral, vegetable, animal, or human kingdom.
Kemmett's precise, to the quick poems are more than oriental,
for he is, in the deepest sense, a New Englander Boston born
and Roxbury raised. His images evoke a strength that is
confirmed by his understatement. I feel as though I know
his backyard, and all the creatures that have passed through
it, and have been captured on his pages. These poems are
original, finely crafted, and each one contains a revelation
shared with the reader."

Peter Kidd, publisher of Igneus Press

Faith of Stone

The cave listens to the night
with a dark ear…
Drops of water echo
in an empty rhythm.

The rock within dissolves
a second at a time,
deeper and higher until
the sun pecks through eroding walls.

From the blinding sky
far back in the shadows
bats dream their upsidedown knowledge
into rocks.

The mountain has been informed.
The stones of the inner core
accept their fate:
know of the wind and rain.

The mountain
is equal to the truth.

William Kemmett
from *Flesh of a New Moon* (Igneus Press, 1991)

Martin: Earlier you mentioned being sensitive to the human condition
as a tenet of the press…addressing it in diverse ways. Talk
about your poetics at the time you brought out Wally's book.
What were your thoughts about American poetry at the time
and has your poetics or outlook changed since then?

Kidd: That's a great question. In terms of Boston poetry, I was at
loggerheads with many of the poets because they all thought
the poem was a product of the mind, and I thought it was a
product of the soul. And so the battle was on and waged. It
came to a point where one poet, Rando, said I wasn't even a
poet but a social humanitarian. As for poetics, from the get-go,
it was the study of the minimalist school. Start with the ability
to focus your consciousness through a single image, so a lot of

my early poems were tiny little poems unto themselves. I will always love minimalist poetry…there is so little time for the epic poem…what with family and work…and I learned to get in and out of a poem. I probably beat minimalism to death… until I realized I could string these images together into stanzas, then *skein* out the stanzas into longer poems, and that has evolved to the point where right now, I've been actually going with a poem for 11 months and it's probably around 140 pages with 117 poems considered part of it…which is quite a change for someone who started out with a single image.

Martin: Let's stay with the minimalist/image period of your work for a moment. Do you see your exploration of this style connected to and/or as an outgrowth of the strand of modernism called Imagism launched by Ezra Pound in 1912 through a poem written by Hilda Doolittle that he sent to Poetry Magazine.?

Kidd: I am thinking Amy Irving began the magazine *The Imagist*, Pound and HD were certainly components of it. I think the modernist movement was most likely an attempt to morph the poem into a new set of language laws, overthrowing the Victorian laws of rhyme and meter. And, in fact, was effective, and led to other offshoots like Objectivism. I have always been drawn to HD, we share some similar metaphysics with her Rosicruceanism and my early immersion into the Grail and the story of Parsifal. I think of HD much like I think of Bach. They were clear examples of Hermetic initiation, spatial relationships. I am afraid I find myself in a minority in terms of Pound's and Eliot's contribution to American poetics. So much of the emerging poetry passed through Pound in that period prior to WW2 it would be useless to try and marginalize him. But I tend to think of both he and Eliot as Neo-Classicals. I tend to favor the Whitmanic stream of American poetry, poets like Hart Crane and W.C. Williams. Not just the furthering of the American voice, but the act of reaching up into the cosmos and bringing down the divine into the human. My minimalism grew out of a humility and consecration of a single simple impression or observation being highlighted. It was born of wonder of how less can be more. It was born out of a sense of the surrounding multiplicity and the question of can a single image stand alone in its midst? As my minimalism grew into longer poems, there was always this sense of layers and negative space, which better reflected how the human mind and soul work, on many different levels simultaneously. Certainly I am aware of how linear time works, but my perception is it does not relate much to the subconscious and the unconscious, both enormous sources of poetry and awareness. Also, I'm sure my minimalism was a response to the growing masses of workshop poetry and writing programs which hyper focus on the construction of a poem, the craft. I learned as a landscape designer long ago, the only kind of craft that interests me is learned through constant repetition of just writing and using one's ear to refine. I must confess I am drawn to more experimental poetry.

Artifact Insertion

The Quarry

where
this time of year
everything is slippery
and the stone is brittle
the equipment breaks down
driving the costs
up

Peter Kidd
from *Bear Stew* (Igneus Press, 1996)

1

Walt's Kid(d)

and yes it was
an immaculate conception
perhaps the only thing
in my life
that is immaculate

when I see people hold hands
sparks fly from their fingers
in sandals toes visibly curl

I'm registered with the government
as a solar powered
generation plant

the NSA leaves me alone
after putting 3 agents
into the mental ward

liberty is hard work

last week
I reduced the macrocosm
and the microcosm into a whole

even my truths and conclusions
have a tendency
to evolve in dynamic fashion

my father taught me a trick
how to catch Blake's Tiger
by the tail

if you find me lacking

in metaphor
it's on purpose
my only narrative
is
this instant

there is no need for a decoder ring

I pay alimony
to 12 harlots
on a handshake

my mission is to alienate
most poets
for their lack of simplicity

screw your vocabulary
learn to dwell
inside your words

is it true your beta-alpha
manifests
upside down

whole grains
you say
whole souls
I reply

my father changed head wound bandages
and still had the clarity
to celebrate life

are you displeased
when you buy
the wrong floss

Dr Williams
my cousin
married Floss
there is a stream
in American Literature
where a handful or two
have taken
baptism

we all meet there
at
unappointed times
to discuss the alchemical formula
of conjoining soul with body.

1/29/14

Peter Kidd
from *Human Condition* (poem in progress)

Martin: Definitely, moving from a single image to an epic charts the
           change in your work. Now we have a number of plates in the
           air: the start of Igneus, the first poets to be published by the
           press, Igneus as a cooperative press, and your poetics over
           time. But now I want to veer back to an earlier statement you
           made and that is the distinction you made between a poem
           coming from the mind and a poem arising from the soul.
           What do you mean when you say "soul?" What is "soul" to
           you?

Kidd: At the concrete level, the soul is memory and the inner and
           emotional world. On the metaphysical level, it is passion
           and involved with feeling. But I always had a sense that the a
           priori for me was this inner welling up of enormous feeling,
           which is not to say that I play down the role of the mind.
           However, I didn't think the mind was the source or the point
           of origin for the poem. I consider the mind the "tool" to
           construct and shape the initial push.

Martin: Is feeling something broader or more inclusive than emotion?

Kidd: I don't think there is a whole lot of difference. Feeling is a word we've brought closer to the pavement than emotion. It's less psychological…more humane. It is something you can talk to children about, and they'll understand what you're talking about. And I think a big key is that it (feeling) embraces empathy…something that leads to a relationship outside of yourself as well as to yourself.

Martin: For you, does the soul or your soul exist prior to existence. Is there a Peter Kidd prior to Peter Kidd? Is there a Peter Kidd soul after Peter Kidd. What are we talking about here?

Kidd: Well, I'll come out of the closet. You know, I've always thought I was one of the 12 Bodhisattvas around Vishnu at the Mother Lodge, and I'm still up to that. I don't think there is anywhere else to go. I'm reaching up and grabbing the divine cosmos and dragging it down. I'm not a transcendentalist. I'm an incarnationist.

Martin: Also re-incarnationist. I remember that walk we took through a mosquito patch in the woods when you defined your position in life. Remember?

Kidd: The walk in which you worried your head would grow in size like a beach ball?

Martin: Yes, the inflatable head stroll through a corridor of pines and into the vortex of mosquitoes…until we reached a country road and you took a toke on your…

Kidd: Herbal experiment.

Martin: Yes. Herbal experiment and you confided to me that you had made a conscious decision to go through your present incarnation medicated to ensure you would return again. Is this part of your idea and sense of soul?

Kidd: Absolutely! I consciously like to leave a little unfinished business, particularly with those I love dearly, you know.

Martin: So the Wheel of Birth and Death is a good thing for you?

Kidd: Yeah, yeah.

Martin: You're not trying to get off of it?

Kidd: Yeah, and Bill Kemmett would say, I'm an evil person – not only because I want to come back, but because I want to bring all you guys back with me by leaving unresolved issues.

Artifact Insertion

Witness

Mind pervades everything is a sentence with clout
Uncertainty is a principle
Cogito ergo sum and the double helix
remain hot news items
We polished off a bottle of Pouilly Fuisse
enjoying the play of mythical children from frosted steps
Are butterflies reincarnated philosophers
Do trees deny the wheel of birth and death
What's your present velocity and location
I've shot pool like David Hume
(*Send the paparazzi to the front(s)*
Send the presidents the monarchs the dictators
The millionaires and the religious leaders too)
It's more than getting one's paperwork in order
or forging the moon's blood work
to obtain the Mind's birth certificate

Great history shakes with the awareness of what has been lost
Pure reflection did explode
See Internet See Spot run
Through equations and livid insights
we encode multiple oblivions
Before it started to thunder
we collected raindrops in pearl pails
There were ghost planes in the sky/homeless soldiers
When consciousness slips on a noose of flowers
eye is not so bad or mad a witness

Richard Martin
(*House Organ #77*)

Martin: Well, I understand that and thanks for that country stroll
because I grew up with the Catholic version of soul –
immaterial and judged up or down by actions and behavior
during one's life. Up or down in terms of heaven, purgatory,
or eternal damnation in hell. Not everyone gets to merge with
Oneness. There's no room for coming back for a second try.
Maybe get right this time.

Kidd: Which is crazy. Christianity doesn't comprehend the power
of grace, which is one of its tenets. The power of grace – I like
that better than karma (the eastern notion of karma) – the
idea, if you make a mistake you just own it and you can have
a fresh start with people…you know…just don't let the lower
ego build a fort around your mistakes. Own them…laugh…
and move on.

Martin: Say you're sorry.

Kidd: Yeah, say you're sorry. I'm human. What I find as I get older
is that imperfections are what are so artistic and lasting. The
imperfections of people and things. Total perfection is auto-
mechanical. I like the human quality …that we're all leaking
a little bit out of our eyes.

Martin: OK…with our imperfections let's get back to poetry and poetics. Poetry appears to be in many camps today…the big one, as Charles Bernstein calls it, Official Verse Culture, which includes poetry sanctioned by the American Academy of Poets or as Joel Dailey says, the American Academy of Armchairs and the various awards linked to "official" poetry – a poetry that more than likely includes many MFA programs and what they're preaching to students, and the rest of the scene, from poets clustered in magazines like Fell Swoop or in the Igneus catalog…the perpetual underground of the unnoticed. Exclusivity bubbles through the veins of American poetry.

Kidd: Yeah, I think it is healthy that you mention that. Frankly, I think every type or manifestation of poetry out there - regional poetry, schools of writing – Black Mountain, Beat, Language, MFA etc…on and on… create and generate quality work regardless of the type, mediocre work regardless of the type and crap. It's my experience when a press or magazine centers on a region, school, or type of poetry exclusively, they go dry very quickly. They don't attain longevity because they're not involved in the evolution of the poetic and that's a great mistake. Again, the reason you might not get into Igneus is that you're not diverse enough.

Martin: So how many poets have been published by Igneus…how many books are available?

Kidd: I've published 58 books since 1990…58 in 25 years.

Martin: And those 58 books reflect your vision of poetic diversity?

Kidd: Because I made my living as a landscape artist and designer, I've always thought of Igneus Press as a landscape – one that includes all kinds of elements and components with specific elements compositionally arranged in sequence or juxtaposition with other specific elements or components like a visual artist would do. As a landscaper, I collect my materials, get them to the site and place them into a landscape composition. Igneus is a poetic landscape from the seventies until now and some 40 years later the landscape is growing in complexity into new and exciting dimensions…one with more layering…layering on layers…exploding the genre… crossing boundaries. More than just ekphrasis…but poets and poems crossing into and breeding with other art forms and bringing enrichment to each. So I think we're just starting to hit our stride. My feeling early on was that people who were constructing poems… a lot of them came from workshops and MFA programs…there was an essential sameness to them…a flatness…and honestly those programs are no different than many academic programs…To become a professional, in this case a professional poet, is humiliating to the poet and the process. You have to become a Genghis Khan shit sniffer to get through and who wants to become that, especially when pabulum is the result…the sophisticated end of the oligarchy, you know.

Martin: Speaking of oligarchy….I find it interesting that when one thinks about postmodern writing, writing since 1945… writing we've come to associate with Black Mountain poets, the Beats, Language poets, etc. …who were all outsiders to the university to begin with, then eventually a number of poets from the outside settled into the university and Academia.

Kidd: They gradually got usurped.

Martin: Yeah…so the chunks of poetry outside the university walls… Igneus…Fell Swoop….etc.

Kidd: Archetypical chunks.

Martin: Yes, these archetypical chunks floating around like air masses in the body poetic…address if you would their direction…

what about our generation of poets, who quite frankly, very few have been read or are known about…where are we headed?

Kidd: Look, we have an understanding that our greater commitment is to the poetic itself. Inclusive of that is our times, the surrounding politics, changes in time and metaphysics, changes in the nuts and bolts of the publication world…changes the electronic and technological age has brought us that have made things more doable. We're not dependent on some small formula. It's always been my opinion that people who are studying or trying to be canonized – reading or taking off on what it took to be postmodern – will blow it completely. Evolution is evolution…So we change, time changes, the poetic changes and so will the criteria of what has substance. I don't think you can work off the recipe for being a well-rounded, respected postmodern. It won't be applicable…you're going to have to have the computer and technology involved.

Martin: So, it's being present in one's time and open to new forms of expression and exploration.

Kidd: Yes, and what is unique is being in your own time, which I think is absolutely right, and to get to that point in ourselves where we are secure enough to move on…and like you were saying…why is it so many people we like are somewhat, in a traditional sense, obscure. But we're not obscure to each other. We were fortunate, and we constelled with 4, 5, 6, 7 core poets that we have had 40-year relationships with and great accessibility to one another. I think that, in and of itself, is unique. Within that primary constellation, each of us have other constellations and those constellations have come together (in some manner) to form a truly diverse constellation. We kind of know who swam against the current, kicked ass, became experimental and innovative. We don't feel responsible to 200 year old language laws. That's not our ilk. We want to play with things. See what the potentiality of language can be. How can we cross pollinate with music…How we can cross-pollinate with painting.

Artifact Insertion:

Advice

Brief through the simple
Confusion: transition
To river of thought

You know what Pound said
About this type of figure
Of speech: Don't do it

River is a natural object –
Thought an abstract one
Both have origins

Meander
When put together
Collision of worlds

Sounds
Vortex waterfall
Wormhole

Rules then
For composition:
Who needs them

Richard Martin
(published in *Chronogram*)

Martin: Let's talk about one Igneus poet who swam against the current
            for a lifetime, a poet Igneus has published a number of times,
            Vincent Ferrini.

Kidd: The old man.

Martin: Let's talk about the old man. I can't claim to know his work like you. How did you meet him?

Kidd: Yeah, it was a great experience for me to know him. I have had two major older generational poets in my life. Neither were mentors – they were peers and recognized that…as I recognized that…One was Bob Kaufman, the old Beat poet, and the other was Vincent Ferrini, who was part of that daemon with Charles Olson and the whole Gloucester scene. I first met the old man at the Boston Center for the Arts. I was sitting with a 100 people or so and this little bitty guy with a head full of white hair and wide brimmed black hat, plus 5 inches of manuscripts steps to the podium on the stage. And he plunks the manuscripts down on the podium and looks up at the audience and says: "I've got enough material here to blow the roof off this building!" He gave a fantastic reading. I loved it. Afterward I started to walk on the stage to talk with him and he pointed his finger at me, wrote down his address and said: "Write me." So Vincent and I started our correspondence and there exist hundreds of letters between us. These letters can found in my archives at Kent State and in his archives at the Cape Ann Museum. They cover a 30-year relationship. He was just a big brother and good guy. He ruffled everyone he had ever met in his life. He was the ultimate "shoot yourself in the foot" poet. He pissed off the postmoderns. He pissed off the moderns. I mean he'd write to Clayton Eshleman and misspell his name. Ferrini was the ultimate…well you met him. I took you to meet him and you know what happened.

Artifact Insertion:

THE MYSTERY

We are not attuned to perceive certain

wave lengths of sound & sight

too low or too bright for

humans
the daily

      crucifixion

the music in everything

          enclosing

the resurrection

      of the known, the unknowing, & the knower

Vincent Ferrini
from *MAGDALENE SILENCES* (Igneus Press, 1992)

The First Intimation

Where is the Heart –
forgotten in a place
before you were born
& it is the closest to you
the beat of your primal bonding
asking you to get in touch with
& stay there
      It is the only voice that can save you
if you obey its rhythms

it will heal you
Forget everything that ever happened to you
dive into the heart's holy water
& let its love for you breathe
give up everything
that is not in tune
with the art of your heart
which is so deep inside
you –
forget
who you are and where you are
drink from your heart's well-water
it is where miracles come from
& the cadence of perfect Being

Vincent Ferrini
from *THE MAGI IMAGE* (Igneus Press, 1995)

Martin: Ok, let's talk about that meeting for a second. It was the day I earned an unexpected Ph.D.

Kidd: That's right. Ferrini broke his recipe. He was committed to awarding only 12 Ph.Ds. But after we drove to his place and spent the day with him, he decided to break his paradigm and awarded you the 13th Ph.D.

Martin: It was a great honor…but I'm a little fuzzy on the events that led up to it.

Kidd: It had a lot to do with your discussion of Blake with him.

Martin: Oh, yeah, now I remember. We both loved Blake, but I wasn't too high on the Blessed Virgin, which came into the discussion somehow…More or less I saw Blake grounded in the transcendence of being here, bringing the contraries together through Imagination. I didn't need an eternal zone. We're in it. Or something like that. Anyway, we went back and forth and started quoting from "The Marriage of Heaven and Hell".

Kidd: And don't forget Ferrini's self-portrait of himself as Christ decked with grape leaves and his own little laureate thing hanging in his bathroom – how that enflamed the conversation. You got him going. Remember, he started pounding on his desk with great emphasis and as a result shattered his eyeglasses.

Martin: Yes, it was all a matter of timing and coincidence. His glasses were on top of a *Time Magazine* and on the cover was a picture of Jesus. We went back forth over the energy of eternal delight…following the crooked path… and were at loggerheads on some issues. At the point of his glasses shattering, and his angry rising, he looked at me and said: "You've just earned my 13th Ph.D."

Kidd: Yeah, he said to me sometime afterwards: "What about this guy, Martin?" We had a ball other than the 2 ½ hours it took for us to have his glasses repaired.

Martin: Great fun. And he is another example, like yourself, of a poet owning his own independent business and/or raising a family, and going through all the ups and downs, and still persisted with pushing the poetic envelope. He owned a frame shop, didn't' he?

Kidd: He was a framer who carved driftwood and built frames from them.

Martin: And again, you owned and operated a landscaping business for 30 years, garnered a number of awards for your business, plus raised 4 kids, and in between published 58 books. I think of Dailey in New Orleans in the same boat of responsibilities and editing and publishing *Fell Swoop: The All Bohemian Revue* for the last 31 years.

Kidd: And Rich Blevins is a professor and poet.

Martin: And until recently I was a principal in the Boston Public Schools – the energy of the day job.

Kidd: And we all knew to keep them. The reality is you don't want to put pressure on your poetry to provide dollars. It's a high art and should be left that way.

Martin: It's an art of acceptance…of readiness to receive.

Kidd: Absolutely, you have to be ready to climb right up on the cross, spread your arms and cross your legs, in case there are not enough nails, you do what I call the C-R-U-C-I-F-I-C-T-I-O-N.

Martin: We'll close on that. Thanks, Pete.

Kidd: You're welcome.

See: www.igneuspress.com and Online Bookstore/Igneus Press at www.igneuspress.com/category/online-bookstore for publishing history and books for sale.

INTERVIEW WITH BILL KEMMETT
PORT ST. LUCIE, FLORIDA
APRIL 29, 2015
WELLFLEET, MA
AUGUST 6, 2015

RM: Bill, we've been having some great conversations over the last couple of days. It is great to be here in Florida and staying with you and Jackie in your Southern estate. It is a magnificent place – a beautiful garden of exotic plants and flowers engulf your home. Plus the weather is warm and friendly – a welcome relief after 6 months of brutal cold and snow in New England. As I mentioned the other day, I'm working on a book that will include interviews with poets and artists. So far, I've interviewed Joel Dailey and Peter Kidd. In May, I will interview Tom Haines, a terrific artist living in Binghamton, New York. Now, armed with cigars and cognac, let's talk poetry. First, talk about how you first came to poetry.

BK: Well, when I was younger, I was mostly interested in writing songs. And I found that the songs I did write were more like poetry than songs, so to speak. My songs were rejected. However, a number of publishing companies noted that I wrote and sounded more like a poet than a songwriter.

RM: So from an early age you were writing poetry before you called it poetry. Song lyrics that edged into the sound and rhythms of poetry.

BK: Yes, I was influenced early by rock-n-roll like many of us were. Initially, I came directly out of Pop music – Frankie Lane, people like that. But I never envisioned myself in the music business. I just entertained the thought of writing some songs. And when I got rejected, I decided that maybe it was poetry that I was looking for, rather than writing songs.

RM: So what was your early poetry like? What were some of the first publications of your work?

BK: Believe it or not, my work was first published in religious
             magazines.

RM: Really?

Artifact Insertion

Ode to Mercy

Why do I offend thee,
   my God? Because it's in
my nature to be willful?

Let me take the time
   to listen. The trees are
full of song.

Not with just insect
   and bird, but the sound
of its own limbs moving
in the soft breeze
   that comes and goes with
every reason to just be.

There is a blossom
   to this joy. Teach me
my Lord to emulate the way

of what just is. Not
   as if I'm not, or that
I am, but because you are –

always present like
   the wind teasing around
the one branch that

will not bend. . .

William Kemmett

BK: And also my work appeared in magazines with a focus on nature. And from that point in my career, I became interested in Eastern philosophy, particularly, a Zen kind of thing after reading some poets – Jesuits, actually. I gravitated toward Haiku, Haibun…Eastern poetry and form.

RM: Talk about where your Eastern feel for language and thinking came from?

BK: Well, I always thought that humans should be naturalized. Wait. Let me start that over again. I don't want to see humanized nature. I do want to see naturalized man, and I found the Orient, particularly the Japanese, were into poetry representing my sense of things.

RM: So from the start of your poetic life you had an affinity for the East, a philosophical bent for observing and seeing into the natural world.

BK: Yes, I did. I found I was comfortable contemplating nature. Plus, because you're a human being you have to contemplate nature as a human being. However, the more that I could get the human being out of the contemplative equation the happier I was. I enjoyed the brevity of Eastern philosophy, particularly when it came to poetry.

Artifact Insertion

Final Poem

It's one minute
to twelve on the last
day. The moth is
still as the air
in a bell just before
the hammer falls. Also
what is striking:
the silence
when the neutron collapses
into the cell
that has no reason
to divide itself.

                    William Kemmett

RM: In other words, you don't have to say a lot, but you have to say it well.

BK: I think the Japanese poets – Yosa Buson, Matsu Bashô, Kobayashi Issa, for example – do that very well.

Artifact Insertion

Walking in Fog:
The Trees Loom Suddenly Up;
Some I've Never Seen.

A Melting Snow;
Gently Lowers the Stiff Bird
Into a Spring Grave

Near the Road House:
Exposed by the Desert Wind –
Old Pump Handle.

Under the Bar-stool;
The Shadow of my Footrest
Moves Another Inch

Sunday Junk Yard;
The Watchdog Yawns Steam
At the Falling Snow

William Kemmett
from *Flesh of a New Moon* (Igneus Press, 1991)

RM: OK, so Eastern philosophy, particularly manifested by Japanese poets, influenced your early work. What other poets fed your evolving poetics?

BK: Well, I wasn't really "feeding" on many other poets during that time. If you were to ask me which poets influenced my work later on, believe it or not, it was the Confessional poets – Sylvia Plath, Ann Sexton,

Robert Lowell. I liked the idea of the confessional mode. But I don't like any exclusionary poetry. Never did and never will. I feel more comfortable with an infusion of different kinds of poetry. I like many Eastern European poets – Charles Simic, Zbigniew Herbert and Miklós Radnóti to name a few. And though we've been talking about Zen poetry, I can't say that I'm tremendously involved with the study of it. I read anthologies of contemporary poets when I read poetry. But I don't concentrate on any particular school of poetry. If, however, I decided to concentrate on a school and/or specific kind of poetry, it would involve Eastern European and Zen poetry.

RM: So you know what you like but remain open to the diversity of types and approaches to poetry. Now, let's talk a bit about your publication history. What was your first book?

BK: *Riverbank Moss*, a book of haiku, published by Stone Soup.

RM: What year did it come out?

BK: I think it was 1978.

RM: Was Jack Powers involved in the publication of the book?

BK: Jack Powers encouraged me to let him publish that collection of haiku.

RM: How did your connection with Jack Powers and Stone Soup evolve?

BK: OK, during that time, I was thinking about taking some poetry courses. Boston University offered courses but they cost a great deal of money. I was married and had a family. A friend of mine suggested an alternative route. Instead of being influenced by BU or anyone else, he thought I should go to where the poets resided and met. I looked in the newspapers, particularly local Boston newspapers, and found Stone Soup. I started to go to the readings Jack hosted on Thursday nights. I liked it. I made some friends and met people of my own ilk. I immersed myself with poets and picked their brains – not quite fellow poets, because I didn't really consider myself to be a serious poet at that time.

However, I was strongly influenced by my interactions with some of the poets I met and that was the beginning of taking myself seriously as a poet. I used to do a lot of poetry readings and people at Stone Soup found my work a little bit different than what others were writing at the time. I started to look forward to my jaunts into Boston and Cambridge and being with a community of writers. It did me a lot of good for I was not part of a community of writers to begin with.

RM: And you were associated with the Stone Soup community for quite a long time.

BK: Yes, a good many years.

RM: Talk about the Boston/Cambridge poetry scene during your time in Boston.

BK: Well, there were many young poets at the time – rebels – people coming in from various coffeehouses. They were rebellious, in a sense, anti-poets. I found that refreshing after being with some who took themselves as serious poets. I found the young poets to be more interesting. They were in rebellion against the whole system – anti-academic – no need of any prior knowledge of any age of poetry with the exception of Hip Hop and performance poetry. However, if originality is a case for poetry, some of them had that.

RM: Who were your poetry buddies at Stone Soup?

BK: Well, I did bond to some degree with the poets at Stone Soup, including Jack Powers, not so much because of his poetry, but rather because of his ability to organize poetry. Then, of course, my friendships with W.E. Butts, Peter Kidd, James de Crescentis and you were part of the Stone Soup experience.

RM: Yeah, we were all connected at some point. I came late to Stone Soup from my work in Binghamton as the founder and coordinator of the Big Horror Poetry Series. Right away, I dug Monday night in Cambridge, getting together with you, Wally, Peter, and Deac at the Field – often before coming to the Field you hit the Bradford Café to write – for some beers and sharing our latest work with each other. Then off to the poetry scene, first at Green Street and eventually at T.T. Bears. After the readings, we went to Mary Chung's for the General Gallbladder special. What a period! We all had families and jobs. No one had an academic job. And so, there was this one night to get together and share work written the week before. Was that your understanding and/or how you saw things?

Artifact Insertion:

Indian at the Bradford Café

The Indian sitting in neon-
light at the bar needn't say a word.
His somber license assures a seat
on either side of him.

It is November, 1992. A full
cycle of industrial progress since
any camp-council talked
of language loss. Pilings have been
balanced with the fire-water
of the twisted dance; sky-scrapers
raised with the tight-rope
of the reckless. I look at him
straight out in the second it takes
to span centuries of trespass: and he
knows in that moment all there is
I would try to bridge.

He goes to the juke
and rolls two quarters
into a saxophone that breaks
through by never reaching
for what is gone.

William Kemmett

from *The Bradford Poems* (Igneus Press, 1996)

BK: To some degree, yes. But besides writing poetry, I had an interest in teaching it. That interest took off when I was contacted by the Rockland Public School System. They were teaching haiku to students (second and fourth grade students) through a book of haiku I had recently published. They invited me to offer a few lessons to the children to see how I would organize and present haiku-type poetry to younger students. I found the work very interesting and the initial few days turned into my becoming the poet-in-residence at Rockland for six or seven years. I eventually worked in all grade areas, including the high school. During my residency, I found that I liked poetry well enough to consider teaching it, perhaps fulltime. I needed to take some time off from my job to get a degree. I opted to go for a Masters of Fine Arts degree at Vermont College. With a degree, I could not only teach in high school but in college as well.

RM: The other night we were talking about what you wanted from an MFA program due to the fact that you were a published poet with a unique poetics. We hit on our dismay over the proliferation of MFA programs and more young poets flocking to them. You mentioned you pulled back from some things associated with the MFA. Can you talk about that?

BK: I wouldn't use the word "dismay" in referring to MFA programs. I gained what I could from the MFA program at Vermont College. Some people can actually benefit from them. And I was one of them. What I pushed back on was groups of people getting together and forming cliques and schools of thought that turned into publishing opportunities. I think if you're good at what you do, your work will rise to the top.

RM: So for you, there are benefits to the MFA degree but also things to be wary of and/or avoid.

BK: Some people – and I think I won't throw any names out there – have benefitted tremendously by getting involved with a specific poetry community, i.e. school. But I haven't attended to that. It's not that I'm against it. I'm just not interested in being involved with any school of poetry. I like to pick and choose…cherry pick – people, poetry and styles that I like.

RM: Would you consider yourself a recluse in the poetic world?

BK: I'm a known recluse. I'm a very hard man to reach. I don't associate much with others, outside of my very close personal friends. I don't send work out to be published unless I'm asked for work. That may sound vain but it's not; it's just my way. But if a friend asks for some work of mine, I will offer some. So, it's true from time to time you will see some of my poems in print. But I don't seek publication.

RM: So you're truly free as a writer. You talked the other night about entering a trance when you write. Talk about that.

BK: Writing poetry is therapeutic for me and also sparks my creative juices. As for a trance, I may be just sitting in my chair, thinking about what I might like to get into, and all of a sudden, I'll get off into a certain thought process, and when I come out of this so called trance, two or three hours have passed, and I have written a number of poems. It seems to me as if the poems were written by somebody else.

RM: I had the good fortune to bring out your book, *Black Oil*, via deadCpress. Editing the book had a profound effect on me. My appreciation and understanding of your poetry deepened immensely. It was already pretty high. However, editing requires; moving into each line, allowing it to sink and seep deeply into consciousness. Your ability to observe and contemplate nature, whether plant, animal, sky, rain, ocean, mountains – is remarkable. The clarity, rhythm, detail, and the evolving imagery of your language are masterful as the world of nature not seen or ignored comes to life to restore life. And although your poems mine the spirit within nature and contemplate the beauty and restless of it, your poems also record the foibles and humor of being human and highlight your upbringing in Boston and your family. I've heard you read many times and those gathered around you during a reading often break out laughing at a situation or event unfolding in a poem. Talk about the place of humor in your poetry.

BK: Well, I've always thought that tragedy can be written about as long as you do it with a sense of humor and be a little bit self-effacing. I've tried to show that pain sometimes in retrospect can be comical. Hopefully, a "humorous" poem of mine doesn't get too much into confessional writing, but rather shares something that we all share as human beings.

RM: So an event or experience in a specific poem may have been painful when first experienced?

BK: Time heals all wounds. Well, once you move away from a painful experience, you have to look back and see its humorous side.

RM: Are there poems of yours that strike you as funny, maybe not during the writing of them, but as the poem found its path, true humor, whether satirical, absurd or surreal found voice?

BK: Well, several poems come to mind. One is "Sardines." It's a poem couched in metaphysical language but it is also a poem almost anyone can relate to, with a certain amount of pain that can only be laughable. But more importantly, a lot of it is based on experience. For instance, "The Bible Salesman," which is a humorous poem, actually came from me selling bibles for a number of years. I went into many people's homes. Some of them just wanted to talk, to have someone to communicate with…lonely people. I ended up seeing photos of their favorite loved cats and dogs and husbands who had been dead for twenty years. You get to the point where you stop listening to it. Basically, all I wanted to do was to sell the bible or the *Lives of the Saints*. But listening was part of the territory and that is where the humor resided – the fact that I had to sit down and discuss a cat that's been dead for twenty years and/or look at the photos of the great grandchildren and feign some interest. Basically, the nucleus of that poem comes from those experiences.

Artifact Insertion
The Bible Salesman

She had a spider
with a genus too complicated
to remember: Amazonia something
or other. It was as large
as a poodle, and she walked it
on a leash of braided spider-web.

She had it de-fanged and neutered
for its own good, she said. Also
she had half its legs amputated
so she could walk it at a reasonable
pace. She was an atheist, she said.
But bought a bible from me, mainly,
I think because she was lonely
and needed my ear.

This wasn't the easiest sale
I ever made: the spider sitting
on my lap; the endless photos of her
and the spider with her husband while
he was still alive; the photos of her
with the spider at her husband's grave-
site; the photos of her with her grand-
children feeding the spider by hand.
And her with the spider taking a shower
together.

She never explained to me who took
these pictures, and I never asked. She
did buy the deluxe model of the bible
along with the *Lives of the Saints*.

It wasn't too long after that I gave
up selling bibles, and went into
selling shoes; and I was the best
shoe salesman the company ever had.
The owner of the firm who hired me
predicted I'd be good at it: said,
"If you can sell bibles, you can
sell anything!"

William Kemmett
from *Black Oil* (deadCpress, 2010)

RM: Going back to "Sardines," for a moment, because this is another one of
        my favorites, I believe those on a beach outing hurled objects at you as
        you left the beach for the day.

BK: Well, yeah in the poem rocks, bottles and jeers because I stunk up the
        place by opening a can of sardines. (Laughter)

RM: Didn't you offer them to someone by you?

BK: I offered them to a young lady who declined and looked at me with
        disgust, not realizing that sardines have such wonderful properties, and
        it's not the worst thing in the world to dine with me.

RM: I think these kinds of situations find their place in a number of your
        poems. Readers love the human predicaments you've been willing to
        share by living a full and varied life. Why shouldn't you eat a can of
        sardines on a beach day?

BK: Well, you have to remember a lot of the language in that poem is
        metaphysical, and it is based on some lines of truth. But in writing it,
        mostly the imagination took over and carried it to wherever it wanted to
        go. "Sardines," is a very metaphysical poem, actually.

RM: So, you're not trying to describe or record "literal" events in the poem?
        There are other bigger and deeper aspects and ideas simultaneously
        going on in the poem.

BK: Usually, that's the case, but I can't stay I'm not also looking to capture "literal" events. Sometimes, that is the case, too. But when I'm writing poetry, I let the poem take care of itself, whether or not it reflects some Eastern European philosophy or Zen philosophy. Basically, its metaphysical language, and the language takes me where I want to go. However, the poem writes itself. First of all, all of my poems, if you look at or study them, have ghosts of form, whether it's a sonnet, or a haiku form like Haibun, which is sort of like a sonnet with haiku moments in it. Again, I let the poem take me where it wants to go. I never sit down and think that I'll write this or that. Sometimes the poem fits into a form; sometimes it doesn't. I let the poem itself decide where it wants to go.

RM: What do you mean by metaphysical language?

BK: The elaborate conceit; irony – what is born of the mind rather than experience – a blend of reality and fantasy. Sometimes, one taking in the other. Everything is possible if the imagination is free to go there.

Artifact Insertion
Sardines

I'm getting back to basics and saving money.
I'm at the beach eating sardines.
I open a can with a jackknife, and cut my finger.
I don't bleed much, but flies are buzzing through the
smell. I offer some. People move their blankets
up wind. A girl close by ties the top half
of her bikini and changes position.
She declines sardines straight from the can.
I tell her about the benefits:
rich in protein and oil for the fair skin.

She calls the lifeguard.
He needs to see my membership pass.
"It's a lifetime, I don't need a card."
He escorts me to my car through a press of onlookers.

"What's going on?" they want to know.
"Sardines," says the lifeguard.
I nudge my car through the crowd
until they're behind and speed away
leaving a trail of flying dust and stones,
all the while showing my finger of defiance.
"Sardines!" I shout back
through a hail of rocks and beer bottles.

William Kemmett
from *Black Oil* (deadCpress, 2010)

RM: So humor, nature, ghost forms, metaphysical language are all part of the
        journeys your poems go on as they write themselves and become what
        they are. Now let's talk about the influence of family on these poetic
        journeys. How has growing up in a large Irish family in the city of
        Boston influenced your work?

BK: Boston, of course, is a predominantly Irish town even with all the other
        denominations as part of the fabric. Basically, during my youth, there
        was a barroom on every corner. You couldn't walk 20 feet without a
        barroom greeting you. And so the Irish culture was like that. From
        the time I was 16, I spent many hours in bars, which help to establish
        some roots for my poetry. My father was an alcoholic; my uncles were
        all alcoholics. But that was the way of life at the time; nobody thought
        anything peculiar of it. It was a culture based on alcoholism or I should
        say alcoholism caused by the culture. My mother probably had more of
        an ear toward me than anyone else in the family. But she could never
        figure out why I would waste my time writing poetry. She said to me one
        time: "Why don't you write songs? You have the melodies and the ear
        to write music, which would certainly be lucrative to you, but not only
        to your benefit, but to my benefit as well. She also said that Aunt Rose,
        her sister, had read all my books and thinks they are all mumbo-jumbo.
        (Laughter).

RM: I get that criticism. When I showed my mother my first book – the
        hospital poems – she said, after reading a couple of them: "Don't show

this book to any of our friends." But I can see the influence of family in your work. You have written poems that reference your uncles and barrooms and other members of your family, including your wife. In fact, weren't you working on a set of historical family narratives a number of years ago? But before we go there, here is one from my "hospital" book that I kept away from family friends.

Artifact Insertion

Rachel

He had just finished telling me
how the boys (he always called those
in the army boys) used to stick
their arms through windows
on their way to diner
and bleed to death
while the cook watched
the government stew harden into adobe brick,
and swore that the damn psychos
never made it to chow on time.

It was when he said
this civilian psycho job is a breeze,
you leaned over the side rail
he was adjusting
and bit through his thumb,
until your teeth were a lover's knife
in the bark of his bone.

Richard Martin
from *Dream of Long Headdresses: Poems from a Thousand Hospitals* (The Signpost Press Inc., 1988)

RM: OK, then. Did you write family biographies at some point?

BK: No, I did put some time into some family narratives but they all wound up as poems. I was encouraged by some friends to write down the biographical information because they thought my background was too rich to let my life and family experiences to slide by. But for some reason anytime I start to write prose, it turns into poetry. I do actually have a few poems that are prose poems. But for the most part my prose turns into poetry.

RM: I think that your friends urged you to pursue narrative and biography because besides being a great poet, you're a great storyteller. You can command a gathering all night long with story after story. Those of us who know you (keeping in mind that you're a recluse) and your work appreciate how some late night stories have found a path into your poems – more or less as seed of a story, not pure biography. Again, the seed opens and takes the open road.

BK: Well, that's correct. And anybody that knows me, as well as they can know me, realizes that there is a grain of truth in everything that I write. But sometimes, the poem takes off on a flight of its own that has little to do with actual biography.

Artifact Insertion
Heavy Metal

I ate chips of paint because
  of the odd taste, while my nose
pressed against the frost
  of the blue window. My little
brother didn't eat lead
  at all. Didn't need it.

He grew wavy hair, and could
  catch a football like a pro,
powered up on nothing: the modern
  day Hiawatha. Going to school
empty like the jade
  in deep sea waters.

I was prematurely toxic, writing
   thoughts as only one who stomps
roaches who have evolved to be
   crush proof. My brother is proud
of my simple truths and shows
   my small book of poems to his
friends. Thugs, everyone, but hip.
   He says "lead" and they say,
"absolutely, what else?"

They high-five at what they
   perceive to be talk only
they can wink at. Fish oil mixed
   with colors smoothes the pull
of lead. Roaches love the taste
   and thrive on the spirit
of past lives.

It's all about who chewed wood
   and who didn't. My brother's
friend, the one who is clean, did
   not eat lead, despite the neat
bullet holes drilled right through
   the rear plate of the hot Mustang.

I thought I heard myself ask,
   "Who wired the horses?"
But the smoke remained in a slow
   circle of only a thought and
the pause provided a window past
   the john to my 1995 Taurus
with the gas-saving motor and
   the rear-view slant to the blue
exhaust of distance where I
   learned another language
to keep my family far from this
   kind of blood to skip
at least one generation.

Prime Time

"What'll ya have?" Pabst Blue
  Ribbon. It's the Friday night
fights, and the uncles and the
  father would make their bets,
and jeer the beer commercials
  between rounds. They drank Pick-
wick ale. Punkie Callahan could
  stay up and watch the fights
because of his enthusiasm, and
  I was his friend. He was trans-
fixed and became a student of all
  the moves. He would cut the air
with left hooks and grunt with
  each body blow, and predictably
he became a fighter in the Navy.
  Never made it big – just an x-
pug. He could have been a good
  one, but had no punch. Now in
the county hospital, he doesn't
  say much, but says the same
thing twice, "get em up, get em
  up." His favorite nurse makes
the rounds every night. Each time
  she walks by his room and fakes
a jab. It's the only kindness
  anyone ever shows him, and he
responds with a duck and a block.
  He is as dry as a five-cent beer
mug. Today he fingers a pet mouse
  he keeps in his pocket. With an
extra scratch on the head he will
  purposely not feed it ever again
until it stops struggling once and
  for all.

William Kemmett
from *Black Oil* (deadCpress, 2010)

RM: So, here we are at the end of the interview. Is there something else we could talk about in a 30 minute interview that we've neglected?

BK: I would just like to say that I have a handful of close friends and value those friendships: Peter Kidd, the late Wally Butts and his wife, Stephanie, Dick Martin (yours truly), Deac (James de Crescentis), the late Bob Synder, and his friend who is still alive, Peter Laska, which you could call a friendship from a distance.

RM: It's quite a group and all have benefitted from being your friend and the multiple interactions that have taken place within group. Thanks, Bill, for the interview. Now it's time to enjoy the Cape.*

BK: The only way to enjoy the Cape properly is with a good cigar and a glass of brandy.

Artifact Insertion
It Only Hurts When the Music Stops

My wife left for the afternoon
  shift, and in the absence of
her presence I scream terror and
  joy. The cat runs for cover,
but soon pesters for another
  gourmet fix.

If I had a song bird I'd open
  his cage just for the excuse.
The choice between me or the cat?
  You'd have to ask my wife.

But a saving grace: he is old
    at ten and I live forever, because
the sand in my watch has legs
    and the gears of a universe.

And now I soften the
    random evening with brandy,
while the fur of the sleeping
    cat takes on the odor
of a forbidden cigar.

William Kemmett
from *Black Oil* (deadCpress, 2010)

*Interview completed in Wellfleet, Cape Cod on August 6, 2015 due to a
smart phone malfunction in April in Port St. Lucie, Florida

Page Nineteen

Interview with Tom Haines
Hampton Suites Hotel
Binghamton, New York
May 11, 2015

RM: I'm in Binghamton with my great friend and artist, Tom Haines. Tom is the most undiscovered artist of the 21st century and late 20th century. (He's laughing at me). Undiscovered, because he so modest and hides his work away from the public. But Tom, seriously, I love your work. Talk about what you're doing right now as an artist.

TH: Right now as artist I'm not doing anything. I'm hoping to do some sculpture this summer, some painting – landscapes, and some interesting bottle people – something I dropped long ago that I thought was pretty interesting. I'm also thinking about doing some welding found-object sculpture, which is something I always liked. Right now I'm just at a point where I'll have the time to do everything that I dropped years ago. And so, I'm happy to be thinking about it all at least. And when I did art and do art, I typically like to work from the inside out.

RM: What does that mean?

TH: Well, it means the inside is my imagination; the outside is the visual world. I'll start with a blank canvas and be looking at something. OK, when I paint, a lot of times, it will look as if I'm obviously doing a landscape. But if you looked at the landscape I was doing, and then look at the landscape I painted, you'll see that they're pretty different.

RM: So the work is not representational.

TH: It's expressionistic, and there's a big difference between – well, it's representational in that you can see that it is something – that it is a landscape, which means it's representational. But it isn't like say the

Impressionists. They were actually doing scientific studies of what they were looking at. What light did. I'm not about that. I'm more like and all my stuff is more like what Van Gogh did. He was more about starting with the landscape and taking off from there, which for some is the first, the beginning of modern art, where the subjective person takes off from the thing. Like Tom Robbins in *Still Life with Woodpecker*. He's looking at a Camel pack and the story comes from that.

RM: So you use whatever object is in front of you and interact with it via your subjective, imaginative faculties.

TH: Yeah. Yeah. An approach that allows me to paint – it's the brush strokes, it's the exertion behind them, it's a bunch of different stuff. Sometimes I'll start with a blank canvas and see what will appear. My most interesting work tended to appear on the canvas and then I chased it and many times caught it. That's one way I do my stuff. Another way is to start – and I mostly did this when I painted with oils, which I hope to be doing again – with a blank canvas and remember something – like I remember a time I was on a beach in Mexico, sitting around a fire on mushrooms and talking to my girlfriend and these people who made jewelry. So I did a painting of that –thinking about that years later – of my girlfriend standing by the fire and pointing up to the sky while this other guy feeds the fire. It was just out of my head, but I liked it as a painting. Another time, I did a painting of a nude Picasso and a waitress at the diner, the one by the dam, what is its name?

RM: Park Diner.

TH: Park Diner and that painting just came out of my head.

RM: Picasso in the nude?

TH: Picasso and this waitress on the South Washington Street Bridge, just kind of leaning back talking to each other.

RM: Naked? (Laughter)

TH: Yeah (Laughter). It just came out. I just painted it, saying: "Hey, this would be cool and this would be cool…" And it just developed into that painting. And a lot of my work is like that, including the famous one that used to hang over your dining room table.

RM: Please don't mention that one. (Laughter) I had to go into therapy because of it. Many people (relatives) had to excuse themselves from Thanksgiving dinner after an eyeful of that one. (Laughter)

TH: Pardon me; it was a giblet (Laughter). But I'm saying that painting just appeared in my head, and another one….

RM: Hold on. You have to talk about that painting. But first let me give you my sense of it. First, I remember seeing you at work on it in your studio in Johnson City. I had stopped by and we smoked a joint while you continued to paint. I was mesmerized by the colors – the motion, the fluidity of the colors. It had a Van Goghesque green sky above two brown figures – one chasing the other.

TH: Right. Brown and Red.

RM: Everything was flowing, and under the influence, I was absolutely taken by the painting. And you, being the person whom you are, finished it and presented it to me as a gift, which I hung prominently in Boston in my dining room until I began realize more about those figures in a more sober mind. Now, please telling me what's going on in the painting.

TH: Well, what is going on is this: you have two men running through a field – one guy has a black beard from that cough drop box, you know, the guys with the hats – the guys from the Netherlands.

RM: The Smith Brothers – Smith Brothers Cough Drops

TH: Yeah, Smith Brothers, and one of them is running and looking back over his shoulder and this other man is running after him. And it is just what it is, whatever it is. It's my father and me. I have no idea. It was just one of these subconscious/unconscious images that just appeared to me. I find that the most interesting. It's interesting because it's a little disturbing. (Laughter)

RM: It was disturbing because this little man, who looked like Dr. Miguelito Quixote Loveless, the villain genius, from *The Wild Wild West,* didn't have any clothes on and his tiny penis was clearly exposed. (Laughter). Family members over for a feast, after checking your painting out would excuse themselves from the table, go to the bathroom, only to find when they came up, they were confronted by Billy Artim's painting of my poem, "A Terrible Dream of Words," a poem displaying severed hands in a wastebasket And that was Thanksgiving Dinner at my apartment. Then one day after looking closely at the painting, I decided the jig was up, that I needed help and a painting makeover. (Laughter). You took the painting back and replaced it with another. Still it was a beautiful painting.

TH: Yeah, but back to my point that there is a certain way that I paint and that is from the inside out to explain my initial thinking on my work.

Artifact Insertion

A Terrible Dream of Words

Now the boy can't even write yet he dreams of being a Poet. The first day of school when asked what he wants to be after accountants department store manager trainees computer specialists fast food chain operators have had their chance he gets up and says: "POET!" The next thing he knows he is in this small dark room his hands tied to a chopping block and with one swift blade stroke they are severed into a grey waste container. "That's the end of that fantasy," he hears the principal say. On the bus the kids make fun of his bandaged stumps and when his parents read the note from school pinned to his chest – YOUR CHILD EXPRESSED AN INTEREST IN BECOMING A POET they grow disgusted and send him to his room without food or water for one week.

"He must learn we will tolerate none of that nonsense," his father says. "Yes, this is certainly true," his mother says. During the week of banishment the boy learns to manipulate a pencil with either set of toes composing lovely sonnets and short open verse by the third day. Back in school the teacher asks again what he would like to be saying: "There are plenty of jobs in society for a boy without hands." Again he says: "POET!" And pulling off shoes and socks with his teeth displays his remarkable talent to the utter consternation of the teacher who later claims in a disability hearing it was at that moment heart palpitations came upon her. The small room again and this time a brown lunch bag of toes attached to the boy when he returns home. His mother faints from anger. His father carries him to his room without a word. Two weeks without food and water. The boy is determined and by the tenth day of confinement has written by mouth his first book of poems: POET RETURNS HOME FOR THE LAST TIME. Back in school the teacher shows him employment brochures that list jobs where hands and feet are not required. "Do any of these occupations interest you," she asks. Again he says: "POET!" And as he struggles to get a pencil in his mouth he is shot by a classmate who dreams of becoming a murderer for a large manufacturer of wordless commodities.

from *White Man Appears on Southern California Beach* (Bottom Fish Press, 1991, cover art by Tom Haines)

RM: Well, hold on.

TH: Imagination…inside/out…I mean, we have the physical world – mental world – imaginative world.

RM: That's right and I think that in your paintings there is a kind of magic in your figures. Many of our friends have your paintings hung in their homes. Very often the characters/figures in them appear weightless and dancing in the middle of the painting. They've lifted off the ground. Spirits going someplace and you don't know where exactly. Children are on to this. In many early drawings my childrens' figures float all over the place – above clouds, below clouds. This is not to say your paintings are childish in any way at all…

TH: No, No.

RM: There's an imaginative subconscious release in them.

TH: Yeah, that's great. I'm glad you brought that up because I've been
        drawing and making art all my life. I started drawing when I was two-
        years old – lots of stuff, and I drew all the time, so did my brothers and
        two sisters. But they stopped drawing and I continued to draw. And
        one of things I had for a long time – from childhood into adulthood –
        was flying dreams…the flying boy…the whole thing, which is pretty
        much Peter Pan. The idea of flying is part of the freedom of being an
        artist. It's tougher to do in your sixties. It's tougher to do in your fifties
        unless you're like Picasso and continuing to make money you know –
        making art I should say – which allowed him to make his next piece of
        art or painting. Yeah, the flying dreams.

Artifact Insertion

Blackberry Pie

I'm sitting in the cool
summer kitchen of childhood
with the dark fruit
picked from lime green stalks
beautiful
dangerous as tropical snakes
my Mother bakes me a pie
outside below the sunrise terraced hill
Proserpine disguised as Suzy Furman
waits for me.
the history of the world drifts by
in the fecund cumulo sky.
I'm a small being container
with the mighty senses of smell, hearing, and sight.
the crows caw in the forest called Ely Park

it will be years before they come down
and pick the carrion on the road
years before the experience and the demanding soul
will make me what I am.
so I sit
peacefully eating blackberry pie
feeding from the Mother.

Tom Haines

RM: Yeah, but we need to go back and talk about your work – the
        relationship among the imagination, memory, and the subconscious
        – streams influencing the perception of the object you're looking at
        or remembering. I get your notion of inside/out in your work but in
        regard to the outside who sees that any better than you? I've hung
        around you and you're totally connected to the world around you. I'm
        talking about your sense of color here, the joy of it, the nuances, the
        clouds, the trees, birds, mountains, rivers and people that astonish you
        in changing and fluid manifestations of color. Talk about color in your
        work and your feeling for it.

TH: Interesting. I always thought I was a pretty terrible colorist, in the
        beginning, as a painting student in college. I wanted to be a painter
        and after a year and half that's what I decided to become, an artist. I
        just started out trying to remotely get at what I was seeing, which is
        incredibly difficult to do and to this second I don't think I really got
        what's there. I might be in the vague ballpark. I could spend the rest of
        my life doing representational stuff…and really one of the things I'm
        really looking forward to is painting clouds and the figures in clouds,
        and the history of the world in clouds. There are a zillion things to see
        in clouds through your whole life. It's just been, here it is. So my sense
        of color always seems to go back to green and red for whatever reason.
        I've actually done more watercolors in my life than any other kind of
        painting. That's because watercolors are the easiest thing to take on a
        trip. I would go to Mexico for two months and paint. And, of course,
        it's very green down there. I'm not sure where the red comes from.
        I guess the green and red comes in…no…I'm sorry…blue is another

color. Green and blue are the typical colors of being a Taurus, which I read somewhere later, but every time I did stuff it seemed to come up green and blue. And so, when I'm doing watercolors in the tropics – because these are the colors – turquoise too – it was just a matter of learning to look at what was there. I was looking, but in fact I wasn't looking that closely, and I thought, well, turquoise is going to be in the sky. Well, for anyone who really looks, you're not going to see turquoise in the sky except maybe at sunset or something. But you're going to see turquoise all the time in the ocean. Now in Boston or on Martha's Vineyard that's turquoise. The Caribbean is turquoise. It's a muted turquoise or an intense turquoise. But the sky is cerulean, ultramarine, manganese. And then you have all the different colors of sand, and basically color, if you're asking me about color, it's about trying to match up, if you're trying to be exacting, which on some level I am and I'm not. But I like to make an interesting painting and that's at the end of the process because if you haven't made an interesting painting, what's the point? And a beautiful painting I would hope. And beauty, what that is, would take a six hour interview.

Artifact Insertion

Colors

My idea arrived in a blue limousine.
There was little to account for:
sleet hammered the house
a parade of lost souls settled for wind,
uprooted trees, shattered glass.
The oven timer went off.
Using crayons and buttressing resolve
with a box of animal crackers
I started to recolor my mind.
"Perhaps I will even reconstruct it
or build it from scratch
if there's time to use both glue
and scissors," I whispered.

You know add a triangle or two.
Let an apple drop from a fragile branch.
Attach Brazil to the next dream.
I was tired of thoughts and imagery
from an earlier life.
I could shout: *child*.
See boxes of marble placed around the crib.
Hold in my hand a packet of rose petals
moistened by holy water.
There were plenty of days
when saints on the wall
failed to hear the rain
or record the look in my eyes
when the bird in mind
grew lovely black wings.
It's a matter of breath and less definition.
With green I roam into open meadows.
Yellow is my light.
I'm not afraid of using red stars
or growing into a big sky
with some shade of purple.
No more bars or rules!
Trembling when the light in the closet
flickers out.
My mind is the ocean.
Listen to the silver surf still left in my box.

from *Marks* (Asylum Arts, 2002, cover art by Tom Haines)

RM: Well, I do think people look at your work and find your paintings
       intriguing. It's not a one shot deal when viewing one of your
       paintings. Your work keeps drawing the viewer in and the more
       one looks at the painting the more one discovers his/her own
       imagination. Your paintings resurrect, provoke and revitalize the
       imagination. Your paintings give the stolen imagination back to the
       viewer, i.e. the viewer's imagination is released via your imagination.
       This is a fundamental reaction people have to your work.

TH: That's great – that would be wonderful if that happened.

RM: That is happening, OK. It's just that you're out of it. You don't realize it. So, now let's talk about your favorite painters – those who influenced you.

TH: Well, I think the first time I was aware of an interesting image was maybe in the fourth or third grade – something like that. It was an illustration in a book my mom and dad had about the "The Highwayman," you know the poem: "The moon was a ghostly galleon…" by Walter C. Noyes, I think. Or maybe that's a used car salesman on Route 17. (Laughter). He could have been the same guy, who knows? Actually, Alfred was the Poet. Walter, the used car guy.

RM: Come on down!

TH: So we have Bess the landlord's black-eyed daughter and a shotgun was up…the landlord's daughter was absolutely beautiful and she was at the window in the illustration, and if memory serves me correct, they (British soldiers) had taken the shotgun and stuck it between her tits. They were waiting for him (Highwayman) to come back. Bess was the bait and he does come back. They gun him down. Those were the first images I liked. Plus, I thought the poem was great, madly heroic and romantic. I thought they were tremendous and from there I started looking at lots of stuff, in high school, mostly in college. I always thought the watercolors of Winslow Homer were great. Also that watercolorist, whose painting greets as you enter the Gardner Museum in Boston, John Singer Sargent, I like his work.

Artifact Insertion
The Highwayman
By Alfred Noyes
Part 1

The wind was a torrent of darkness upon the gusty trees,
The moon was a ghostly galleon tossed upon cloudy seas,

The road was a ribbon of moonlight looping the purple moor,
And the highwayman came riding–
Riding–riding–
The highwayman came riding, up to the old inn door.
He'd a French cocked hat on his forehead, and a bunch of lace at his chin;
He'd a coat of the claret velvet, and breeches of fine doe-skin.
They fitted with never a wrinkle; his boots were up to his thigh!
And he rode with a jeweled twinkle--
His rapier hilt a-twinkle--
His pistol butts a-twinkle, under the jeweled sky.
Over the cobbles he clattered and clashed in the dark inn-yard,
He tapped with his whip on the shutters, but all was locked and barred,
He whistled a tune to the window, and who should be waiting there
But the landlord's black-eyed daughter–
Bess, the landlord's daughter–
Plaiting a dark red love-knot into her long black hair.

Source: Poetry Foundation
        Collected Poems (1947)

TH: But the biggest influences on my work are Van Gogh and Picasso. I really love Van Gogh. There is so much emotion in his work and his story is a killer. He tries to be a preacher for three years and is an abject failure. His ministry was in the coal-mining district of Borinage in Belgium. They kick him out because his task was to write the best sermon anyone could, and, of course, he can't and he is beating himself up. So anyway they throw him out and he becomes a painter. And he paints for 7 years and paints all these wonderful things, and he was also a botanist. A great story. And Gauguin, I always thought he was great. I like a lot different things – just like a variety of foods. It's the same thing. Art is a huge banquet of ideas and images.

Artifact Insertion

Preachers

The preachers of divine harmony
have just been murdered
by the preachers of ultimate war

You had to have cable tv
to witness it.

The preachers of ultimate war
have just been murdered
by very poor ratings.

It says so right here
in TV Guide.

from *Modulations* (Asylum Arts, 1998, cover art by Tom Haines)

RM: What about Pollack?

TH: Sure, I like Pollack. But I love Picasso. Picasso was the guy. He
        was so protean. Everything he touched he could change. He could
        move from one thing to another like a musician who can play one
        instrument then play all instruments. He was like that, a genius
        piano player. Name it and he could play it. His thing was freedom.
        He remained representational. In fact, he called himself a realist –
        what he saw he was actually seeing. Picasso is intellectually great.
        He was influenced by different poets around him – Apollinaire, Max
        Jacob, Andre Breton. I don't know if read much, he probably did, but
        he worked a lot. He talked to these guys, and they told him, here's
        what is going on. And he took in ideas. Picasso is contemporaneous
        with the Theory of Relativity. A nose being on the side of the face, or
        one eye bigger than the other, all of that is the Theory of Relativity
        in paint. Cubism is literally the Theory of Relativity in paint, which
        was out there and being talked about and also X Rays had just been
        invented – how wild that he was painting the invisible (X Rays) and
        relativity.

RM: How are you making the connection between the Theory of

Relativity and Cubism?

TH: Well, if you look at Picasso at a certain state, I mean there it is. I'm saying in the Cubist period of his work he's addressing relativity, a relative view – the invisible architecture of the X Rays.

RM: Of the observer?

TH: Looking at a person and saying you can't possibly get this image as a static thing. It has to be a moving thing. It's almost like the Doppler Effect. There is distortion – the view is from multiple angles.

Artifact Insertion

Doppler Effect

Sitting in a Camaro.
The smell of love and liquor
on the seats
saxophone tales of New Jersey
on the 8 track.
Jack and his Blues
and Buddha
on my lap
waiting for a friend
outside the LA Times.
Thinking: Buddha's been shot
on 405 the message
flashed on smog alert signs:
JOIN THE TREND
CARPOOL WITH A FRIEND.
Thinking: Emptiness
is serious
I gaze out the window
at the mythology of moths

and orange flowers.
Strangers pass.
AM FM lunch pails
suitcase cassettes
plugged into ears.
And I without a fifth
or patriarch
the mirror of mind
salted with petrochemical dust
lost in the Doppler Effect
of Enlightenment.

from *White Man Appears on Southern California Beach* (Bottom Fish Press, 1991, cover art by Tom Haines)

RM: So it's an object moving through space and time?

TH: Yes, it's an object moving through time and space, but also a lot of time and a lot of space. If I wanted to do a portrait of you, really as dramatic and truthful as I can be in a Cubist influence, it would have to be from myriad viewpoints. It would have to be – obviously people do portraits of people right now – but Picasso was saying I want to paint you from here, from here, from here, and I also want to do you from just remembering you. I want to do all these takes and different moments in time in painting a portrait.

RM: I can understand this within this context: I heard a physicist on the radio the other day while driving and waiting in Boston traffic he described spacetime as a loaf of bread. The front slices of loaf, or spacetime, are the future of the universe. The end piece is the Big Bang and the start of spacetime inflation, and the middle slices represent the changing present. What aspect of spacetime comes into our lens depends on our observation point and rate of speed. Get the observer to the speed of light and things change radically in terms of what is observed. His point in all of this was that the past, present, and future are happening simultaneously. The universe is being born, moving through spacetime, and expanding all simultaneously, if we could only see it in its entirety as we can observe a loaf of bread. I'm a baby, a young man, old man and a dead man, and hopefully, a reborn man (Remember Whitman said he would return in thirteen trillion years) all at once. Thank God for the present and a reduced speed. Does this relate a little bit to what you're saying – observation over time?

TH: Yeah, it's in there though there are a couple of things in the mix besides the Theory of Relativity, though that is in the mix of Cubism. It's also the time when X-rays were invented. So that everything that is invisible – like looking at my leg – nice leg – but underneath if you take an X-ray of it, now you see everything that you couldn't see before.

RM: But if you keep going past the X-ray and you move into the actual atoms that your leg is made of and the protons and quarks etc., all of that, you're moving into the invisibility that exists inside of you.

TH: Right.

RM: You know what I'm saying. Even though we're substantial, we're also not simultaneously.

TH: Oh yeah, it's pretty miraculous that my leg doesn't just float off. But, here's what Picasso is doing, he's painting the invisible. He painting all the pins in all the architecture. He's building a whole new way of seeing existence; that's my point about relativity. It's a new view, a totally new view. It's taking the Renaissance and everything on the table, which he is very aware of as a wonderful painter, and just tipping the table over. It's like we're starting again, doing something absolutely radical. And it was great, and he was enough of a creative person to accomplish this. I don't know, Cubism was 1902 -1914, something in that range. And at the end of WW I, Picasso is painting classically, marries this woman, Olga, and paints beautiful paintings – gorgeous paintings, and so much more – sculptures, found object stuff that he creates. He and Braque created Cubism.

RM: So you love, Picasso.

TH: And I love the freedom of the Abstract Expressionists in America, and other artists before them. John Marin, for example, who was a twenties-thirties painter. I really love his work. Some Dali stuff, I dig, although not as much as I did when I was in high school…because he's not the end all, but he's still interesting. I've been in museums and seen stuff and said who did that, and then, WOW! it was Dali. He's pretty easy to spot but sometimes he isn't.

RM: All right this is great but we running out of time and I want to hit on a couple of other things with you.

TH: Sure.

RM: Talk a little bit about Paris, because I have some paintings you did in Paris when you carried an easel on your back… paintings of buildings and bridges…

TH: L'lie de la cite.

RM: It would be great to go there again. So your Parisian paintings are up in my house. But here we are in Binghamton. And walking around Binghamton is walking around your house and home because you have renovated so many buildings in this city. You've restored them through your company Tom Haines's Renovation and brought color into the city. Talk about that.

TH: Well, when I started I thought of myself as sort of a Potemkin painter. I wanted it to look like something was going on in Binghamton. So, if you came down into Binghamton, you could no longer say the place is terrible, it's depressing. When I walked into Binghamton and I really started looking at the buildings, I thought these are beautiful buildings. They're really interesting. But people weren't looking at them or looking up at them because there was nothing to look at unless I painted them and painted them interestingly. When I painted the buildings, I never repeated myself. I painted to make each building as interesting and unique as possible. The city wasn't into that. City officials told me to paint by being cognizant of the buildings next to each other. I told them I disagreed with that view. Each building needed to be painted so it's interesting to look at as an end in itself. It's sort of like clothing. I might be wearing something that's interesting and the next person is too and so on, as opposed to everyone wearing the same uniform.

RM: Like the building color evident in New Orleans.

TH: Yeah, New Orleans is wonderful. And I guess my love of color comes from 5 trips to Mexico and being there for a couple of months each time. I've also been to Jamaica a couple of times and to Dominque.

RM: Bermuda also displays buildings with a variety of colors.

TH: I've never been to Bermuda, but I've been to the Caribbean quite a bit.

RM: So color for Bingo buildings, instead of painting them grey to match a grey sky.

TH: Yeah, Binghamton city officials had actually two colors for me – grey and black. You're kidding me! Black in Binghamton!

RM: Yeah. We already have the gun to our heads.

TH: Give me the bullet, come on. So, I wanted to paint the buildings so people would be interested in looking at them, and I think I did.

RM: Did you take photos of every building?

TH: Not of every building, no.

RM: Do you have a collection of photos?

TH: I have some, sure. Mike Gaul, my good friend, who is unfortunately no longer with us and who read in our the Big Horror Series, used to take some pictures of my stuff. Mike was another Binghamton painter, along with Michael Kelly.

RM: Do you have access to his photos?

TH: Yes, Mike gave them to me. Plus my mom took some pictures.

RM: Is the former McLean's Department Store building your masterpiece?

TH: Yes. For starters it's a great building. It's a cast iron building by Isaac Perry who is one of the three big architects around here, and not just around here. He had a big hand in the design and building of the State Capitol. So I started out with a great building to begin with but they had painted it terribly. In the 19th century, cast iron buildings were painted to look like masonry buildings. I'm not sure why, maybe because there were so many cast iron buildings. Well, I thought that was insane in a rust-belt town that was dying and trying to come back. What's neat about the building is that it is cast iron. I painted it a patina green. I painted it so it would look like it was copper. It did patina-out but not exactly into copper, but into a cool combination. I got all kinds of shit from the city but people passing by gave me the thumbs up.

RM: Absolutely. The building is magnificent. One building that is close to my heart is the one you painted in red brick and used some of the money from it to start Bottom Fish Press —the press that published *White Man Appears on Southern California Beach*. In 2016, the book will celebrate its 25th anniversary. I'm talking about the old Fair Store Building. Talk about your press and how my book came into being.

TH: OK. First, let finish about the colors of the building, and how they came about. The Fair Store building is a building on the river as you cross the bridge into Binghamton, it is the first building on the left.

RM: Crossing the Chenango River?

TH: Crossing the Chenango, coming into downtown Binghamton. They were actually six separate buildings in my initial proposal, and I thought of keeping with my basic idea of doing each building in its own unique colors. But the person in charge from Blue Cross and Blue Shield that owned the buildings said no to that. He told me he was too conservative for that approach. I wanted the buildings to look like something out of the Amalfi coast in Italy. So, I said ok, and said to him that I see you're wearing a conservative red jacket, grey slacks, cream-colored shirt and tie of such and such, and so the clothing he wore that day became the colors of the building. The buildings came out fine and look fine today. Well, it was a big job, and I made some good money back then. I put ten grand from the job into Bottom Fish Press. That's part of the story. Remember, we went down to see the publisher who originally had decide to publish your work, in Manhattan, what was the name of that press?

RM: East Coast Theater and Publishing Co.

TH: OK, you wanted me to do the cover for it. I experimented with some watercolors, a beach scene and a couple of rubbings. Then I did a bigger painting of it and we finally ended up with a cover.

RM: That's right. It's coming back to me. I have the original cover for the book hanging in the foyer of my house. Time is screwing me up some. I thought the whole book project with East Coast had blown up before I met you and your brother, Billy, in Tom and Marty's Bar by chance. It had been years since I had seen Billy and really didn't know you at all.

TH: No, we went down and met with the publisher. I remember thinking what this guy says sounds great but is he being realistic. He had kids, a business, and was building a house upstate – a typical New Yorker. Type AAAA….And then for whatever reason, it didn't come off.

RM: Yes, it didn't happen. The press gave it shot under the conditions and even guaranteed a hundred books to be delivered prior to a book party reading at Swat Sullivan's. Two days before the reading the books hadn't arrived. Then I get a call from the publisher's wife saying that her husband had a breakdown of some sort and had left the house and was driving around somewhere in Queens.

TH: So, I said why don't we do the book and Bottom Fish Press came into being. I started work on another cover. And one day, I just looked at one of the brushes I had been using on the Fair Store and said, "God, that looks like a face with bristly red hair." I've always been into things appearing as something other than what they are. So I thought it would be great to have this face close to the plane of the book with a little beach scene built behind it. I know the book party proceeded without a book. But we eventually had a great book party. Remember, we were at my house the day the book arrived.

RM: Yeah, and we ran out of your house when we saw the FedEx truck.

TH: Yeah, at first, it went by my house and then came back.

RM: You had a pen in your mouth and must have bitten it or something because your mouth was bleeding as we reached the truck. The guy opens up the back and there are all the boxes of books. The guy considers our excitement and asks: "Pornography?"

TH: You bet.

RM: Thanks for book, Tom, and for this interview. May many more enjoy your original art and take a stroll through Haines Village.

Artifact Insertion

White Man Appears On Southern California Beach

1

So it's my day off from the drug store
and I've managed to rip off a few amphetamines
'cause Sammy-boy the pharmacist is such a puke
and the day before was so FUCKING! SPACED OUT!
ON ALL THE COCAINE! AND SHIT HE DOES!
he stepped out for a breath of air
'cause there were not many customers
except a few old ladies you see everywhere in Santa Monica
old and rich as hell
wandering into shops
to check out the latest ivory trinkets and antique horseshit

till they eventually make it to the DRUG QUEEN
for some talcum powder for their old salt-rusted skins
and a few dull minutes of staring at bottles
of Jean Nate and Oil of Olay

IF YOU CAN DIG THAT!

On the day of my speedDEMONheist
I am stocking vitamin shelves
right in front of Sammy's highass counter
near the little entrance way
that leads to the feudal walls of Drugdom.
Sammy's job is such a push over
his most exerting task
is the number count of valiums and libriums
or any new tranq some wimp salesman from Squibb
or Holy Dow says is GOOD SHIT! with few contraindications
and will really calm those nerve endings
having wild neurotic guilt parties
in the skins of frantic stressed Americans.

FOR SURE…

While all the time the fat safe drug kings and queens
stuff tranquility bucks
into mansions pools elaborate security systems
(putting the poor stupid ferocious guard dog
in the unemployment line)
soothing their own Blue Blood Dendrites in redwood hots
with some slick babe
driving their Silver Royce down a stretch of
DESERTED GUARDED PRIVATE PROPERTY
hiring some imported Hindu swami to guide
create their meditations of Obese Nirvana
and if these fail?

Well

JOG THE BALLS OFF
CRUSH MAGNESIUM PILLS IN THE MORNING O.J.
GET TO THE EXECUTIVE TOWER WITH A SPEECH
FOR SUBHUMAN EAGERBEAVER MANAGERS
TO INSPIRE THE MANIC CHEMISTS UNDER THEIR COMMAND
TO CREATE ANOTHER MINDLESS DRUG FROM THEIR ALCHEMICAL

F $ A $ N $ T $ A $ S $ S $ I $ E $ S.

from *White Man Appears on Southern California Beach*, Bottom Fish Press, 1991, cover art by Tom Haines)

INTERVIEW WITH JAMES DE CRESCENTIS
MARCH 5, 2016
BOSTON, MA

RM: It's good to see you, Deac, and thanks for making the trip from the South End to West Roxbury. As you can see, your paintings and collages remain in prominent places throughout my home. In fact, the place is a mini-museum of your work. Over the years, Eileen and I have bought your work and received some as gifts thanks to your generosity. Eileen has one of your large paintings in her office downtown. So, we're James de Crescentis fans. Welcome.

JdC: Thank you for your patronage and friendship over the years. It's good to be here today.

RM: Now, a number of years ago, two of your paintings were featured in the Luxembourg literary/art journal, *Estuaries*. I wrote a brief introduction to your work for the European audience. I entitled that introduction, "At the Altar of Color." In it, I described your work – your paintings – as "necessary ecstasies for the eyes." And the artist, Tom Haines, has noted "the perfect beauty of his colors, clarity of his line, and energy." Let's get at these "ecstasies;" talk about your development as a painter.

JdC: I started working as a painter in 1969 and was basically just fooling around. Then there were many years when I didn't paint (1982-1991.) I was in Bowling Green, OH, working on my MFA in Creative Writing and then in Rochester, NY, until 1987. Poetry and teaching were my focus during that stretch. I returned to Boston in the summer of 1987, and I'm still here. In 1991, I went to an art show featuring younger artists and was very moved by their work. I decided I needed to paint again. When I returned to my apartment, it took me 45 minutes to find where I had packed my brushes. I had some white latex paint left and some black paint from the time I put a prose poem on my door, enlarging it using an opaque projector. I had a piece of sheet

rock which I had cut down to pop into the door to prevent people
from seeing what I was doing. So I had brushes, paint, plus a little
red and green acrylic and thought, OK, what am I going to paint. It
was around midnight and I spotted the sheet rock; I had emptied the
paint roller on it and this left it with some random white patterns.
And I thought, perfect, and began the process of creating a painting,
a painting a lot of my poet friends became very interested in and
fascinated by.

RM: What was the title of the painting?

JdC: "Breaking The Lightbulb Of Song," which is also the title of one of my
        prose poems.

RM: In your new book?
JdC: That's right.

Artifact Insertion

Breaking The Lightbulb Of Song

A light would go off in his head whenever he left the
house without his machete, and he wondered how he'd cut
through the thick reeds like a panther stalked by angry
men. The evening is electric with drugs, fires break out
in slick back alleys, assault weapons go off in a
spray of random death, an aftertaste of violence
permeates the very soul of resistance. The house usually
feels like a prison, a cave of light gone berserk during
some misguided spell, candles waiting in purple, or a
fast shift of colors rushing through the body.

He finds a cloud to ride downtown before the demolition
ball breaks the skyline, no one knew the architect spoke
about paying off all transparent dangers, like some rich
crash down this spiral blush of kissing the knee too many
times causes a rash move of fingertips towards buttons,
which are everywhere, might be the babysitter.

James de Crescentis

from *Pounding The Door Into Gray* (Igneus Press, 2015)

RM: We'll get to your new book in a little bit. But for now, what other materials have you used in the creation of your paintings?

JdC: OK, here's a little tale associated with another painting. I was returning to my apartment one very humid Fourth of July, and there happened to be a dumpster outside my building. I took a peek into it and there at the bottom was a piece of ¾ inch plywood. It was the only thing in the dumpster. I thought it would be too difficult to remove. So I went upstairs to my place and had dinner. Around midnight, I decided I wanted to paint. Plus I had a bottle of white wine in the refrigerator that I had forgotten about. I went back to the dumpster for the plywood and with some work I got that "fucker" out of it and carried it upstairs. I had very limited art supplies, but managed to create a painting titled "Ultimate Grasshopper."

RM: I thought the original title was "Kermit on Prozac."

JdC: No, that was one of the paintings featured in *Estuaries*. Don't you remember? You gave me the title for the painting. It was a fairly good size piece and when you saw it you said: "Ultimate Grasshopper, Deac." I thought it over, and remembered as I struggled to get the plywood out of the dumpster, it was more or less surrounded by grasshoppers. So everything in the title is kind of related.

RM: So the work we're talking about now could be labeled abstract expressionism. But, I also noted in the "Estuaries" introduction: "de Crescentis brings new evocative dance steps to the dance of abstract expressionism."

JdC: Yes, the paintings we've been discussing are in that vein. But people see things in them.

Artifact Insertion

"I have seem ultimate grasshoppers, frogs on Prozac,
battalions of comets, the birth and death of galaxies,
the sky through a squashed grape and the grand
parades of vivid wraiths through green seas struck
by lightning in his work. Critics have mentioned
lively jungles, herds of black horses, dragons,
and travelers lost in blizzards."

Richard Martin
from "At The Altar Of Color" (Estuaries, 1996)

RM: Tell me about it. Your abstract paintings pulsate with forms and
       transformations. Talk about the creative process that allows your
       work to be so rich in dimensions and possibilities.

JdC: I'm not painting like that anymore. Now I work mostly in the
       daytime.But for many years, and for many of the paintings, the
       process of creating them would start late, around 11 PM or so. To
       be honest with you, I drank about eight Sam Adam's during the
       development and creation of a painting. When I cracked open the
       fourth beer is when I mixed the paints. And everything happened
       after that.

RM: So are you saying you had to have a little buzz on, Deac?

JdC: More than a little one.

RM: Wasn't rock-n-roll also part of the late night process via headphones?

JdC: Yes, I had a "joggers' belt to hold a discman, and I would dance
       around my apartment. And the whole time I was preparing the paints
       I had the music turned up really loud. I grew into the evening. Once
       I started the painting, it went really fast. I would finish around 4 AM,
       have a snack and go to bed.

RM: So it would be accurate to say a "mania" or maniacal dance was underway in your studio on many nights after 11 PM – more or less whipping yourself into some visionary stance, sight or position.

JdC: Yes, I created my own maniac episode.

RM: And you had the space, the studio, to wander into the night with a paintbrush in your hand.

JdC: Yes, I wandered.

RM: Did your involvement with abstract expressionism evolve or grow from previous work and interests? What artists do you admire and/or were influenced by?

JDC: I would have to say my influences were Pablo Picasso, Willem de Kooning, and of course Jackson Pollock, the latter showing me the freedom of how paint can be applied to whatever I was painting on.

RM: So now that you have stopped painting at night and have moved into the light, let's talk about what you're up to during the daylight hours.

JdC: It essentially means that I start with a cup of coffee and on my board I have a sheet of heavy watercolor paper. This paper can be saturated, and hold a lot of paint etc. I start by taking a sharpie and draw a couple of things. I'll keep adding through the day and sometimes over a period of several days. I've slowed the process down. On a recent piece after drawing with the sharpie, I took a bottle of black ink and pen and drew some more. Black ink is darker, more pronounced than a black sharpie. But then I got bored with it and dumped the entire bottle of black ink and completely covered it. I rushed the work into the shower. Water creates a very nice accent as most of the black ink comes off. I'll let the drawing sit around for a few days to dry. When I looked at the work, I thought what if I mix titanium white acrylic so it becomes like a wash. Then I took a sponge brush and covered the entire piece. But now, shit man, the whole thing is white. So I threw it in the shower again. This time the top of the drawing is mainly black ink but little remnants of white adhered to the drawing in a very subtle manner. At the point, I stopped working on the drawing. The process is so much different than painting at night. Those big paintings were done in acrylics and oils, moving basically from acrylics to oils. With the daytime drawings I'm into sharpies, markers, and ink. When I get bored I explore other mediums.

RM: So is dumping a bottle of black ink over a drawing and then putting it in the shower a deliberate choice, a spontaneous reaction, or just an accident?

JdC: A combination of them. I had to do something when it was all black or all white before it dried and set. The accidental beauty resides in what the water washes away and what remains on the paper. After it completely dries, I saturate it in the bathtub again. I then clamp it between two boards so that it then dries flat. There is a certain risk to this procedure, but that's part of the mystery like a chance encounter.

RM: How productive have you been in the daylight?

JdC: I have a new one started on watercolor paper, 22 inches by 30 inches. I bought oil based paint markers to work on it – black and silver ones. I've started out with an abstract drawing with these markers. This drawing is a much bigger version of the black and white drawings I have filled sketch books with. So it's on my board now and every morning I look at it and add something. I can't tell how many sharpies I've destroyed pounding them into the paper.

RM: All of this work, both at night and during the day, takes place in your home and studio in the well-known Piano Factory in the South End of Boston. You've lived there for quite some time.

JdC: That's where you met me in 1981, remember?

RM: That's right I came to Boston in 1981.

JdC: Yes, you were the unexpected visitor to my studio.

RM: Right, I was with Joel Dailey.

JdC: Yeah, he asked my permission if he could bring you to my studio. He came in with his girlfriend at the bus station and I was there to meet him. You were sort of standing off to the side, wearing a pair of moon boots. It was a horrible winter. And Dailey said: "This is Dick Martin; he's going through a hard time. And I said: "Sure, bring him along."

RM: That was a pretty special encounter. We hung out, drank some beers and shared some poems.

JdC: It went to about three or four in the morning.

RM: You encouraged me to send my "hospital" poems to the NEA.

JdC: I gave you the address. You were very skeptical at first, but I made you take it. Then when I got my rejection notice from the NEA, I looked down the award list… there you were – Dick Martin, Avon, New York. I said that motherfucker! He got the grant on his first try.

RM: Help me out. Have you been living at the Piano Factory since 1981?

JdC: No, I lived here from 1980-1982 and then left for graduate school. I picked up my MFA at Bowling Green. After that I lived in Rochester and came back to Boston in 1987.

RM: The Piano Factory is not what it used to be, is it?

JdC: That's an understatement. It's not even close to what it used be – a home for working artists – an affordable home. We had an agreement with the landlord that ran out in 2014, which protected the original gallery. We were advised by our attorney to start negotiating with the owner. He always wanted to move the gallery and put in a Lobby in its place. We spent a year negotiating and we now have a new gallery. Once the new gallery got put it, the lobby went in and then the place went crazy. I view the courtyard from my studio. They cut down two beautiful pine trees in the courtyard and dismantled the theater in favor of an indoor pool and fitness center.

RM: Did all this happen because the agreement with the original tenants expired?

JdC: Yes. The agreement that we won in negotiation ran from 1999 through 2014.

RM: The Piano Factory isn't for artists anymore?

JdC: No, it's not.

RM: For students, right?

JdC: Students and also young high-end professionals. They pay ridiculous rents to live here and stay about a year or two.

RM: So the community of artists has been more or less pushed out due to higher rents.

JdC: The community of artists is essentially gone.

RM: That's regrettable but a few of you are left and continue to be productive. You hosted some great art openings, readings, and parties in the old gallery as the Director of the Gallery, parties that often migrated to your studio and continued through the night. Thank you for all of it. But with the time left I want to switch to your new book, *Pounding The Door Into Gray*, from Igneus Press, a collection of prose poems written some time ago.

JdC: I ran the original gallery in 1995, 2008, and 2010 through 2013.

Artifact Insertion

Pounding The Door Into Gray

I scrape the floor like the rent in my nails. My lungs,
away from the rain forest, slip into forbidden nights.
It seems as if all the animals are dying, packed in sand,
not feeling any muscle spasms.

I dance in the stairwell of cobwebs without killing any
living spiders, so they collect again. Dangling down all
nearby factories, this shaft is dangerously low and can
wreck itself with nets.

I bend into the cave of light, and separate these
transparent bones. Throwing evidence, a sliver fingers
the moon and waits downstairs. This is how the electric
walks, splitting this temple called home.

James de Crescentis
from *Pounding The Door Into Gray* (Igneus Press, 2015)

JdC: I wrote the poems 24 to 25 years ago.

RM: But they don't have that feel to them. They are immediate and present.
       I read them again the other day and I came away with a feeling of the
       "madness of sanity" moving through the poems. Images melt into
       each other and/or leap over each other, yet reality – the reality of the
       streets is described and often the violence in them but not in a typical
       fashion, the phrasing…the structure of the poems is unique. The
       poems come at the reader, demand engagement.

JdC: Thank you. The poems are not light hearted nor for the light-hearted.

RM: What lies behind the creation of them…the process etc.

JdC: Well, the process is very similar to how I paint. Again, music played a part. I wrote these poems with headphones on. I interacted with the music and the music may have generated some of the images. Basically, it was spontaneous composition. I turn on my computer, look at the blank screen, and start writing. There were written fast without much editing, at times no editing at all. I wrote them when I had an apartment facing Tremont St. and my view was very urban with a rhythm of danger.

RM: The streets are clearly manifested in these poems. In the opening poem of the collection, "Breaking The Lightbulb Of Song," a person leaves the house with a machete.

JdC: That image was not generated through music. It came from a poster I bought when I went to visit Joel Dailey for Mardi Gras 1989. The poster shows a panther moving through reeds with men stalking it. I took the image from the poster and threw it into the poem. I grab everything.

RM: That's interesting…the notion of spontaneously grabbing images from anywhere and letting them leap and associate with each other as the poem is written…a grand accumulation. However, there are fragments of description, i.e. defining an event or situation…some anchor for the reader in the flow of imagery.

JdC: It's a combination of effects – imagery amid description.

RM: Crashing into each other?

JdC: That's right. I'll send you the review written by Richard Wilhelm (poet & artist) and published in the Somerville Times by Doug Holder. The review stated that "he is smashing narrative, disrupting any kind of narrative." I wrote some of the poems during the time I was working at the Lindermann Mental Health Center on a locked unit in Boston. I did the 4 PM-midnight shift. Just by observing them, I moved into a persona representing them. When I use "I" in the poems, it is not me.

RM: Sure, Deac, I knew it was you. Everyone always says the "I" is not me. (Laughter).

JdC: I guess I thought I was a staff member and I actually was a patient. (Laughter).

RM: Joking aside, I agree with the reviewer's comment. Narrative is getting smashed, as well as tables and other things in the poems.

JdC: You're referring to the poem, "Warehousing The Corpses," which mentions a table and a puzzle on it?

RM: Yeah.

JdC: That image came about as a result of being on duty one night. I was monitoring the hall and there was a room at the facility where patients could go and work on puzzles and other things. I happened to be walking by when a patient working on a puzzle in the room got so frustrated that he just flipped the table over, pieces of the puzzle flying through the air.

Artifact Insertion

Warehousing The Corpses

I want to break the table in front of me so it looks like
a puzzle flying in pieces all over the badly painted
room. Then the attendants will take notice and run in
shouting these restraints are ready to clip your wings,
which have been singed often enough but we'll do it one
more time for the paycheck bounces into Commonwealth
River, and it's hot outside.

In here, the pulse moves faster and faster. I cry out
for cigarettes I forget to buy earlier, and the boom
box's frenzied headphones take their pause. They have
been stirred up by a new system and keep eyeing the

furniture with that kindling intention in mind. This
crowd marches on and all their delusions, worked out,
don't matter.

James de Crescentis
from *Pounding The Door Into Gray* (Igneus Press, 2015)

RM: How long did you work in psychiatric health care?

JdC: Twenty-four years all together. The Lindemann was an agency job.
When I worked there for two years, it was a sprawling unit with sixty
patients.

RM: Well, we are getting short on time. One last question: What is the
relationship between the poet and painter in you?

JdC: It's a constant struggle. I go back and forth between the two. However,
visual art has more or less taken over. I don't write as much as I used
to. There was a period when it was just the opposite – more writing,
less art. Sometimes both have been operative at the same time – a
period of equalization. That remains the ultimate goal for me – to
write a poem and then switch to painting.

RM: Well, as a fan of your poetry and patron of your art, I'm glad you get to
both. Thanks for spending some time with me to today.

JdC: Thanks, Dick. It is always good to see you.

INTERVIEW WITH JV MILLER
PROPRIETOR OF ARTFUNKLE
APRIL 22, 2016
CLARION, PA

RM: I'm sitting in the backroom of ArtFunkle with JV Miller, writer, poet and proprietor of ArtFunkle in Clarion, PA. JV has turned off *Cannon* so we can talk about his recent book, *What Else Do You Want?* published by Lavender Ink Press in collaboration with the admired literary magazine, *Fell Swoop: The All Bohemian Revue.* JV's book has taken the reading public by storm, selling numerous copies and garnering praise from savvy readers. The book centers on family – mother, father, uncles, brothers, and grandparents. JV, talk about your book. It seems at times almost autobiographical, keying in on your family's experiences. What's going on in *What Else Do You Want?*

JV: Well, thanks, Richard. *What Else Do You Want?* is a book of short stories, quite a few of them I wrote a number of years ago – 20 years ago, but some are much more recent than that. The original story ("What Else Do You Want?") comes out of or came about from the notion everyone has a story to tell. I mean everyone has phenomenal things that happen in their lives which they can or could turn into amazing narratives if constructed properly and in a language accessible to others. The older stories – the ones which I say I wrote a couple of decades ago, when I first wrote them I thought these were really funny and a bit sad. And then, just a few years ago when the book was coming to fruition, becoming a real object, and of course, I had to dive back into the stories, edit them, reconstruct to some degree, my view of them changed. Once I moved through the editing process, I thought these stories are really sad stories. Maybe as I get older, the sadness percolates to the top more than the humor. Well, I think the humor is still present in the stories, at least I hope so, but there is something else there now. People pass away, as happens to all of us as we go through time and interact with others, our family and loved ones etc. *What Else Do You Want?*, the title story of the collection is a free form poem and the rest of the book is structured as five typical short stories. The free form poem, the last piece in the book, is about my dear father who is a main character in the book. He was a depression-era child, so his idea of quality food was quantity– more food meant better food. So that story (poem) is about that experience, which we often had. The story encapsulates a particular day when we went to a chain restaurant for an all you can eat lunch buffet. For my dad, that is all you had to say – all you can eat. Dad would say: "All you can eat? Well, I can eat a lot and it's cheap too, so let's go."

Artifact Insertion

'Well, I'll tell you what,' he says
'You,
and me,
and Sue
will go out
to the Ponderosa.
On Saturday
they
have a breakfast buffet.
It's beautiful!
I've got a coupon
that's good
till the twenty-sixth.
A dollar off
on each
breakfast.
That's what
I was
Just checking'
'Breakfast buffet, huh,' I say
I'm less than enthused…

'So what do they have there?'
she asks

He smiles
knowing
glowing
holds up
an open hand
palm towards him
& with his other
index finger
he counts
off digits
'They've got bacon,'
The index finger
goes back
'They've got eggs,'
back goes
finger two
'They've got sausage,'
the ring
finger
bows
'They've got waffles,'
the pinky
is forced
to acknowledge
'What else do you want?'
he says
thrusting out both
open hands
like Christ
imploring
the minions…

from *What Else Do You Want?*
J.V. Miller
(Lavender Ink/Fell Swoop, 2013)

RM: I found the book to be quite sad in effect after reading the stories. However, humor infiltrates the sadness in the characters' lives through funny and bizarre scenes. For example, the story about watching a Sunday afternoon football game with your dad and your brother, and your dad goes pretty crazy watching it, and hurls insults and slurs at the players and pretty much every race on the planet. It's pretty funny in seeing how wildly mad he gets about a football game. But then as the story and stories reveal the father through his years as a worker at IBM and also your grandfather and what they had to do to earn a living, the humor is tempered. Life is tough, dirty, and dangerous in American factories. Your stories also capture the immigrant experience – your grandparents coming here from Ruthenia. Talk about your sense of the immigrant experience and how it informs some of the stories.

JV   Well, certainly, it's somewhat universal – people come to America because they want a better life and expect a better life, and in some cases they do get one. My grandfather's job was atrocious, and coincidentally, many years later, I got a part time job at the same place where he had worked.

RM: We're talking about IBM, right?

JV: Yes, IBM, but this was not white collar IBM; this was very blue collar IBM. My grandfather dipped metal panels into vats of chemicals all day long. It was not only physically demanding but meant he spent the entire time breathing in nasty solvents and acids and corrosive cleaning agents. I got a temporary job at the same Plant decades after he retired and ended up doing the same thing. These intense chemicals would slop over their vats whenever I'd dip one of the heavy metal baskets into them. On my first day on the job, there was this old guy who was about to retire and he said that he knew my grandfather. My grandfather was his mentor when he started the job. So he liked me because of the family lineage and connection to my grandfather, which had to be 40 years prior to my taking the job. So he showed me the ropes. On my first day, chemical "slop" splashed over the vat and I felt this burning sensation in my stomach. When I looked down, the bottom third of my shirt was completely gone. So I said, "Hey man, look at this, what am I dealing with here?" And the old guy says: "Don't worry about it. Tomorrow I will get you a uniform so it won't happen again." This is a little encapsulation of my first day. For my grandfather, this was his day to day experience. He thought that he had a great job compared to what he had back in Ruthenia, a part of what is now Slovakia, living in the mountains – very poor and poverty stricken – and the fact that you could get a job, and all you had to do was work your ass off every day and you'd get enough pay to eat and buy a home, was gold to my grandfather. This was America and it was golden to them, but at the same time my grandfather was ingesting nasty chemicals into his body. He had neurological problems. I mean he was getting beat down, beat down, but he didn't see it that way because it was so much better than what he left. Everything was great. So the immigrant experience is certainly a theme in the book. I think many people can relate to the same thing. It happened in your family, maybe, you know first generation, you come, and at some level you're leading a better life than where you lived. But there is a price to pay even though things are comparably better here than in the country you left.

RM: Yeah, the sense of what was left behind and what America offers adds power to the book. The reader, in terms of the grandparents, gets to know them in both worlds. I'm thinking of your grandmother in another story, "What We Have Left", and how she reflects about her life as a little girl in the "old" country, and how the values and experiences learned there carry forward in America. I mean the way she carries a bag of cash into the hospital to pay for a heart operation for your uncle. It baffles everyone in the hospital. Nobody pays cash. When a hospital administrator tries to explain health insurance to her, she says something like: "I'm the insurance for my children." That's beautiful and the book is full of such telling moments. The story, "Scooch," is one of my favorites in the book. The story centers on your disabled brother and his friends who are off to a hockey game with you. They sit down for dinner prior to the game at the home of one of his friends and the conversation they get into is masterful in its humor, sensitivity and honesty.

JV: Yeah, my older brother, who passed away recently, was disabled. There was a time when the word "retarded" was not a bad word. He was retarded and he was in a class with retarded kids. But he was always at the top of his class. Terminology changes; now he would be called functional, which is a really crude thing to say. He was functional because he could drive a car, get a job, a low end one admittedly, but basically he could work and support himself. He lived at home and he needed help with certain things like paying bills. But with a little supervision he got by, and because we were an old school style family – parents and grandparents all living together – everyone helped to take care of him. He was a great great garrulous guy, and when he was in a good mood, he was the best possible person to be around. He got very enthusiastic for certain things, one of them being hockey. We lived in an upstate New York town, Endicott, and in Binghamton, there was a hockey team. The area was known as the Triple Cities – Binghamton, Johnson City and Endicott. So one day my brother was looking for something to do and a hockey game was the answer. He didn't know anything about hockey, but he would get so jazzed about the game. He would bring this little bell to the game and when the home team scored he would shake the bell. He got together with his friends from his school days – who were also in the class for the disabled – the retarded kids – and we would all go to the games together. Well, before one game, we went to dinner at one of his friend's parent's house. It was a very sad situation. The mother was into her seventies and the husband had passed away. So there are many factors all going on – small house, difficulty with bills, dead father, disabled son. The mother is simply hobbling along with all these factors but trying to find some laughter and joy in all of it.

RM: The circumstances come alive in the story but then there is the conversation of your brother and his disabled friends around the dinner table. Your brother is joking and kidding a friend incessantly about hot peppers and others at the table are talking and/or fixated on something. Everyone is having a good time and not focused or aware of the context of the situation. They are in the moment. The dialogue among the disabled friends is kind of funny.

JV: I appreciate you saying that because there is jocularity in the conversation among them. Actually, it's pretty absurd and taking one step back someone might accuse me of making fun of my brother and his friends. But I'm not making fun of them. We're all dealing with the same kind of stuff. Yes, everyone is teasing each other but not in a mean way. This is how we keep the language going and move through things. We joke to each other, we mock each other. Things are tough; life hurts, but we're going to make a joke about it hurting. We're not going to give into it. But it is a conversation around the dinner, and on the cover of the book, there are various images of food. Food is big, a foundational aspect in our lives. And food is big in "Scooch," and in this case old Slovak food – halupki, pigs in a blanket. As I got older and the older people died off, I never had this kind of food, and it was a real treat to have it – so that's in the story. And then there are some food types not desired by all, even those who haven't tried them.

Artifact Insertion

"Yeah what do you say, Nick? Bob's anxious to get some hot peppers, aren't you, Bob?" Nick's staring spell breaks. He moves his head and looks at Joe.

"Well, come to figure Joe, I don't think that my mother has any of those hot peppers here in the home. At least I've never haven't seen any. She might have them here, Bob, but I don't believe she has any of them here in the home."

"Keeee….keep those danged things away from me. They're hot going in and ho….hotter coming out, by the gee!"

from *What Else Do You Want?*
J.V. Miller
(Lavender Ink/Fell Swoop, 2013)

RM: I never felt when reading the story that the characters were being made fun of. You captured the excitement and joy of your brother and his friends having dinner together and getting ready for a game. It reflected their lives. But it was funny, the laughter is not at them but with them. Throughout the book, the dialogue is authentic to the characters' lives and situations and description of the various settings in the stories puts the reader right there. So this brings me to the writers that have influenced your work. Who are they?

JV: I wish I could answer that. I really can't. Many of us say we don't read as much as we should. Just recently, I was reading William Saroyan. This guy – and I'm not pretending to put myself even near him, in terms of his direction, however – is where I'm going. He writes about his family and the people around him, and also his work-a-day life. It is something we all can relate to. Every day presents a story, and if you have the time to sit down and write it or tell it so much the better. The realities of life often block that opportunity for many. But I've also written some other types of things – novels with a pop culture or pop reading bent. Tom Robbins comes into play here. I was reading him way back when and I thought man I want to be like him, imitate this guy, because he's hilarious. So I wrote some stuff, not intentionally imitative, but Tom Robbinsesque. Ok, roll your eyes, but more importantly I like to blend styles.

RM: You're not stuck in one approach, style, or way.

JV: I don't think so. I read all kinds of different stuff and it all flows into this pot of people. There is no one writer or group of writers that I could point to as outright models. I wrote one novel while reading Umberto Eco's, *Foucalt's Pendulum*, and I found that I was playing off the same things he was playing off. Reading him highlighted in some ways things I was grappling with. So Eco was a big influence for a period of time. But really, it is all a stew to me.

RM: I think all writers interact with other books and texts. Sometimes they're just talking back to or answering another author. Some writers are like diving boards for other writers into the unknown and new. So let's talk about your novels. I read *Beef* and *Bug*. What is the title of the really long one?

JV: Relative in terms of length is the word, for they're all quite long. *Beef* was the last one I wrote.

RM: What was the first one you wrote…the longest one of all, I believe.

JV: It's entitled, *Yin Yang Do Do & The Gas Attack Ensemble.* I drew on my martial arts background for this one. I teach karate, and there was a time I was very into that. So I had a martial arts instructor who became one of several main characters in the book. Time travel and social criticism also figure into the novel. I'm an over the top social critic. I'm a leftist politically and that comes through in the work. Indictment literature is what one reviewer called my work. We won't name names (Laughter). I think his name was Martin. And I admit to that; it is in your face. There is some soapbox to it.

RM: Now wait a second. I have to pick up on the indictment literature statement. Let me veer to *Bug* for a second. In that novel, the 20 billion or so insects on earth are portrayed as one conscious bug living out their lives in the manmade toxic environment that they will survive but not the human agents who have damaged and killed the environment. Unlike your short stories, in which the characters are so real that they walk off the page and take up residence with the reader, the characters in *Bug* are foils for the author who kills them off without mercy. Pretty funny, however, and thus indictment literature. The dumbasses that we are get what we deserve.

JV: You're right, that's why I mentioned some of the Robbins' influence. *Yin Yang Do Do* is similar in style to *Bug*. It is a very very long book. I sent a draft to XJ (Joel) Dailey, *Fell Swoop* publisher, great poet, great editor, and a wonderful friend. Joel saw things he liked and things that needed some work. He suggested cutting out the fat, shorten it and overall tighten it up. At the time it was 276 typed pages long. So I told him fine and that I would get back to him with a second draft. A couple of months went by and Joel called to check in on my progress. I told him that the draft was now 1200 pages long (Laughter). So, he said: "What are you talking about. I told you to tighten it up." So I told Joel, and this will probably sound like a cliché, that the characters said no to me because there was so much to report on and consider. Consequently, the book got longer and longer. And just recently, I went back to the book (written in 1992) to see if I can play with it some more and maybe tighten it up a little. The problem: I cut massive things out but then massive things jump back into it.

RM: So what you're saying is that you can go short and long.

JV: Yeah, but I really like the novel form. It's just fun. I'm playing around and having a great time. I feel like I don't have to edit myself or be critical. I'm just out there, into the form, and having a good time. This is not to say I don't love what I'm doing in the short stories. The short stories are certainly more accessible and traditional in a narrative sense. I think people can really relate to my short stories. I love my family and the fact that they're providing me with characters and stories to tell is just great.

RM: OK, let's talk about your poetry. I've seen you perform in public and you're a terrific performance poet. How did your poetic style evolve?

JV: Well, we have to go back to Binghamton and the Big Horror Poetry Series you started. The series brought amazing poets in on a regular basis. It was great experience to be part of the series as a member of the Binghamton Community Poets. It was there that I first saw some performance poets and thought that the style was very cool and I wanted to go in that direction. So I wrote many poems in that genre. I even wrote a performance piece on the 100th anniversary of Walt Whitman's passing, entitled, "Artificial Turf."

Artifact Insertion

‛So sorry, Walt / but it's the new millennium / and the body electric / has blown a fuse / fission fractured / the song an implosion / I scream / the body nuclear / doing the fusion funk / along crack cut sidewalks / in inner city sewage / vials to go / before we sleep / weep acid rain / tears of treeless terror / my song of myself / an encumbered sperm wail / swimming small circles / beneath Brooklyn Bridge….'

from "Artificial Turf" by J. V. Miller

RM: Who are your poetic influences?

JV: Would it be absurd for me to say Richard Martin? (Laughter)

RM: It would be OK…

JV: I can't even do that with the influences etc.

RM: OK. Let's move along to your work on the Clarion Arts Council. What have you brought to Clarion in terms of the arts since living here? I know your wife, Susan, is a professor at the University. You've been here quite some time. Talk about your literary activism.

JV: Clarion is a small, rural town in western Pennsylvania that tends to be reactionary and provincial – all that negative stuff you want to put on it. But before moving here, due to my wife getting a job at the college, I had never heard of Clarion. So like in many small towns, there were complaints of nothing going on. Nothing is going on because we're not doing anything except complaining that nothing is going on. So let's do something and make something happen. I think the arts are important so I got involved with the Arts Council, drawing on my experiences working with the Big Horror Poetry Series and the Binghamton Community Poets. I thought why not try something here that was similar to what was going on in Binghamton. At the time, the Clarion Arts Council simply focused on Visual Arts. I met the president of the Arts Council at a party. He asked me to start a literary aspect and to bring in some writers and poets and maybe do some workshops. I agreed. When he moved out of town, I became the president (not because I necessarily had the skill set, but if you can find someone to do it for free…then you're hired!). I was President. Whoopee! So I brought in some writers and poets and we had a reading series. It's a bit sporadic due to funding. It's difficult to get any money together to pay anyone. But Binghamton (Big Horror Poetry Series) established and maintained that writers and poets should be paid just as much as musicians etc. In fact, any artist doing any sort of craft or labor should be paid for their work. So we're trying to keep on bringing in writers and pay them. I'm now involved in it all – visual and literary arts, printing, photography. Clarion is a great little town, and like every little town, it is what you make of it. I bristle every time someone says there is nothing going on here. I say: "Yeah, because there's nothing going on with you. You're not making anything happen. What would you like to have happen? Tell me. What do you want to happen and let's see if we can make it happen?"

RM: That's fantastic. For some artists, it is just about their work. For others, it's about being active for all. It's great that your work is centered on the community.

Now what about Artfunkle? It's a funky store of used books, comics, jewelry, paintings, scarves, and crafts. How did you get this business started on main street in Clarion?

JV: As I mentioned, my wife is an Archeology Professor at the University. About 12 years ago, she and a colleague went on a dig in Ecuador. So the husbands went along, myself with Susan, and at the time my business partner, Joe, with his wife Laurie. They were working and teaching and had students to attend to, and Joe and I were doing what husbands are supposed to be doing, sitting around drinking beer while the wives worked. (Just kidding, Susan). So, Joe said to me (we were in Otavalo which is the market center of the entire nation, just rows and rows of artists and crafts and sales people, and we got to know some of them): "We should open a business in Clarion. We should get some merchandise in Ecuador and sell it in Clarion." And I said: "That's the dumbest idea I've ever heard. There's no money in Clarion and the people aren't going to buy things from South America. It's not going to happen." So, it didn't happen. But we still discussed it and about a year later, he came back to me and said: "This business idea is till gnawing at me. So what if we focused on local artists and their work. You're the President of the Arts Council and know the local artists. We could give them a place from which to sell their wares." And I said: "Ok, maybe we can try that. It will be a consignment shop. artists will be welcomed to sell their art and receive a large percentage of the sale price." We struggled to come up with a name for the business. Joe offered: Consignment and ArtFunkel. Now, I like Simon and Garfunkel, but they don't mean that much to me to have a business centered around them. Eventually, we settled on ArtFunkel around the time we had to sign the business papers with our lawyer. For a while, I found the name too cutesy, but I have come to like it a lot. Joe moved out of the area and I now run the place myself. Things have changed over time. I don't need to make money but I do need to pay the rent. The local artist consignment business didn't pay the rent. I've expanded and have a distributor in Philadelphia – a fair trade merchant, which enables me to sell incense and head "shoppy" type of stuff. I don't want to characterize my business that way, but there is a little of that patina to it. However, just before Joe left, it looked like we'd go out of business again, but then a gentleman, a book collector, offered us a load of used books. He was moving to Seattle and so he just donated them to us. It was a sign to stay open. The store is now 80% used books. I also sell some new books and special order books for people. So throw in the incense and stuff like that, plus some local artist consignment to round it off. But most of my sales are used books and I have also expanded to comics. I've given another gentleman a quadrant of the store for the comics and work on a consignment basis with him.

RM: So you are a novelist, a writer of short stories, a performance poet, an arts activist, a small business owner, martial arts instructor and pretty much the de facto mayor of Clarion. I'd like to end the interview by finding out more about the mascot for your business (and maybe your life and work). Talk to me about Killerbasa. (Laughter).

JV: Killerbasa?

RM: Yes, tell me about Killerbasa.

JV: As I get older, I'm hesitant to use the word "elderly" anymore, but there is a man about 80 years old or so who comes into my shop regularly. In one of his many many divorces, as it turns out, he ended up with a taxidermist stuffed Polish Fighting Chicken. So he brings it into my store and says: "Hey John, I want you to sell this for me." I don't really have a market for Polish Fighting Chickens. He sets it down and claims someone will buy it and he wants a thousand dollars for it. I tell him he must be off his meds or something but I keep it anyway. He comes back a few days later and says: "Did that chicken sell?" I tell him no way and that he wants too much money for it. Then he says: "I only wanted a $100 for it." I reminded him that he told me he wanted a thousand for it. So it's like that. I start to think this fighting chicken needed a name. So I came up with "Killerbasa" and the obvious pun on kielbasa and killer because it's a fighting chicken. So for now Killer stays in his role as the mascot of Artfunkle and greets each customer who enters the store. Killer intimidates some customers and others find looking at its butt (I rotate the bird) as they enter the story less than aesthetically pleasing. I don't understand why.

RM: Well, I think the interview should end in an aesthetically strong way. (Laughter). Thanks for sharing your thoughts about your work, activism and business with me. And of course, Killerbasa.

JV: Ok, thank you, Richard

Reader's Notes and Artwork

APPENDIX A

"THE POET AS COMEDIAN: CONTEXTUALIZING DICK MARTIN'S *boink!*"
BY RICHARD BLEVINS

"He created his own Kool Aid reality and was able to illuminate himself by it."
-- *Trout Fishing in America*

On his fiftieth birthday in the final year of the millennium, inspired by a belated reading of Richard Brautigan's *Trout Fishing In America*, Dick Martin realized his plan of fifty days of writing which he would publish as *boink!*, splendidly unaware he had initiated his "antimemoir" on the mutual birthdate of Tex Avery and Jackie Gleason, while sharing his own birthday with Ducky Nash, the voice of Donald Duck. If reading Brautigan's novel for the first time in 1999 was unfashionably late in its afterlife, an overdue book truly and a fact most of us would omit from the conversation about books we've meant to read, it was no problem for the maladjusted memoirist. I am myself writing a decade too late for a proper book review of *boink!*, my roundabout way of coming to terms with the problems and rewards it poses for a reader of poetry, and humor, and humorous poetry--unless, that is, like the late Thomas Bernhard, the reader is humorless and has abandoned poetry or, like Jackie and Tex, one has a genius for comedy and has passed on--, having been boink'd again by re-reading Dick Martin's classic memoir. (1)

Texts that make us laugh, to wildly paraphrase the Freud of *Jokes and Their Relation to the Unconscious* (1905), are problematical to think about. The master's English-speaking lackey Ernest Jones tells us that *Jokes* and *Three Essays on the Theory of Sexuality* were written on adjoining tables, Freud going from one manuscript to the other when a thought struck. (2) If the father of psychoanalysis had known what we know—that he was not a scientist but, in fact, one of the seminal creative writers of the end of the nineteenth century and, with the lesser poet Benjamin Blood, a pioneer of drug lit—he might have written his two books as one grand collage of sex jokes. Dick Martin, publishing *boink!* on the centennial of the publication of Freud's doubleheader, was free, in the way that Brautigan before him was liberated by collage technique, to carve memoir and comedic poetry with a pen knife into his assigned school desk whenever he thought the teacher wasn't looking. Martin invites us to recall that essential part of ourselves we mostly thought we'd left behind to childhood play by virtue of what Freud calls "the rediscovery of something familiar" in jokes.

Although the influence of *Trout Fishing* never reaches the level of voice in *boink!*—

Martin's manic wise-cracker cannot be confused for the disengaged narrator from North Beach—Dick Martin's gaggle of chapters does resemble the collage structure that worked so famously in Brautigan's novel. The forty-seven sections of *Trout Fishing* (which include, but are not limited to, the narrator's memoir of childhood, a cookbook, information on John Dillinger, the narrator's trout fishing trips, news from North Beach, an autopsy report, letters, book cover information, and so-called footnotes, all abandoned in an open-ended ending) are comparable to *boink!*'s chapters (which include, but are not limited by, remembrances of things childhood, query letters to publishers, newspaper articles, a diploma from a radio and television broadcasting school, the list of readers Dick hosted for the Big Horror Poetry Series in Binghamton from 1983 to 1996, ads for books of poems, reviews of books of poems, an interview with the poet, Dick's accounts of various visits to medical doctors and surgeons, the Martin family tree, maps, Dick's astrological chart, a Joel Dailey discography, a bibliography of books published by Peter Kidd for Igneus Press, "chunks" of a novel, and often hilarious footnotes, the ending open-ended). Part of the fun is culling all the good poems from the footnotes, such as:

Remember how perfect the ladder
lay against the moon

Beanstalk and all in our heads
we climbed
out of time
out of space
out of anything to say

We went up and up
into the yellow darkness[.]

And the prose footnotes are as funny as Jack Spicer's. The best poems are two long ones, "How I Became an Elementary School Teacher" and "White Man Appears on Southern California Beach," reprinted here in appendices. A play by "Duck Martian" will give the uninitiated some general idea of Dick Martin performing his poems. (3) Martin sustains his book of pixels and bits like Hans, in the fairy tale, who makes the princess laugh (and gains half the kingdom in so doing) at the line of people sticking to him; we stay glued, wanting to know what he'll say, or do, next.

But the problem with *boink!* is, it's seriously funny. "What looks like a surrealist writing his will and sounds like an irrepressible stand-up comedian is, actually," observed the late

Guy Davenport, "fresh, green, recognizably original poetry." We might expect one of the most prominent critics of our era to recognize Dick Martin's poems, but--and herein's the historic problem--, there is no tradition in our reading for funny poetry (a condition necessitating the "is, actually"). If Dick Martin is "a surrealist writing his will," then his is an American surrealism, the realm of Dock Ellis' no-hit game on acid, a work of art and zaniness critiqued telepathically from Arizona by the cryogenic head of Ted Williams. "Surrealism will be around for a long time," Martin surmises in *boink!*. "It's part of the brain." He is the author of the pure surreal line "A beautiful and incomplete guy, he walked into a disaster of plates," which by definition could lead to no additional sentences in his paragraph. Boink! Rightfully adverse to silly verse, Ogden Nash, Joyce Kilmer, Gelett Burgess, Robert Service, the e.e. cummings of "buffalo bill defunct" and "In Just-/ spring," and defender of the faith Hilaire Belloc, are no help to readers of Dick Martin. Among those writers in Andre Breton's eclectic *Anthology of Black Humor* (1936), Martin is surely closest in spirit to Christian Dietrich Grabbe (d. 1836). Heine, who quarreled with the playwright, dubbed Grabbe "a drunken Shakespeare," and the anti-literate Nazis were told they loved him; but who in America has read Grabbe's plays or Breton's book? The repeat offender Louis Untermeyer's *A Treasury of Humor* (1946) was the mainstream anthology to Breton's underground stream. However, the household-name cutups of the previous turn of the century are no help to those of us who read Dick Martin. Perhaps, the Joyce of the *Wake* or John Lennon's two little books of poems sounding like Joyce via Edward Lear nudge us toward making sense of the nonsense verse of the unforgettable Lear and Lewis Carroll, but Martin was not born with a runsible spoon in his mouth. Our very own Crispin laments the linguistic dilemma in *boink!*:

Words are too heavy.
They've grown fat
with centuries and mouths.

Any one of them
could flatten us
into a railroad penny

Go ahead
lie down on their tracks
and see what I mean[.]

Neither does Martin's delivery seem to owe debts to the more recent "occasional" poems of joel oppenheimer, Jonathan Williams, Anselm Hollo, or Bill Shields, although I shelve my copy of *boink!* in an unalphabetized place of honor beside their books, Dorothy Parker's traditioinal-verse quips stuck in sideways. There is a striking physical resemblance between Dick Martin and the Jorg Kolbe black and white photograph of Bertholt Brecht (German Federal Archive, 1954).

Edward Dorn was tasked by his teacher Olson's obsession with his teacher Pound's *Cantos* to write *a poem containing history*, which he subverted by humor ("Entrapment is this society's sole activity--& only laughter can blow it to rags."). *Gunslinger, the historical poem containing humor* Dorn invented, may be the closest predecessor to *boink!* Dealing cards at Slinger's table, Dick Martin proposes "Television is the olive in the martini of chain reaction," a line Dorn would have traded on. By comparison, the emergent distraction of funny cowboy poems is merely another noisy fight down the bar. Martin's brand of humor, like the late master's, is determinedly social. Only the clinically mad tell jokes to themselves, and even then Artaud kept on writing for the stage. As neurotically self-absorbed as *boink!*'s speaker is, Dick Martin is paradoxically one of our unblinking social critics—and part of the power of his book derives from his relentless re-estimations of his fate as a plastic card-carrying member of the popular culture it has taken a century for late capitalism to manifest. The title he chose for the book, and its cover, are a well-aimed shot to the noggin of the slapstick comic as well as an impudent shout ("Boink!") from the Pop Art balloons of Roy Lichtenstein and cheap imitators. When I read that sour-faced old Baudelaire, in his study of laughter, posits the comic as being "visibly double" (showing both its art and its moral) and, at the same time, "transparent" (written in accessible language), I immediately thought of Dick Martin. A poetry written at the table of our impulse to make people laugh, and a poetry written at the table of the compulsion to write poems, startles when they become transparent in one volume, *boink!*. Conversely, and to the detriment of a talent like Martin's, a readership as vast as Amazon may be too lazy to go between two tables, content to know a memoir is a memoir, humor is humor, and I don't buy books of poetry anyway. I have witnessed Dick Martin, in response to the academic equivalent of this audience, climb the nearest table at a poetry conference in New Hampshire and shout—"But how about *me*?" Everything in the auditorium clarified. If comedic poetry has the power to strip the bride of literary culture, Dick Martin's work is a reminder that we inmates are allowed to use only Swintec Clear Cabinet typewriters made of see-through plastic (the new transparency is self-censoring) for sending messages outside.

In *boink!*, Martin practices most of the types of jokes that Freud classifies and today's humor theorists, such as Jerry Aline Flieger and John Morreall, start from. He is capable of composing loving vignettes of his late father, and sweet poems about the kind of "Love that makes the divorce lawyers go away." George Meredith, the earlier expert on modern love, observed in his essay on comedy that "The reasonings at which we laugh are those we know to be false, but which we might accept as true were we to hear them in a dream." Here's a virtuoso passage of the dreamy poet joke, another type:

> In heat, we headed for San Francisco with enough coin to get a room at the YMCA. The Y was gay and I nearly tumbled out the window in our fourteen-story room finishing Hesse's *Narcissus and Goldmund*. I was a period piece without even knowing it. Blissful ignorance. On the run in America and a Hesse fanatic. Horny, too. Digging Goldmund's escapades into sensuality, after the anti-body, repressive days of Roman Catholicism. Yet the monk, Narcissus, was part of me too. I had done time in a seminary before breaking out into being a dropout in New York's public university system. The holy man motif is a basic archetype in young men. And for me, the dialectic of spirit/body was still unresolved and out of whack at the time. Star date: the "Summer of Love" and I remained a virgin. ("Oh, behave, baby!").
>
> So as I crossed the room reading Hesse, I tripped on throw rug and split head first for the big wide-opened window on the far side of the room. Chance had me catch a knee on the window sill and my freefall to the concrete below was canceled, a potential freefall from 14 stories up. Still my body got far enough out of the window for the woman in the tenement across from us to yell: "DON'T JUMP!"
>
> O those hazy lazy days of summer.

To dwell overlong on the poetic achievement of all this funny business risks spoiling the occasion of art, the viewer becoming conscious of Harold Lloyd's prosthetic hand and neglecting to follow the movie, or thinking about Edward Lear's big nose (and, wow, Freud's lit cigar!) when you read "The Dong with a Luminous Nose" to the grandkiddies. To spare me from trying to unscramble the sentence I've just written...*When we read Keats extending his hand in the poem, we boink on Lloyd's gloved hand, only to wake up shaking-- Dick Martin's hand, "Friends!"...*, I'll give the memoirist the flood light for the last laugh, and return to my seat in the dark to enjoy.

"Customary Strangers"

I was reading poems about his mother
when the tractor-trailer burst into the yard
and crushed my hosta plants.
His mom could shoot a mean game of pool:
always wore a red party dress (décolleté)
when sinking the eight in the side
and thinking of the Sunday pot roast.

I knew the trucker had been drinking
in a small town with a single bar
run by a man with a bullet
lodged in his jaw
who kept a python in a shed
with a John Deere mowing tractor
and mementos from the days
his son played with toy explosives
before joining the army
to destroy bridges of bad ideology
springing up in the world
like fleurs du mal.

The trucker insisted there was a road
inside my house
and if I consented to hop in his truck
he'd let me shoot holes
in deer crossing signs
as he roared down my living room
blowing retreads and tripping
alarms in the canvases
of two twentieth century masters
I'd stolen while drunk on wine
from a rich girlfriend.
I felt no remorse about the theft
suspecting from my days in the factory
I had missed a turn or two
and with a hatred for customary strangers
maps or the desire to go back
probably had detoured onto a path
littered with failed campaigns
and remnants of escape.
Things beyond the ken of poems
doused with twilight
and pinned on the backs of human targets.

When the trucker yanked on his horn
it was my chance to find out.

Notes:
A pdf version of *boink!* is available free from the publisher at <www.lavenderink.org>.
As I worked on this essay, I became acutely aware of a surprising number of jokes about
two tables. Two examples will suffice here:
    --A man walks up to two tables in a bar and asks them: "May I join you?"
    --Two tables walk into a bar. The first one says, "I'll get this round." His friend replies,
"Okay, next drinks are on me."
It is our good fortune that "Pieces of Furniture," a play by the Athenian comic poet Plato
Comicus (d. 416 BC), survives only as a title, or there would be even more jokes about
tables dating back centuries before the bad joke of Greek Revival furniture you couldn't
sit on which my grandmother bought at a good price.
Duck Martian is one of the pseudonyms this latter-day Pessoa publishes under; see also
Ant McGoogle, Al Pants, and others. No relation to Clarence "Ducky" Nash (see my
essay's opening paragraph).

from *House Organ*, Number 90 Spring 2015

Appendix B

Sponsored By:

"Dick
"Brick!"
Genius

IndependentPressParty2 04/21/05

Dick Martin
40 Sozeter Rd
Westbury MA
02132

APPENDIX C

Fell Swoop:
The All Bohemian Revue
1983-2017

edited by XJ Dailey, Editor-for-Life

ONE FELL SWOOP: Normandi Ellis, R. Stephen Posey, Ed Shushi (translated by Joel Dailey),Gordon Anderson, Mark Chadwick, Richard Martin, Randall Schroth; James Haug.

2 Fell Swoop: James Magorian, Lucas Wells, Gordon Anderson, James de Crescentis, Richard Martin, dan Raphael, Randall Schroth, Joe Kapusta.

3 fell swoop: Gordon Anderson, Richard Martin, Robb Jackson, Randy Signor, Dave Kelly, James Haug, Andrei Codrescu, Dave Morice, Dave Kelly, Ed Motorcyle (poems arranged by M. Chadwick & J. Dailey.

4 fell Swoop: Fielding Dawson, George Chambers, Roger Kamenetz, Elizabeth Thomas, Normandi Ellis, Elizabeth Thomas, Sylvia Kelly, Richard Martin.

Five Swell Foop: The Aztec Guide to Water Sports!: Gordon Anderson, Flung Hi, Joel Dailey, Ruhl, Noah Fence, Horace Voice, Arthur Winfield Knight, Joel Dailey, Clara Talley-Vincent, Richard Martin.

6 Fell(ed) Swooping: the 'wrong planet' issue!: Ed Dorn, James deCrescentis, Normandi Ellis, Gordon Anderson, Richard Martin, Robb Jackson, Clara Talley-Vincent, Alphonso Perky, Heidi Furr, Joel Dailey, Randall Schroth (cover by Joe Martin).

ANGRY RED BLUES   Fell Swoop#7: S. Zivvit 57 (translated from the Martian language by Joel Dailey).

8 fell Swoop: The All New Exciting, Necessary & Fun Ultra-Special Victimization Issue!: Fred Schwartz, Elizabeth Thomas, John Gery, dan raphael, Richard Martin, X.J. Dailey, Ellen diNormus, J. Garmhousen, Gordon Anderson, Father Richard Martin, Randy Michael Signor, Thomas Costello, Donald Levering, Edward Mycue.

9 FELL S' Woop: Chris Toll, A Concerned Guy, Clara Talley-Vincent, ex-Ray, "Fast Eddie Whirlpool, Richard Martin, R. S. Posey, Joel Dailey, J. Garmhousen, J. Vassily Milos, James de Crescentis.

Fell Swoop Ten: Pat Nolan, Donald Levering, oppenheimer, R.R.Odell, Richard Martin, Mark Salerno, Clara Talley-Vincent, Paulette Hinderboggen, Sheila E. Murphy.

Fell Swoop 11 & 12: Anselm Hollo, Normandi Ellis, Randall Schroth, Keith Veizer, Buck Downs, Derek Pell, Joel Dailey, Sheila E. Murphy, John M. Bennett, Richard Martin, Gordon Anderson, Bonnie Spillway, Ted Berrigan, Sandle Castle, Ruth Pettus, Richard Sober, David Beaudouin, Damon Norko, Daniel Linenstruth, Tom Diventi, Chris Toll.

FELL SWOOP the 13th: Thomas Jasins, Elizabeth Thomas, Brett Evans, w.j. austin, J. Garmhausen, Richard Martin, Anthony Robbins, x-ray, Richard Collins, Joel Dailey, Cliff Dweller, J. Millos.

FELL SWOOP 14 & 15 – BIG HORROR READER: Karen Corinne Boccio, Barney Bush, W.E. Butts, Andrei Codrescu, Tom Costello, Tom Kolpakas, Joel Dailey, james de crescentis, Rachel Guido deVries, Dave Kelly, Michael Kelly, Kate McQueen, Richard Martin, Milloz, Bern Mulligan, Jerome Rothenberg, Knute Skinner, Phil Sweeney, Elizabeth Thomas, Lloyd Van Brunt. Art: Tom Haines. Cover Art: James de Crescentis.

SIXTEEN FELL SWOOP(S) – NEOSWOOP: Lisa B. Herskovits, Dennis Formento, Paul Weinman, Richard Martin, James Gawron, Buck Downs, Normandi Ellis, Joel Dailey, Chris Toll.

MINIGOLF – Fell Swoop 17: Anselm Hollo.

FELL SWOOP EIGHTEEN – THE PROFESSIONAL DOG GROOMING ISSUE: Chris Toll, Lisa R. Mednick, Pat Nolan, Richard Martin, Judson Crews, Greg Boyd, james de crescentis, Nico Vassilakis, Philip Hughes, Stephen Toth, Pat Nolan, Gordon Roy Anderson, Richard Martin, Joel Dailey.

FELL SWOOP NINETEEN/TWENTY: Dennis Formento, Clara Talley-Vincent, Bill Myers, Normandi Ellis, Doug MacCash, M. Kettner, Richard Martin, Duck Martian, William Talcott, Barbara Bush, Kate McQueen, Judson Crew, Justice Howard, Bill Myers.

TALES FROM THE HOME PLANET is Fell Swoop 21: Chris Toll issue. Front cover and drawings by Richard Sober.

DONT MISS Fell Swoop 22: Richard Martin, Alex Rawls, Bill Myers, Kirby Olson, Marcia Ann Pollo, Clara Tally-Vincent, Mark Chadwick, Skip Fox, Doug MacCash, Chris Toll.

FELL SWOOP 23: Normandi Ellis, Buck Downs, Alex Rawls, Lisa Kucharski, EXIA, Richard Martin, Kate McQueen, Bill Myers, Anne M. Giovingo, Anonymous, Dan Nielsen, Michael Estabrook.

The Nolan Anthology of Poetry – Fell Swoop 24: Pat Nolan issue.

FELL SWOOP 25: Richard Martin, Robert Head, Robert W. Howington, Skip Fox, James Haug, Philip Hughes, Doug MacCash, Skip Fox, Richard Craig, L. E. McCullough, Dan Neilsen, Jeffery Little, Milos, Pete Lee, Philip Hughes, Judson Crews, Chris Toll.

BIG DADDY'S BOTTOMLESS TOPLESS FELL SWOOP NO COVER ISSUE #26, 27: Bill Myers, Greg Boyd, Kimberly J. Bright, Pat Nolan, clayton brooks, Marlon Niedringhaus, Judson Crews, Brett Evans, Alex Rawls, Todd Kalinski, Martin Kirby, John M. Bennett, Steve Doloff, Jeffery Little, Bob Heman, Jay Marvin, Dennis Formento, Bonnie Spillway, Ann Marie Bourgeois, Chris Toll, John Elsburg, Suzi, August Franza, James Tolan, Jerry Benjamin, Robert Head, Cynthia Copeland, Sarah Rosenblatt.

FELL SWOOP 28 – POETRY FICTION BULLSHIT: Richard Martin, Ann Erickson, L. E. McCullough, James Tolan, JV Miller, Red Shuttleworth, Michael A. Griffith, Randall Schroth, Dennis Formento, Michael Leddy, Bill Myers, Jilly Schaefer, C.F. Roberts, Judson Crews, Elizabeth Cook, Duck Martian.

Channeling Olson: FELL SWOOP 29: Randall Schroth issue.

FELL SWOOP 30: Richard Martin, JV Miller, C.F. Roberts, Camille Martin, Greg Fuchs, Glen Bach, Robert Rhine, Chris Toll, Kimberly Bright, R.O. Hood, elliott, Kevin McGowin, Anne Trumbore, Brett Evans, David Gray, Joel Dailey.

YOU'RE OUT OF MY MIND (but so am I) Fell Swoop 31: Dan Nielsen issue.

FELL SWOOP 32 – POETRY FICTION GOLF BULLSHIT: Jennifer Lee Fader, Richard Kostelanetz, Dennis Formento, Ann Erickson, J. V. Bug, Noelle Kocot, Selena Anne Shephard, T.S. Burroughs, Richard Martin, Hugh Fox.

"Maenad" Fell Swoop 33: Poems by Kimberly J. Bright.

FELL SWOOP 34 – None of the talent (DIET SWOOP) Half the Brain: Richard Martin, Vasyl Milos, Dave Kelly, C.C. Russell, Martin Kirby, Andy Haupert, Dan Nielsen, brett evans, Eric Basso, Michael Phillips, Mark Begley, Doug Dibbern, Rupert Wondolowski, Todd Moore, Marc Swan, Raymond Tod Smith.

FELL SWOOP 35/36: Pierre Reverdy: Prose Poems (translated by Ron Padgett), Camille Martin, Richard Martin, Molly McNett, Robert Kenter, Anselm Hollo, Dan Nielsen, Doug MacCash/Alex Rawls, Greg Fuchs, I. Griffin, M. Phillips, Dave Kelly, John Jenkinson, Dennis Formento, Kimberly J. Bright, Bob Heman, richard wilmarth, brett evans, Ann Erickson, Fred Lame, William Penn Myers, Joel Dailey, Hannah Faith Dailey.

A TUB OF FLOWERING BIRDS Fell Swoop 37: Mark Chadwick issue.

THE SHAKE UP by John Miller – Fell Swoop 38.

TANG DYNASTY: Fell Swoop 39: Brett Evans issue.

time to go – FELL SWOOP 40: Richard Martin issue.

Plastic heaven – Poems & Photos by Camille Martin: Fell Swoop #41

Fell Swoop #42 – nay-pau-loron: a. di Michele issue.

FELL SWOOP FORTY THREE – DIRE POULTRY**CRUCI-FICTIONS**COMFORTING LIT IN A DIM TIME: Richard Martin, Joe Napora, Bob Hemen, buck downs, Chris Toll, Brett Evans, Clara Tally-

Vincent, james mecham, Sheila E. Murphy, Gregory Vincent Saint Thomasino, Gordon Anderson, Arthur Winfield Knight.

FELL SWOOP FORTY-FOUR – THE RETRO—INTRO—SPECTIVE ISSUE: Richard Martin, John M. Bennett, Amanda Gardner, Greg Evason, Brett Evans, Buck Downs, John Lowther, Marrissa Filippo, Bob Heman, Peter Kidd, Gregory Vincent Saint Thomasino, Spencer Selby.

WELCOME TO BANGOK BY JAMES MECHEM: FELL SWOOP 45.

FELL SWOOP 46/47 – The "Look out, you oaf!" Issue: Richard Martin, Petula Dvorak, Greg Evason, Camille Martin, Lewis LaCook, John M. Bennett, Brett Evans, Michael Andre, Sheila E. Murphy, Kevin Kazubowski, Bob Heman, Greg Fuchs, Mark Salerno, Buck Downs, John Stickney, Richard Kostelanetz, Laura E. Wright, Randal Schroth.

NAPKIN APOLOGIES by DUCK MARTIAN: Fell Swoop #48.

SIDE SWOOPED 49 (To WOULD BE CONTRIBUTORS: on the expensive advice of our sleazy backalley lawyers Fell Swoop is compelled to state the obvious: let it be known that publication herein very well may result in utter ruination of one's writing career. Now, we feel better – Richard Martin, Tom Devaney, Jan P. Christensen (with Brett Evans), Brett Evans, Bob Hemen, Paul Long, Hoa Nguyen, Camille Martin, Bonnie Spillway, Jon Powell, William Lavender, John M. Bennett, Steve Hughes, Greg Evason, james de crescentis, B.Z. Niditch, Sheila E. Murphy, Brendan Lorber, Bill Myers, Dave Brinks & Bill Myers, Ryan G. Van Cleave, Dennis Formento, DRINK STATION: INTERVIEW WITH AN ANONYMOUS AM PO.

FEEL SWAY FIFTY – The 'los hormigas' issue: Richard Martin, Andy di Michele, Randall Schroth, Brett Evans, bill lavender, Andrew Winston, Bob Hemen, John M. Bennett, Greg Fuchs, Mark Stricker, Alex Rawls, John V. Miller.

Fell Swoop #51: Richard Martin, Dave Brinks, Matvei Yankelvich, Buck Downs, Jason Lynn, Greg Evason, Dale Smith, Jamey Jones, Russell Helms, Robert Head, Joe Cabeza, Joel Dailey.

Jayne Mansfied's Dog by Alex Rawls: Fell Swoop 52.

FELL SWOOP FIFTY THREE – Poultry You Chew*CRU-CI-FICTIONS*TRIUMPHANT ASPHALT: John Miller, Camille Martin, Brett Evans, Randall Schroth, Alex Rawls, Dennis Formento, Richard Martin.

GET YOUR FUTURE SWOOP #54 RIGHT HEREE: Richard Martin, A. di Michele, Chris McCreary, Bill Lavender, Sheila E. Murphy, Greg Fuchs, Elisabeth Gonsiorowski, Camille Martin, Hank Lazer, Ann Erickson, Brett Evans, Emory Elkins.

PROBLEM 35 by Joel Dailey: Fell Swoop 55.

FOGSOUP 56: The Pensacola Issue: Scott Satterwhite, Allan Peterson, Paul E. Williams, Lance B. Young, Miriam Woods, Fred Long, Paula Mayberry, Ryne Ziemba, Mike Racine, Matthew McCandless, Jamey Jones, Philip Good, Bernadette Mayer, Camille Martin.

FELL SWOOP #57: Richard Martin, Ed Orr, Clark Coolidge, Paul Williams, Jamey Jones, Kathleen Gasparian, Randall Schroth, Chris Toll, Tod Edgerton, Bill Keckler, Aram Saroyan, Jessica Freeman, Robert Head, Brett Evans, Gerry Crinnin.

pentacl by Bill Lavender: Fell Swoop 58.

FELL SWOOP 59: Richard Martin, Carol Szamatowicz, Larry Fagin, clark coolidge, Aram Saroyan, Jamey Jones, Andrei Codrescu, Paul E. Williams, Dave Brinks.

Hoppy Poems by Clark Coolidge: Fell Swoop 60.

Day by Day – poems by Aram Saroyan: Fell Swoop 61.

SCOOCH by John Miller: Fell Swoop 62.

The Brooklyn Stoop – an anthology of Brooklyn poets edited by Anne Moschovakis and Matvei Yankelevich: Aaron Kiely, Betsy Fagin, Brenda

Bordofsky, Brenda Iijima, Brendan Lorber, Brian Kim Stefans, Carin Besser, Christopher Voigt, Dan Machlin, David Cameron, DglsN.Rothscjhld, Edmund Joseph Berrigan, EJ Fugate, Eugene Ostasbevsky, Garrett Kalleberg, Genya Turovsky, greg fuchs, Jacqueline Waters, jen bervin, Joanna Fuhrman, Kristin Prevallet, Lewis Warsh, Macgregor Card, M. Nelson, anna moschovaskis, matvei yankelevich, Melissa Busseo, Michael Ruby, Prageeta Sharma, Rachel Levitsky, Renee Gladman, Tracey McTague, Tracy Grinnel, Trey Sager. (#63 without the number)

Fell Swoop 64 –TIME FLIES BY LIKE A GREAT WHALE by Anselm Hollo. (A talk given in the American Poet Greats Series hosted by Jim Cohn at the Boulder Book Store in Boulder, Colorado, 13 March 2001)

SPEED DIALING Feel Swab #65: Richard Martin, Ron Padgett, Clark Coolidge, Sarah K. Inman, Gerry Crinnin, Hank Lazer, Bill Lavender, Mark Salerno, A. di Michele, Greg Evason, Russell Helms. (cover by Nicole Martin)

Fell Swoop #66.5: Anselm Berrigan, Richard Martin, R. Schroth, Greg Evason, Frederick Long, Alex Rawls, Brett Evans, Jesse Freeman, Andrei Codrescu, Mark Chadwick, Jamey Jones, Philip Good, Buck Downs, Bill Lavender.

The FELL SWOOP Eye Chart Issue #67.1: Richard Martin, Mark Chadwick, Bill Lavender, Tom Weigel, Bill Freind, Jesse Freeman, Gerry Crinnin, Greg Evason, Chris Toll, Marie Kazalia, David Saffo, Randall Schroth.

MUSCLE MEMORY NEVERMIND THE IROQUOIS by Brett Evans: Fell Swoop #68.

Fell Swoop 69 MILWAUKEE SWOOPS edited by Stacy Szymaszek & John Tyson (covers: Tony Stonehouse: Francesca Abbate, Kiki Anderson, Antler, Robert J. Bauman, Jim Chapson, Dave Chirot, PPd'CaCa, Robert Firth, Nicholas Frank, Jesse Gant, Karl Gartung, Josh Gilman, Charles Goldman, Bob Harrison, Charles Goldman, Michael Hauser, Marie Larson, Chuk LeFuk, James Liddy, Jennifer Montgomery, Steve Nelson-Raney, Zack Pieper, Randy Russell, Anne Shaw, Tony Stonehouse, Stacy Szymaszek, John Tyson, Peter Whalen, Karl Young.

Fell Swoop 70: Richard Martin, Greg Evason, Jamey Jones, Stuart Ross, Bill Lavender, Chris Toll, Camille Martin.

POETS at Le Swoopo # 71 (handwritten by the authors and published unedited and indiscriminately by Fell Swoop – in tribute to Dan Saxon's POETS AT LE METRO- March 1964): Ted Berrigan, Anselm Hollo, Randy Schroth, Gerry Crinnin, Clark Coolidge, John Miller, Bill Lavender, Richard Martin, Andy di Michele, Maureen Owen, Chris Toll, Elizabeth Thomas, Simon Pettet, Edmund Berrigan, Ed Sanders, Tom Weigel, Buck Downs, Greg Fuchs, Hank Lazer, Andrei Codrescu, Aram Saroyan, Brett Evans, Jamey Jones, Sheila Murphy, Joel Dailey.

Fell Swoop # 72 – the OH NO! issue: Richard Martin, John M. Bennett, Dennis Formento, A. di Michele, Sarah K. Inman, Philip Jenkins, Dan Freeman, Tom Weigel, Gerry Crinnin, Camille Martin.

Fell Swoop # 73 – Next Door to Samsara by Keith Abbott.

fell Swoop #74…a warm und fuzzy Swoop…:Richard Martin, Jesse Freeman, Susanna Lea, Brett Evans, Camille Martin, Sarah K. Inman, Greg Evason, Randall Schroth, thurston moore, Gerry Crinnin, Buck Downs, Jamey Jones, Mike Topp.

Cauliflower or Bust by Tom Weigel FELL SWOOP #75.

STREET DEBRIS by John Coletti and Greg Fuchs, Fell Swoop #76.

HELP! FELL SWOOP 77: Richard Martin, Camille Martin, Megan Burns, bill lavender, John Tyson, John Landry, Dave Brinks, Mike Hauser, R. Schroth, Robert Head, Gerry Crinnin, Greg Evason, John Bennett, buck downs, John Leon, Jamey Jones.

Parts of the Body – a 1970s-80s Scrapbook by Bill Berskson, Fell Swoop #78.

45 Minutes to Air by Joel Dailey, FELL SWOOP #79.

Louisiana Creole Tomatoes – fell Swoop 80 – 'comehell or highwater issue': Richard Martin, Brett Evans, Gillian McCain, Jamey Jones, Tom Weigel, Jason Lynn, bill lavender, Greg Evason, buck downs.

West Coast of New York by Gerry Crinnin, Fell Swoop 81.

FELL SWOOP 82 - REVVING UP RIMBAUD: Richard Martin, Camille Martin, Ron Padgett, Aram Saroyan, Brett Evans, Chris Toll, Dave Brinks, Tom Weigel, Jesse Freeman.

against news by dik tater (cover and portrait of dik tater by Tom Haines): Fell Swoop 83.

Sunday School by John Miller: Fell Swoop 84.

The Ted Berrigan Issue (cover by paul williams): Fell Swoop 85.

FELL SWOOP 86 – THE EVENTUAL ISSUE: Richard Martin, Dave Brinks, Duck Martian, Brett Evans, Helen Peterson, Peter Kidd, Tom Weigel, bill lavender, Chris Toll, Jamey Jones, Rupert Wondolowski, Gerry Crinnin, dave kennedy, Daniel Peavey, robert head. (cover: Camille Martin)

LIKE I JUST DID – Selected Letters of XJ Dailey Fell Swoop 87 (front and back covers: Hilary Crane-Stern) Photo of XJ Dailey: Joe Martin.

Recent Information by Bob Heman Fell Swoop 88. (Cover collage by author)

FELL SWOOP 89 "The Presidential Polyp Issue": Richard Martin, Ron Padgett, Tom Weigel, Robert Creeley, Matvei Yankelevich, Camille Martin, Randall Schroth, Allen Ginsburg, Philip Good, Bernadette Mayer, Skip Fox, Gerry Crinnin, Jamey Jones, Dennis Formento, Brett Evans. (front and back covers Tom Haines; back cover: portrait of Robert Creeley.

Fell Swoop #90 – The New London School edited by Tom Weigel: Dan Freeman, Rocco Russo, Dave Spinelli, Frederick Vaughn, Colleen Keenan, Davana Grabel, Megan Carlson, Dave Kennedy, Jake St. John, Tom Weigel, Helen Peterson, Emmett Jarrett.

The Rise of the New Media by Duck Martian, Fell Swoop 91. (cover: Tom Haines)

MAJOR SWOOPAGE (#92): Dave Brinks, Richard Martin, bill lavender, Camille Martin, Jesse Freeman, Dave Kennedy, Tom Weigel, Gerry Crinnin, Brett Evans, buck downs, Chris Toll, Claudia Nostril.

fell swoop 93 Souvenir Valium by Duck Martian.

AROUND THE LONGVIEW by Tom Weigel, Fell Swoop 94.

Ant McGoogle's Headlines by Ant McGoogle, Fell Swoop 95. (cover by Chitlynn Dupont).

Uncrucify That Angel Now by Bill Myers: Fell Swoop 96. (cover art by Miriam Schaefer)

Blue Rain Morning by James Jones, FS 97.

FELL SWOOP 98 Poetry Enhancement Issue!!!!: Richard Martin, Chris Toll, Alice Notley, Chitlynn Dupont, Tom Weigel, Gerry Crinnin, Pat Nolan, buck downs, Camille Martin, Brett Evans, bill lavender, B. Finnegan. (cover: Dave Brinks)

Fell Swoop 99 missing

SYNAPSE PICNIC by Duck Martian, Fell Swoop 100. (cover by Melissa Martin)

eskimos at two o'clock by philip Jenkins, Fell Swoop 101.

cells of fancy: poems by peter kidd,   Fell Swoop 102. (cover by "eye5scram")

103 missing

104 missing

Fell Swoop 105 "The Self Review Issue": Richard Martin, Aram Saroyan, Greg Fuchs, Sarah K. Inman, Scott Satterwhite, Joe Longo, Brett Evans, Frank Sherlock, Pat Nolan, Tom Weigel, Bossy Davis, Joel Dailey, Jamey Jones, God et al, Bill Kemmett, Gerry Crinnin, Ted Berrigan, Chris Toll.

Automaton Holiday by Duck Martian, Fell Swoop 106. (cover by Melissa Martin)

NO. 107 Fell Swoop "unsafe @ any speedo: Richard Martin, Jessica Fiorini, Jim Cory, Tom Weigel, Brinks/Mayer, Brett Evans, mark chadwick, Jamey Jones, Peter Kidd,

108 missing

Pisa Can (74) by Brett Evans, Fell Swoop # 109. (cover: Tracey McTague)

THE SAMUEL BECKETT LOOK-A-LIKE ISSUE FELL SWOOP 110: Duck Martian, Dave Brinks, Richard Martin, Gerry Crinnin, Bernadette Mayer, Tom Weigel, Dave Kennedy, Megan Burns, Bill Lavender, Jake St. John, Mrs. Irene Mice, D. Spinelli, Buck Downs,

Upper Level Activity by Joel Dailey, Fell Swoop #111, signed and dedicated to Richard Martin.

FELL SWOOP # 112/113 MADE IN CHINA ISSUE: Richard Martin, Camille Martin, Eddie Berrigan, Tom Weigel, andrei codrescu, Dave Brinks, Chris Toll, brett evans, bill lavender,

114 missing

The Human Bond (Some New Bond Sonnets) by Clark Coolidge FELL SWOOP #115

ABC OF DUCK by duck martian, Fell Swoop 116. (cover by Nicole Martin)

FELL SWOOP #117 THE POST CONTEMPORARY ISSUE!!!!!!: Richard Martin, Rupert Wondolowski, Brett Evans, John M. Bennett, Camille Martin, Tom Weigel, Cheryl Quimba, Clark Coolidge, Jamey Jones, Bill Lavender, Chris Toll.

THE KEEP CALM & CARRY ON (DOUBLE-DOG DARE YOU) ISSUE FELL SWOOP 118/119: Richard Martin, Vincent Spina, Angela Genusa, Buck Downs, Tom Weigel, Dennis Rojas, Chris Sullivan, Jim Cory.

LIFE ON EARTH by Chris Toll, Fell Swoop # 120. (cover collage by Chris Toll)

Mattress In an Alley, Raft Upon the Sea by Rubert Wondolowski, FELL SWOOP 121.

Fell Swoop # 122 In Defense of MFA and Exotic Vacationland Writing Workshops by Richard Martin.

FELL SWOOP 2012 Guest Editor: Megan Burns Fell Swoop 123: Martha Reed, Jean Marie Nunes, Tracey McTague, Jen Tynes.

The Ghost of Richard Brautigan by Ant McGoogle, Fell Swoop #124.

TWO TALES by Coolidge & Fagin, Fell Swoop 125. (cover by Keebler Brown)

Fell Swoop 126 Abstract Hysteria by Duck Martian (cover by Nicole Martin)

tumescent rat by mark chadwick, Fell Swoop 127.

FELL SWOOP 128, 129, 130 The Alien Swimsuit Issue: Richard Martin, Jake St. John, Jamey Jones, Lewis Warsh, Clark Coolidge, buck downs, Camille Martin, Andrei Codrescu, Aram Saroyan, Tom Weigel, Brett Evans, Christopher Shipman, Chris Toll. (cover: dbayar)

FELL SWOOP the 131.6 aka the ritchie martin review: Richard Martin, Stuart Ross, Miles Champion, Buck Downs, Brett Evans, Jamey Jones, Bill Lavender, James Haug, William Pen Myers, Tom Weigel, Camille Martin, Rubert Wondolowski.

The Year I Wanted to Be on Television by Al Pants, FELL SWOOP 132.7. (cover by Hilary Crane-Stern)

Touch Typing in 10 Lessons by Joel Dailey, Fell Swoop 133. 3. (cover by Chu Mee)

FELL SWOOP 134.6 TAKE ME TO YOUR SWOOP: Tom Weigel, Richard Martin, Clark Coolidge, Camille Martin, Maggie Cleveland, Brett Evans, Rubert Wondolowski, Bill Berkson, Bill Lavender.

TIME FURTHER OUT by Tom Weigel, Fell Swoop 135.

VEE VEES by Brett Evans Fell Swoop 135.5.

FELL SWOOP 136-137 for happy children: Richard Martin, James Haug, Bill Lavender, Chris Stroffolino, Brett Evans, Jamey Jones, Pat Nolan, Christopher Shipman, Charles Bernstein, Camille Martin, Tom Weigel, Buck Downs, Matvei Yankelevich, Claudia May Nostril.

FELL SWOOP 138/139….The 'Swoop It Under the Carport" Issue…Mas bliss now in print….Peter Kidd, Bill Lavender, Jim Brody, Tom Weigel, Richard Martin, Brett Evans, Gerry Crinnin, Evelyn Von Scrubb, Paul Dean. Cover by Bob Heman.

ISLAMOPHOBIA by Joel Dailey, Fell Swoop #140.

An Unpleasant Sense of Being Frank by James Haug, Fell Swoop #141, Fall, 2015.

FELL SWOOP #142 (A Swoopological View)…:A GUEST EDITORAL FROM WILLAM SHAKESPEARE…

> Malcolm:
> Be comforted.
> Let's make us medicines of our great revenge
> To cure this deadly grief.
>
> Macduff:
> He has no children – All my pretty ones?
> Did you say all? – O hell-kite! – All?
> What, all my pretty chickens, and their dam,
> At one fell swoop?

Contributors: Bill Lavender, James Haug, Richard Martin, Tom Weigel, Layla Chifferobe, Brett Evans, Stuart Ross, Jamey Jones.

Fell Swoop 142/143 Ozzie Nelson Relapse Four: Richard Martin, Colonel Will Bill Lavender, Stuart Ross, Michael Basinski, Edna Barbell, Tom Weigel, Bradley Evans, Jamey Jones, Gerald Crinnin, Jim Cory. Brently Evans.

Maybe Today after Tomorrow is Fell Swoop 143 by Duck Martian. (no mistake, just misnumbered)

Mambo is Fell Swoop 144, Summer 2016, by Tom Weigel.

Fell Swoop # 145 (shh! the Luddite Lit issue): Richard Martin, Tom Weigel, buck downs, Pat Nolan, Michael Basinki, Al Pants, Edna Barbill, b.evans, Bill Lavender, Jim Cory, Bob Heman, Chris Toll, Trax Buttcheeks

New Digs is Fell Swoop # 146, Summer, 2016, by Ant McGoogle.

FALL(EN) SWOOP 147/148!: Bill Lavender, Tom Weigel, Andrei Codrescu, William Penn Myers, Christopher Shipman, Richard Martin, John M. Bennett, Brett Evans, Michael Basinski.

Interview Without A Vampire is Fell Swoop 149. (Camille Martin's interview with Joel Dailey)

a small bag of balls by mark chadwick is fellswoop 150.

Fell Swoop # 151 THE READY TO SERVE ISSUE: Tom Weigel, brett evans, James "Al" Haug, Richard Martin, Gerry Crinnin, Kyle Flak, buck downs, Bill Lavender, Harris Schiff, Bob Heman. Cover Art: Sir T. Weigel.

FELL SWOOP 152-153: Ted Greenwald & Charles Bernstein, Jamey Jones, Kyle Flak, Al Pants, Pat Nolan, Andrei Codrescu, JV Miller, Brett Evans, Richard Martin, Duck Martian, Mike Sikkema, Bill Lavender, Michael Basinski, Tom Weigel.

THE POCKET RHYMING DICTIONARY, edited with unmitigated joy by Joel Dailey and Clara Mae Nostril, is Fell Swoop 154-155.

Appendix D

And More: Bern Mulligan

The Big Horror Poetry Series ended in May, 1996, after a fourteen year run as a community poetry series – a community series that gave everyone a shot at the microphone and paid featured poets, writers, and artists. In my anti-memoir *boink!*, I acknowledged the Binghamton Community Poets who worked with me to ensure the series flourished and remained open to the variety of voices and forms that compose the poetry landscape. Too often poets reside in camps and fixate on their spot of land. The "Horror" was different. It went out into those "camps," scouted them and invited poets and writers from them into the series. The series treated its audience to performance poets, beat poets, language poets, narrative poets, Native American poets, gay and lesbian poets, community poets and university poets. Thanks to the poets, the audience entered the heaven of bewilderment. They applauded loudly, shouted and heckled, asked questions and partied. Above all, they listened. At times, the readings went on for a couple of days, even though each reading (including an open mike) went for two to three hours. They could get rough. At one reading, I tore the meniscus cartilage in my right knee just trying to find a floor seat.

Now imagine being asked to comb through 10,000 reading objectives, pick your favorites and write comprehension test questions connected to them that could be scored by computer. That was my job in 1982, and because I was situated in the computer center of a local educational facility and completely ignorant about why computers would want to do such a thing, I got to hire (recommend for hire) an assistant. My manager gave me 150 resumes to sort through and enjoy. I decided to sort them by philosophy and poetry. Anyone who mentioned either one went in one pile, the others were tossed in the can. Six souls mentioned philosophy and/or poetry. The most interesting applicant had a BA in English from Colgate and a Masters in English from SUNY at Binghamton. His present job was delivering flowers. Somehow, I knew that this person would help me start a literary magazine for children (which he would edit), initiate a poets-in-the-school program, comb through those damn reading objectives and create state-of-the-art comprehension tests, and be my sounding board for reading workshops for teachers from eight school districts. Maybe, he would even become part of the Binghamton Community Poets. The applicant's name: Bern Mulligan.

Bern Mulligan did become a key member of the Binghamton Community of Poets, serving as its publicist for fourteen years. He also guaranteed that the Big Horror Poetry Series will survive for all those who love poetry for a very long time. It is a pleasure to have Bern share exactly how he has accomplished that magnificent feat.

Preservation Act: Digitizing a Literary Reading Series

All night the sound had
come back again,
and again falls
this quiet, persistent rain.

From "The Rain," as read by Robert Creeley on September 15, 1992
at Mad Murphy's Irish Pub

Introduction

I first met Richard Martin on a job interview in 1983. He looked a little like James Taylor, long hair, moustache, denim sport coat, and cowboy boots. Not what I was expecting from the straight-laced educational organization with which I was trying to get the job. We talked about philosophy, postmodern literature, and my then current job delivering flowers, all seminal topics for an elementary school language arts program. As was the case with everything in my life back then, although our interview went well, it took a couple of months for things to sort themselves out with the higher-ups in the organization, but eventually I got the job, which started a friendship which has lasted more than thirty years. Our on-the-job relationship was a genuine partnership, with Dick as front man and me as the behind-the-scenes detail guy. Not that Dick couldn't get into the details. We spent many afternoons walking around the campus discussing all the minutiae of the project. As Dick once told me, he could think better while he was in motion, so that's how we did much of our planning. But on the days we were holding professional development workshops for up to 100 elementary school teachers, Dick would lead the sessions and I would provide material and logistical support. For the better part of 12 years, we worked together on this project until the annual grant money finally dried up. Dick had remarried by then and relocated to Boston. He became an elementary school principal with Boston City Schools and only recently retired. I became a librarian and have worked for the Binghamton University Libraries for twenty years.

During the first year that we were working together, Dick mentioned that he and a few others in the area had formed the Binghamton Community Poets. Membership changed throughout the years but always included local writers who were dedicated to the idea of creating a space where literary art could flourish. That year he started the "Big Horror Reading Series" at a local coffee house. I remember this because I was one of only three people in the audience for this first reading. Things definitely got better from there. At one "poetry happening" (the Robert Creeley reading mentioned above), 300 people attended.

For 14 years, readings took place at various venues around the Triple Cities featuring nationally and internationally known writers while also providing "open mike" time for local community writers and sometimes musicians. The series received funding from the New York State Council on the Arts, the Broome County Arts Council, and Poets and Writers, Inc., as well as public donations. Many of the readings between 1987 and 1996 were videotaped. In addition to Creeley, some of the writers who are featured on the videotapes include Charles Bernstein, Barney Bush, Jayne Cortez, Joel Dailey, Jim Daniels, Diane DiPrima, Bob Holman, Bill Kemmett, Peter Kidd, Jerome Rothenberg, Patricia Smith and Lloyd Van Brunt. (For a complete list of featured readers by venue and date, see Appendix).

DIGITIZATION AND PRODUCTION

After the series ended in 1996, the videotapes sat in boxes for the next ten years, occasionally being passed between former members. When they came to me in 2006, I knew that something had to be done to preserve them since they were most likely degrading and losing both video and audio fidelity. As Keatinge (2009) points out…

> videotape is a surprisingly fragile medium, with inherent chemical and electromagnetic instabilities, which makes it inappropriate for long term archiving. The two main reasons for this are scientific phenomena known as binder hydrolysis and magnetic remanence decay. (p. 3)

I came up with an idea to suggest a project to the Dean of Libraries. Specifically, I asked him whether the Libraries would accept the collection of videotapes as a donation from the Binghamton Community Poets and allow me to work on digitizing them for preservation and access purposes. After discussing the feasibility of the project, the Dean composed a "Memorandum of Understanding" between the BCP and the Libraries that was acceptable to both parties.

After the MOU was agreed on, I began looking into the best way to accomplish the project. The first step was to obtain the proper equipment. This ended up being more of a "trial-and-error" process than I had first anticipated. Initially, I started digitizing tapes using my desktop computer but soon ran out of space. That's when the need for more storage became clear. Breeding (2002) notes that

One of the challenges of digital video that becomes apparent very quickly involves the vast amounts of storage it demands. From text, to still images, sound, and full-motion video, multimedia options form a continuum of increasing needs for storage and bandwidth. Video, by far, is the media with the largest storage appetite. (p. 32)

Tapes ranged in length from one to two plus hours, which translated into about 2.5-7 gigabytes (GBs) when digitized. With the average size about 5 GBs, this meant the 68 tapes (66 to start but two more were discovered during the course of the project) would need nearly 350 GBs of storage for the raw footage alone. After several fits and starts and experiments with different equipment, we eventually settled on a videocassette player/recorder, a dedicated computer loaded with conversion software, an external hard drive, and a dual-layer DVD burner. (We decided on the dual-layer burner after the first attempt at conversion of one of the two-hour tapes resulted in a file more than the 4.7 GB limit of a single-layer DVD.)

The project involved a steep learning curve (how to digitize VHS tapes, then edit and produce DVDs) and a lot of work (the actual digitization and production). Since this was a "one-horse operation," the equipment was kept in my office, which was fortunate since it allowed me to work on other things while converting and editing the files. Initially, I thought the project would take six months. As it turned out, it took more than three years. This was due to a number of factors: bugs in the software, hiccups in the hardware, and the necessity of being in my office during the digitization, which meant days I could not carve out two-hour chunks of dedicated time were "lost" days.

Phase One involved attempting to convert the videotapes to DVD-quality MPEG files. The videotapes were in ok shape, but many had glitches and dead spots and several others were not originals but copies, further adding to loss of video and audio fidelity. I was able to convert all but one (67). The video quality was enhanced to a degree from what was on the tapes, but not much. More importantly, however, for a reading series like this, the audio quality was enhanced significantly, so the sound on the digital versions is much better than on the tapes.

Phase Two involved producing individual DVDs from the MPEG files. This required another equipment upgrade, as more storage space (a terabyte) and "rendering" capacity were needed, and a completely different focus on my part. I had to look at the reading events in a new light and decide how best to edit and produce them as DVDs. The videotapes were literally "raw": they started when the camera had been turned on and continued without interruption until it was turned off, which meant there was often video of silent microphones and audio of irrelevant crowd noises and conversations. Editing these out made the DVD much better than the videotape. I also had to learn how to create menus and chapters, which turned out to be the most difficult aspect of the entire project. The software was not intuitive about this, to say the least. After pouring over the technical manual and after a number of attempts, I succeeded in creating a simple menu that worked and was able to produce DVDs for the majority of the events. But there were approximately ten that remained recalcitrant and could not be written out to DVD. With the assistance of our Director of Library Technology, they were finally produced.

COPYRIGHT COMPLICATIONS

Once all the DVDs were produced, the topic of copyright surfaced. As McDonough and Jimenez (2006) observe

> We need to know what we are legally permitted to do with any given video resource; for scholars this is a matter of knowing whether they have sufficient use rights to accomplish and report on their studies, while for archivists this is a matter of knowing whether they have sufficient rights to engage in the activities necessary to keep the resource accessible. (p. 177)

During the series, readers either gave verbal approval to being videotaped or tacit approval by just reading. There was nothing surreptitious about the camera and everyone knew they were being recorded. But the Dean asked if the group had collected any signed waivers from readers concerning copyright of the material they read during our events. The answer was no. After consultation with University Counsel, it was decided that the DVDs had to be treated as if there were no copyright agreements with the readers. Use copies were made of the DVD masters and after further discussions with the Dean, it was decided that the best place for them to be kept was in Special Collections. Although this arrangement protects the DVDs from any possible copyright infringement, it also curtails their accessibility: they can only be viewed when Special Collections is open.

CONVERGENCE EXPERIENCE

In order to draw attention to this rich collection of readings, the Dean and I came up with a pilot project in which individual segments would be excerpted, reformatted, and mounted in a digital repository with a built-in viewer. The video segments would then be associated with the print titles from which they originated via our catalog. We did this for about 12 excerpts in the pilot. This created a truly unique "convergence" experience for our patrons, as the catalog record "came alive" and they could see and hear an excerpt from the book before they even took it off the shelf to read. Unfortunately, we lost access to that digital repository and are no longer able to show these video excerpts in the catalog.

PRESERVATION AND FUTURE ACCESS

In addition to the use copies made of the edited DVDs, backup copies were also made of the MPEG files. However, as Corrado and Moulaison (2014) note

> While having a well thought-out backup and disaster recovery strategy is a key component of any digital preservation program, having backups by itself is not enough to "ensure ongoing access" and cannot be considered a digital preservation strategy. (pp. 3-4)

After several conversations with the Director of Library Technology, it seems the best solution for us is Rosetta, our digital preservation system. However, it has only been used to preserve still images and text. Preservation of the Big Horror Reading Series DVDs will be the first time it will be used for video and so will be a beta test for this format.

The first step will entail converting the DVDs into ISO files. ISO files are disc images that contain all the components of the DVDs, including the menus and chapters. The ISO files will then be ingested into Rosetta for safekeeping. If necessary in the future, the ISO files can be converted back to DVDs that retain all the properties of the original discs.

Making the readings more accessible is a little more involved since Rosetta does not contain a built-in viewer. Two possibilities exist: either integrating a third-party application (e.g., JW Player) into Rosetta, which could play the readings and would be password protected; or separating the delivery from preservation and streaming the readings to the campus, which would also be password protected. Both would require another reformatting of the DVDs, possibly to AVI or WebM. Either way, it will add a dimension to the access situation (the physical DVDs will still be available for viewing in Special Collections) and potentially allow more students in creative writing classes at Binghamton University to see and hear some great readings.

REFERENCES

Breeding, M. (2002). The challenges of converting to digital video. *Information Today, 19*(7) 32-33.

Corrado, E.M. & Moulaison, H.L. (2014). *Digital Preservation for Libraries, Archives, and Museums*. Lanham: Rowman & Littlefield.

Keatinge, R. (2009). *Causes and measurement of videotape decay* [White Paper]. Retrieved from *http://sportsvideo.org/main/files/2010/08/video-tape-white-paper.pdf*

McDonough, J. & Jimenez, M. (2006). Video preservation and digital reformatting: pain and possibility. *Journal of Archival Organization, 4(1)*, 167-191. doi: 10. 1300/J201v04n01_09

APPENDIX

Big Horror Reading Series DVD Master List (by venue and date)

Swat Sullivan's Hotel
May 6, 1987 Barney Bush/Jerome Rothenberg
November 11, 1987 Adrian Clarke
April 28, 1988 Diane DiPrima
May 21, 1988 Elizabeth Thomas/Joel Dailey/Dave Kelly
March 15, 1989 Phil Sweeney/Pierre Joris/Milton Kessler
April 25, 1990 Phil Sweeney/Lance Henson
May 23, 1990 Michael Kelly/Ann Goldsmith
June 20, 1990 Richard Martin/Jerome Washington
Vintage Swat's (compilation)

Benlin's
January 22, 1991 Tom Costello and Friends
February 12, 1991 Milton Kessler
February 19, 1991 Open Mike
March 19, 1991 James Haug
March 23, 1991 Dick Martin Book Party
April 16, 1991 Jackie Warren Moore/Mary Slechta
April 23, 1991 BCC Writers
May 21, 1991 Ritch Keppler/Suzanne Cleary/Donald Peterson
June 11, 1991 Lloyd Van Brunt/Wally Butts
June 18, 1991 Wail Poets
August 6, 1991 Elizabeth Thomas/Joel Dailey/John Miller
October 15, 1991 Tom Costello/Bern Mulligan
November 19, 1991 Bob Mooney/Tom Bailey/Phil Brady
December 17, 1991 Zack Grabosky/Gerry Crinnin
February 19, 1992 Sylvia Kelly
March 10, 1992 Igneus Press (Peter Kidd/Bill Kemmett/Wally Butts)
April 7, 1992 Back Fence "The Lost Reading"
May 12, 1992 Liz Rosenberg/David Bosnick
May 19, 1992 Safiya Henderson Holmes
June 9, 1992 David Adams

Mad Murphy's Irish Pub
September 15, 1992 Robert Creeley

The Tazmanian Embassy
October 13, 1992 John Bartles
November 10, 1992 Greg Boyd/Patricia Smith
November 17, 1992 John Vernon and Friends
February 9, 1993 Tom Costello/John Miller/Mike Finn

The Amsterdam
February 16, 1993 Edwin Torres
March 16, 1993 Mike Gaul
March 23, 1993 Dorianne Laux/Todd Beers
April 13, 1993 Dirksen L. Bauman/Jerry Mirskin
April 20, 1993 Sylvia Kelly/Michael Czarnecki
May 18, 1993 Bob Holman/Jim Martin
May 25, 1993 Gerald McCarthy
June 15, 1993 Jack Dann
June 22, 1993 Kate Rushin
July 20, 1993 Gerry Crinnin
July 27, 1993 Other People's Stuff
August 17, 1993 Paul Dean/Cosmo Calabro
October 12, 1993 Bernstein Cancellation Show
November 9, 1993 Betsy Robin Schwartz
November 16, 1993 Ingrid Arnesen/Mary Beth O'Connor
December 7, 1993 Charles Bernstein
April 12, 1994 Doug Paugh/Jim Laviska
April 19, 1994 Elliot Richman
June 14, 1994 Steve Kowitt/John Miller
June 21, 1994 David Bartine
July 19, 1994 Tom Costello Farewell
September 13, 1994 Keith Gilyard
September 20, 1994 Tish Benson
October 11, 1994 Phil Sweeney
October 18, 1994 Barry Silesky
November 22, 1994 Richard Braco
March 21, 1995 Binghamton University Creative Writers/Bob Mooney

April 18, 1995 George Zebrowski/Pamela Sargent
May 16, 1995 Richard Martin/Joel Dailey
June 13, 1995 Ed Ochester
June 20, 1995 Jim Daniels

Java Joe's
October 14, 1995 Tino Villanueva

Amp's
May 4, 1996, The Last Big Horror Part 4 (featuring Barney Bush/Milton Kessler)

POEMS BY BERN MULLIGAN

Rain

> *Western wind, when wilt thou blow?*
> *The small rain down can rain.*
> *Christ! That my love were in my arms,*
> *And I in my bed again.*

> Anonymous, 16th Century

Rain pours down
and pours down.
This is not a small rain:
it makes the ground swell
and the trees bend;
it is incessant.
It seeps inside buildings;
it dampens thoughts
and chills bones.
It is narcotic and infectious.
It makes you yearn for
someone, something
to curl up beside.
It is an invitation

to sloth and indolence,
but also
to reflection and introspection.
It makes you think
how lonely life would be
without people;
how lonely life is
with people;
how glad you are to accept
the unevenness of your life,
in all its neurotic splendor,
in the hope that
someday it will change,
and the world will change,
and the rain will fall
not from a blank sky
but from one
with a purpose.

One Fell Swoop (Issue 14/15, Spring 1989)

Swat's June 6, 1990

The voice began. The room was half full; most people were
listening and drinking; some were smoking. The room, as
always, was hot and smoky, but the fact that it was late
spring and the windows were open made it better. Sounds of
the street, cars and buses, sifted in through the green
translucent curtains and became part of the story. Also
sounds from the bar, voices, laughter, a ballgame, could be
heard. These things had not been planned, but they were
there nonetheless. They were part of the story.

The voice began to describe the room itself: black tables,
wooden or red and blue metal folding chairs; dark wood
paneled walls, silver radiators, green linoleum, orange

light, white ceiling with panel missing, happy birthday
banner, shamrocks for different beers, p/a speakers,
microphone. A man up front reading to a room half full of
people sitting at black tables with graffiti etched in them,
listening, drinking, smoking, talking.

They wondered where this was leading, the voice describing
the room and its occupants in the late spring evening as
street and bar noises sifted in; then it stopped.

Fascination

I am sitting in the past;
I am playing a game.
I am fascinated by the game,
the silver balls making their ways
through the maze on the blue board,
but I am also thinking about the future,
about a time when I might
think back to this moment.
I am trying to win the game,
yet I am also aware
that I will remember playing it.
When I think about this moment,
I will remember the smell of chlorine
from the municipal pool behind our house,
or more precisely, our neighbor's house,
where I sit playing my friend's game
on his back porch overlooking the pool,
thinking how wonderful it is to know
that I will remember this moment.
I cannot recall with any certainty
what happened next,
or even who won the game.
But this one moment
is as clear to me now

as if it had just happened:
I know that it happened,
and I knew I would recall it
in other times,
in other places,
vividly,
with a certain fondness.

Wail! Magazine (Vol. 4, No. 6, Summer 1991)

In September the Squirrels Inherit the Park

The leaves have not yet changed,
but they have a pale cast;
mushrooms thrive;
it is a time of decline,
decay,
of pulling the essence back in
after the long effort to produce:
everything is spent.

Concourse 8 (Spring 1994)

November Grey

Dreariness
distracts from
self-consciousness;
nose runs
despite efforts
to stop it;
snow sifts
through greyness
whispering
more, more;

roofs reflect
color of sky:
if loneliness had a form,
it would certainly be
this godforsaken day.

Untitled

Would you call this
the late fall of our love?
Wind blows cold,
light darkens early,
ground waits for final freeze.
I don't think
I can
weather
the winter
without you.

Concourse 8 (Spring 1994)

Back to Menelaus

How he yearned to rest his eyes
on her lovely face:
the eyes so fine and bright,
the skin so soft,
the cheeks pronounced,
the lips chiseled into a bow
only Eros could make.
How he longed to run his hand
along the voluptuous curve
of hip or breast.
The jealous rage he felt,
the rage upon finding her gone,

left with the outsider,
left him beside himself,
calling on kith and kin
to follow the lecherous road to Troy
and lay siege upon the town
to recover the stolen gem.
What could have run through his mind
when he walked into the temple
of the Goddess of Love
and found her earthly reincarnation
waiting for him?
Could he believe her to have been guiltless
in this episode of lust
or a party to the transgression?
The face that launched a thousand ships
come face to face with the one
who had loved and lost,
no more repentant than the day she left
but unbelievably, even more beautiful.
His eyes could not get enough of her,
and love came in through the eyes to the heart.
No words spoken, only gesture,
a hand extended in her direction,
impunity granted where none asked for,
no talk of trespass,
only the long journey
back to hearth and home.

The Cafe Review (Summer 1999)

Knowing

Empiricists believe
all knowledge
comes through the senses.
Then my knowledge of you

couldn't have been more complete.
I took you in via
every available sense,
the look of you,
the sound of you,
the feel of you,
the smell of you,
the taste of you,
in quantity deserving of
such a specimen.
I came to know you
as well as I knew myself,
better perhaps.
I knew you in
an elemental way,
beyond thought or description.
To be deprived of you now
does not diminish
the lasting impression
I have of you.
I can say
in all honesty,
I knew you.

APPENDIX E

Industrial Loop
Joel Dailey

Lavender Ink/Fell Swoop

120 Pages; Print, $15.00

The world is on the edge of falling apart. Our phones are tapped; our emails hacked. Our wars are long and expensive; our veterans are treated like crap. Giant storms and fires ravage our cities and towns. People have taken to the streets to protest the killings of unarmed black men. We're addicted to what our screens tell us. Congress is broken into rich and powerful lobbies. The media primes us for the next disaster. Terrorists hunt us in malls and schools. I'll read your blog, if you read mine. The poor remain poor. The middle class looks for a raise. The infamous 1 percent and Wall Street think things are just fine. There are polar bears on our front lawns. And our immigrants would prefer staying here.

Thank God for popular culture, TV, and omnipresent corporate advertising. Things aren't as bleak as they seem. There are plenty of pills to take, new cars to drive, new celebrities to follow on Twitter, and more formulaic shows to watch through weary eyes. Still there seems to be something amiss as if we – the ordinary we – have become our own daily reality show. It might help if our poets, "the unacknowledged legislators of the world," as Percy Bysshe Shelley stated, would put the whole fragmented mess into perspective i.e., shed or share critical light on our challenges through an unfettered language up for the task. Unfortunately, many of our poets ("legislators") are occupied in sanctioned narrative prosody and/or networking their way to awards and acclaim.

One individual who has chosen a different path, at times a reclusive one, but innovative in the recreation of poetry, is New Orleans poet, Joel Dailey, the esteemed editor of the influential literary magazine, *Fell Swoop: The All Bohemian Revue*. In his latest volume of poetry, **Industrial Loop**, Mr. Dailey, in five mind-altering sections – *Suspicious in Florida*; *What's Wrong?*; *The Art of the Hot Dog*; *Better Yet*; and *Upper Level Activity* – operates on and plays with language in its multifarious forms: word play, puns, snippets of speech (formal/colloquial), and newspaper, magazine and internet headlines and advertisements. In doing so, he painstakingly reassembles our language-exhausted American polis and world into other than it is and maybe what it could be.

In first verse of the poem, *What It Would Look Like If You Were In Space* (*Suspicious in Florida*, p.40) Dailey writes:

The social fabric covering the furniture is
　　tearing at the
　　　　　　corners
Differently, indifferently
Down at the inconvenient store the visually
attractive (bubble
　　　butts)   form a conga line
Footloose or footless　　there's Footlong

The last verse of poem states:

All this infrastructure generated to pacify
　　the animal within
Indispensable or indefensible
A burglary happens every 18.3 seconds here
　　in the Land of the Break In
I'm trying to break out

A view from space changes the ground perspective. The social fabric, that which unifies us as a people is tearing at the corners. We're becoming undone. *E pluribus unum* is showing signs of wear. Are different segments of the society engaged in different ways and responsible for the process of social disintegration or is it pegged to historical forces and the arrow of time? The poem won't say but encourages the reader to enter into it and spend some thought time, some composing time. Are "bubble butts" a symbol of beauty, a sign of obesity or both? Are all the conveniences we take for granted inconvenient to our growth? Have we copped to pacification? Crime is all around us. It's time to break out and poetry will show us the way.

In the poem, *Doff The Sombrero (What's Wrong? p.52)*, the first thirteen lines of a thirty-one line, single verse poem present:

Dear Fun Lover, in order to prevent a
　　disruption of service here's
　　　　　to your square footage
For the first time ever the presence of water
　　on Mars confirmed
　　　　　　　(a la clank) by robotic touch & taste

Our robot, velveeta fluent
Looking young   purposeful   in
  trendy bicoastal shirtpocket
        protector
A product of poor moisture management, our
  Genius In Rez craves
          Sequencing (a la car dent)

At first, readers unaccustomed to Dailey's unique and idiosyncratic use of language may avert their eyes and minds to the default status of what do these lines mean. Bringing in one's ear into the process is essential. Reading a Dailey poem out loud is a treat. In the lines quoted above, Mr. Dailey does not permit a wayward syllable into the construction. Sound attends to energy and meaning. Poems flow or as Charles Olson states in *Projective Verse*: "…a poem is energy transferred from where the poet got it (he will have some several causations) by way of the poem itself to, all the way over to the reader. Olson continues to say: "…the poem itself must, at all points, be a high energy-construct and, at all points, an energy discharge." And how is this accomplished? Again, quoting Olson, it occurs by: "the Head, by way of Ear, to the Syllable/the Heart, by way of the Breath to the Line."

Joel Dailey knows his Olson and is fearless in his play of presenting his poems as high-energy constructs and discharges. Boom! Take the first three lines of the lines above. The phrase "in order to prevent a disruption of service" comes from the "causation" of the endless messages from the phone or the electric company that we all receive. Dailey will have none of this, prevents the assumed closure, and sets the line sparking with "so here's to your square footage." *Square footage* discharges the concept of property. What about a property? Who has it and who doesn't? The American experience of property goes back to the Pilgrims' swindle of land from the Native Americans. It's the American dream, after all. Who can say if Dailey intended to mock property acquisition and/or predict how the "sparks and discharges" in his poems (part of the joy in reading his work) will affect the minds of his readers? We do know, however, that our robots exploring Mars resemble "cheesy" retro-NASA engineers (circa moon shoot) before the *Genius In Rez* fancies sequencing (a la car dent). Yes, it is good to laugh. Laughter is a sign of comprehension.

In the *Art of the Hot Dog* section of **Industrial Loop**, Mr.Dailey offers a set of poems that will ensure he never receives awards or due acclaim from the Academy of American Poets, but just maybe, the poems will put him on the short list for a McArthur Genius Grant.

In the poem, *To The National Reply Center* (p.72), dedicated to Arnold Ziffel,* Dailey reveals the influence of Ted Berrigan's poetry on his. Give a listen:

At 10:29 AM CST I day dream (blue dinghy) of
    new procedures
      everyone can follow
  A dash (hi Andrei hi Anselm) of Foreign
    Accent Syndrome
Mixed with advanced untreatable cases
  a tidal wave of 'sports
       logoitis'
  A faux leather bound comprehensive American
    Literature cheese
      Concordance

In the first verse of a three verse poem above and by the dedication to Mr. Ziffel, Joel Dailey establishes that he is the connoisseur of a Master, a satirist, an ironist, a comic, an irritant, a literary critic and an original. The lines clearly reflect Berrigan's commitment to the immediacy of the self in the world by reference to the actual time of day, a penchant for mentioning or writing to his friends (in Dailey's case Hi to Andrei Codrescu and Anselm Hollo), and a genius for collage and arranging lines for an "unintended" or discovered effect, all hallmarks of Berrigan's oeuvre. However, the new procedures Dailey dreams of (*nonstandard language techniques?*) and that everyone can follow pose ironic challenges: a dash of Foreign Accent Syndrome, advanced untreatable cases, sports logoitis (a common condition where clients see their logos smaller than they actually are), and an American Literature cheese concordance. The first line of the second verse stokes and frames the irony (universality of the procedures) for the reader: "Clearly there is no time for character development." True enough. For it will take time to absorb and commit to these "new procedures." As for the "American Literature cheese concordance," Dailey challenges the reader to decide if "cheese" in this case, refers to the Big Cheese Canonical Ones of American Literature, silent but deadly gas, or an alphabetical index of favorite cheeses to serve when hosting famous author book tours.

Unlike Charles Olson and the Black Mountain School and Ted Berrigan and the second generation of New York School poets, Joel Dailey is not affiliated with a specific group of poets, although his work exhibits an affinity with Language and Flarf poets. In his essay, *Poetics of the Americas*, Charles Bernstein writes: "Poetry can be a process of thinking rather than a report on things already settled, an investigation of figuration rather than a picture of something figured out. Such ideologically informed nonstandard language practice, I call ideolectical…" Mr. Dailey's poetry resides here.

Linguistics defines "idiolect" as a person's individual speech patterns. In terms of writing, Dailey's poems are unique figurations (patterns) created through "nonstandard language practices" that foster multiple meanings or not as his poems play upon the page. In many ways, his poems, the verses within a given poem, and between the lines in individual verses model the Joseph Cornell epigraph at the opening of **Industrial Loop**: "How does one know what a certain object will tell another?" Joel Dailey's poems have lines of communication open among them but what they are saying to each other is up to the individual reader. However, Dailey never allows or is interested in turning poetic expression into purely theoretical constructions. He wears a hard hat to work. As he writes in *Industrial Loop* (p. 34), the title poem of the collection:

> Anyone who talks about "street cred" doesn't
> have any
> We find this comforting
> I read the trades   I follow the
> Trends   I stalk celery

Mr. Dailey lives in the streets of language. He is on the scene as: "The carpet remnants of civilization are being hauled out the front door." (*Not Now Maybe Later*, p. 36) Dailey gathers the remnants, especially the linguistic remnants and fragments in order to create a complex view, a shattered mirror perhaps in which to see ourselves renewed and grabbling with undefined and open possibilities for inhabiting the planet through language-inspired epiphanies. Or in Mr. Dailey's words, as he writes in *Regis Philbin at 80 MPH* (p.81):

> Around the Clubhouse Turn it's Easily
>   Confused
> & here they down the stretch   neck
>   & neck
> It's Perspective & Easily Confused
> The winner is Perspective   Perspective
>   by a nosehair

*Arnold Ziffel was the pig on the situation comedy *Green Acres* and the son of Doris and Fred Ziffel. A unique feature to the book and part of Joel Dailey's love of mixing popular and high culture together to suit his vision. Of the 79 poems in the book, 51 of them are dedicated to individuals and friends including Ralph Kramden (*Best Casseroles Ever*), Derek Jeter (*30 Things to Put You in a Good Mood*) and Marge Perloff (*Son of Flarf*).

Reviewed by Richard Martin

APPENDIX F

New Digs

Ant McGoogle

Acknowledgements

Ant thanks the usual suspects and those who refer to themselves in the third person, excluding those running for political office, celebrities and professional athletes. *George is getting angry.*

Cover Art: Melissa Martin

UNIFORMITY IS NOT THE FINAL FRONTIER.
RICHARD MARTIN

for William Bronk

Constant Love

Love gets old, loses a few teeth
Wears a bracelet that reads – Help me!
Love remembers youth – the dawn
Of beauty

Meanwhile the mind stokes
The eternal
Into restless energy
Love is reborn

QUIET DOWN

Words were having quite a party
In the brain; a few
Were drunk and disorderly.
None of them heard the sirens
Outside his house.

PARABLE OF LIGHT

One day the fire drops
Out of the body
And heads for town.
Everyone feels the heat.
"The fire is back," everyone says,
After the sun comes out.

Events

The mail came
addressed to no one
in particular.

The phone rang
but nobody
answered it.

Whoever knocked on
the door and rang the bell
was not there.

The glass half empty
remained so
for the entire evening.

There is nothing
in the refrigerator
someone claimed.

Holes in socks
mustered courage
and accepted the condition.

Voided checks
littered the floor
unceremoniously.

A coffeepot witnessed
the impatience
of the vacant cup.

The hollow impression
of time
went unnoticed.

Mishap

He fell through a hole
in language

Someone told him
there were many

Ones that offered travel …
new worlds …

Others fostered the past
of dust and light

He stood up
as flames licked higher

He called to words
to gather around him

EPISTEMOLOGICAL DISPUTE

The logic of others
before and after oneself
is irrefutable
to many

The rest claim
in loud and vigorous voices
they are the only world
as far as they know

STUFF

The mind needs space

To become empty

Or is it better said

The goal of the mind is emptiness

Space was once thought to be empty

At least that was the prevailing idea

Then came the startling news

Empty space is full of stuff

Just like an empty mind

It's a contradiction

Dualism

We come back to what we left behind.
There's the body walking in the weeds of time.
It's a ghost now amid stark trees.
The moon sees it but can trace its outline
From memory anyway.
Once the body returned to a place imagined
After it imagined the place it could return to.
Now the earth sings to the body,
Displays its rocks and deep fires
While we hover.

Royalty

Some days after making up
Who we are
We grab a hat or scarf
And enter the day

The day has been waiting for us
In its own disguise of rain
And wind or whatever
Suits the occasion

New Lease on Life

The great thing about rising from the dead
is to get back to work and get busy doing
what we were doing without the fear
of not being here

Taking Sides

We raised the banner
Of inexplicability
Is what we did
And apologized to no one

They admired us
From a safe distance
Sold their wares
And believed in their answers

TRUST

Still the cardinal
On a tree branch
Outside the window
Singing

Knows the metaphysics
Of the situation
As well as the physics
Of flight

Odyssey

The journey was conceived
In great silence
And with great imagination

It would cover many miles
And call on light
To monitor the distance

Everyone would have a shot
On saying where it was going
Debates raged about incessant motion

There was really no place
Or known reason for the journey
To stop anywhere

Somehow the journey knew
Where it was going and headed there
Without stopping

FANFARE

Again squirrels zip through
And across the branches
Of hemlock trees
In the backyard

The phenomenology of clouds
Highlights their actions
In grey light
It is Easter morning

Crocus have come and gone
Without fanfare
The time to awaken
Is constantly present

Big Secret

*

Love appeared as a statue
"Take it," he said
"It's for you."

*

The house of parrots fell under suspicion.
Neighbors peered through windows
at the show in muted light.

*

Her body covered his like a lampshade.
He offered to bring an umbrella of shadows
just in case.

*

He had a little too much to drink
and swam across the ocean and back,
which one he can't recall.

*

There was a time every particle in space
had a known position,
according to the best scientific imagination.

*

Planes roared overhead.
Cats played tag with the wind.
Everything had some hop in it.

*

No one would say
if he had been reborn or not.
Apparently, it was a big secret.

Not Quite

Is there identity in the multiplicity of soul
Nothing bubbles into concept
A blueprint of stars arranges the sky
Air and the body are fabrics
Time performs on stage

We are an array of personal pronouns
You and I are the mind of sunlight
They engage raindrops from the highest peaks
He races to the end of a sentence
How she loves the varieties of now

HOME IMPROVEMENT

Eventually words believed in themselves
and excavated the mind

Things were now things
and dug their new digs

RICHARD MARTIN is a past recipient of a National Endowment for the Arts Literature Fellowship for Poetry, founder of The Big Horror Poetry Series (Binghamton, New York, 1983-1996) and a retired Boston Public Schools principal. He lives in Boston with his family.

CPSIA information can be obtained
at www.ICGtesting.com
Printed in the USA
BVHW02s1328260718
522572BV00005B/10/P

9 781947 980044